Explore

My life searching for lost locations in the Bible

By Robert Cornuke

Koinonia House

Explore: My life searching for lost locations in the Bible
© Copyright 2019 Koinonia House Inc.
Published by Koinonia House
P.O. Box D
Coeur d'Alene, ID 83816-0347
www.khouse.org

Author: Robert Cornuke
Editor: Amy Joy
Cover illustration by Dean Packwood

ISBN: 978-1-57821-780-9

PRINTED IN THE UNITED STATES OF AMERICA

My daughter Shannon is a fiery shooting star who continually lights up my life. Thank you, Shannon, for being the igniting spark for me to begin the long process of writing this book. This one is for you Shani.

Table of Contents

INTRODUCTION

The passage of time is cruel to archaeologists and historians, to any who hunt down the remnants of the civilizations that perished long ago. With each passing century and millennium, archaeological evidence succumbs to the ravenous appetites of erosion and oxidation. It's always a joy to uncover an ancient artifact that has survived the vast arsenal of nature's destructive elements, and it's especially exhilarating when that unearthed object holds a holy pedigree. When this happens, I stand in awe at what the special relic reveals about history, the Bible, and my own faith.

In its most basic, unflattering terms, the science of archaeology is simply a tedious search for durable rubbish. I don't describe myself as an archaeologist as such, because I do not dig up small patches of dirt with a hand trowel and brush. That type of dedication is for academics capable of tedious foot-by-foot research. In simple terms, I describe myself as a *trained police investigator*, and I use the skills I acquired during my years in law enforcement to track down clues which may lead to the discovery of lost places with a biblical lineage.

To date, I have participated in more than seventy international expeditions in my efforts to track down elusive lost artifacts and locations described on the pages of the Bible. In other books, I've described the holy objects and sites themselves, but this book focuses on the adventures I've had in hunting them down. In the following chapters, I will chronicle many of the exciting, and often dangerous, expeditions I've made during my thirty-some years of worldwide searching. I have often trespassed into dangerous, forbidden lands. I've trudged across many blistering deserts and climbed the icy flanks of great mountains. On five separate occasions, I was arrested while traipsing around Muslim countries - countries swirling in geopolitical controversy and a general distrust of anyone carrying a Bible. I am thankful to our gracious God for His tremendous protection over me in all my exploits (and some painfully close calls).

My primary goal has been to seek out the accurate geographical positions of real places described in the Bible, locations where common dirt was once transformed into holy ground through an encounter with the Divine. These searches include the landfall of Noah's ark, the Exodus route, Mount Sinai, the Ark of the Covenant, the anchors from Paul's shipwreck, the true location of Solomon and Herod's temples, and the hilltop where Jesus was crucified (Golgotha). In all these searches, I used the Bible as my compass and my guide. Conversely, I have cautiously avoided the mangled mass of popular traditions, which often have lured researchers in the wrong direction because they are so prolifically corrupted by misleading information.

I invite you now to join me on some of these demanding and perilous journeys as we follow the directional clues penned upon the scrolls of time and Scripture. We will enter step-by-step into the forgotten chambers of history, where faint whispers from the prophets of old will guide us along our way. Our quest will be to solve ancient mysteries and decipher secrets of the Bible, because we all know that secrets can't be kept forever!

For there is nothing hidden which will not be revealed, nor has anything been kept secret but that it should come to light.

Mark 4:22

CHAPTER 1

I WAS A COP

As long as I can remember, all I ever wanted to be was a policeman. I grew up in Van Nuys, California, in a typical baby boomer neighborhood where small, boxy homes were crammed into an expansive grid of urban sprawl. Down the street from me lived a tall, soft spoken police lieutenant named Bob. After his shift, Lieutenant Bob would park his big old black and white police car in his driveway, and many days I would appear as he drove up - a small boy waiting in excitement.

That police car was so imposing to me, with its draping round 1950s style fenders and a growler siren mounted on its roof. I know my eyes widened when the lanky man stepped from his cruiser, and I saw that long-barreled revolver slung on his hip. Without a word, big Bob would offer a slight nod in my direction, which was his way granting me unspoken approval to climb into his police car. I would quickly clamber onto the cigarette-burned and coffee-stained front seat and just sit there for hours, listening in rapt attentiveness to the police calls on the radio. Without moving, that black and white cruiser transported me into an exhilarating world of cops and criminals. The crackling words filled my exuberant and fertile mind, and it was I who chased down stolen cars and fleeing bad guys.

Many years later, I realized my dream when I became a police officer with the Costa Mesa Police Department in Southern California. I worked as a patrol officer for several years, then as a motorcycle cop and finally, a crime scene investigator (CSI). Eventually, I graduated from the FBI Homicide Institute.

I admit, there's some truth to those stereotypes about cops and donuts. Some mornings after a long graveyard shift, when the sun was straining through the coastal haze, I would find time for a routine cup of coffee at a small donut shop on 17th street. On several occasions, around 7 a.m., or so, I would find a wide-shouldered, big man standing next to his car all alone in the parking lot. He lived in nearby Newport Beach, and he liked to frequent this particular donut shop about the same time I did. He wore an Irish tweed cap on his head and held a steaming cup of coffee in his huge fists. His name was John Wayne. We often talked together about what had happened during my shift. He loved hearing stories of the night's activities and, just like me as a small boy, he too liked to stand by my police unit and listen in on police calls.

Once Mr. Wayne told me that his life was completely scripted, and while he was sometimes shot or killed in the movies, it was just an act and he always went home unharmed. He often said that the police were his heroes because we weren't acting, and real harm could come to us at any moment from unexpected circumstances. He liked to say that my job was *unscripted*. In my job, the bullets were real, and the potential for death skulked around every corner. Ironically, it was not that long after one of my morning meetings with the Duke that I was involved in one of those "unexpected circumstances."

THE BURNING TRUCK

One late afternoon, while working in plain clothes as a crime scene investigator, I heard a radio call reporting that a man had set his pickup truck on fire in his front yard. I had no clue that this odd event would ultimately change my life. The call was not directed at me, of course, because I worked on crime scenes at that time and didn't take general patrol calls. I was right around the corner from the burning truck, though, so I radioed "9-10" to say I would take the call. I turned down a narrow neighborhood street and, sure enough, there was a pickup truck parked on a front lawn, totally engulfed in a ravenous ball of fire.

I parked my all-white police car directly in front of the house, got out, and walked up the short driveway through a curtain of sour smelling haze. The black smoke burned my eyes, but I could see well enough to discern a blurry man behind the front screen door of the house. I rubbed my watering eyes and made a few more steps in the man's direction, trying to focus on him through the screen door. Then I stopped. He stood about thirty feet away from me, a half-empty bottle of vodka dangling from one hand, and a rifle propped up in the other. The barrel was aimed directly at my forehead.

"You a cop?" the man grumbled. Then he slurred, "I'm gonna kill a cop."

The day had started out like any other, if anything could be considered "normal" on that job. Many shifts were just long days of drudgery, with one call after another followed by the tedious filling out of reports. Many shifts involved incursions into the darker corners of society. On occasion, a circumstance would erupt that sent a sour shot of adrenaline across my tongue, while my heart pounded wildly against my ribs. This was one of those days.

On one side of that screen door stood a man whose mind was saturated by alcohol and strife. On the other side stood me. His finger locked onto the trigger while he struggled to keep my head positioned in the metal v-groove on his rifle sight. I thought about reaching for the semi-automatic 9mm under my sports jacket but decided against it. Instead, I slowly—if not meekly—stammered out, "Hey man, I am no cop." He seemed to relax a moment, and I turned to walk away.

The calm lasted only a few moments. Maybe he saw the yellow light in the back window of my unmarked unit, or maybe he spotted the barrel of my shotgun peeking up from the dashboard mount. Whatever connection he made, he must have decided that I was law enforcement, and gunshots erupted through the smoke.

"Pop pop pop pop!" The man unleashed the hell hounds that had been crouching in his wounded soul. If he'd been sober, his aim might have been better. As it was, a fusillade of sonic-snapping bullets shot past me and I sprinted to my car. Something stung my leg just before I dove behind the steel body of the cruiser, and I thought I had been shot. Happily, it was only asphalt spraying from bullet impacts. I pressed my back behind the shielding bulk of the car axle as a barrage of bullets flew past. Across the street, puffs of stucco blew into the air, shingles popped up and windows shattered. Shredded tree leaves rained down from the canopy of branches above me.

When under extreme stress, a rolodex of bodily reactions kicks into high gear. The heart races to pump more oxygen to the brain. Surges of adrenaline prepare the body for the strength needed in a confrontation. Eyes widen for greater peripheral vision, and nostrils flare to suck in the air needed to operate the body's survival mechanisms at optimum efficiency. I added one additional method to my survival system that day; I sent up a short prayer.

A raging fire still consumed the man's truck, and over my shoulder I watched as the black funnel cloud tilted in the wind. It seemed as if a demonic tornado had stopped to sip up the flames, and I felt certain that a fire in the man's heart roared as hot as the charred truck. I later learned that the man had been arrested for drunk driving on the previous night. He had lost his job over the crime, and his fed-up family had left him alone and distraught. Uncontrollable rage overwhelmed him and demanded recompense, and his plan was simple. He would kill a cop for what had happened to him, and I was the sacrificial beneficiary of his reprisals.

I hunkered behind my car while the man unleashed his fury, still in danger but at a distinct advantage. I had good cover, and I would be alive at the end of the night if I didn't do anything especially stupid. I waited until I heard a metallic "clank," which told me his spent rifle clip had dropped to the tiled floor. He'd have to reload, which gave me a few seconds to open my car door and reach for my radio mic. I pulled out the grey, coiled umbilical cord attached to the radio, and I forced out the words "44 290- 998" into the receiver. The first five numbers were my call sign, and the dire proclamation of "998" alerted all other cops that shots had been fired. I grabbed my shotgun and yanked it free from its clamshell mount on the dash.

No music from any composer ever sounded so beautiful as the sirens that wafted through the hazy sky. The posse soon arrived. A crowd of curious onlooker began to grow, and newly arrived officers set up barricades to keep them back. There was no loss of excitement, though, because the enraged man kept shooting. Firetrucks arrived, and when I saw an ambulance pull up at the end of the street, I hoped I would not be its next occupant.

The hostile situation lasted for hours. I tried to convince the shooter to come out and give up, but the vodka kept a-flowing and the bullets kept a-flying. The shooter communicated through the screen door with incoherent rants punctuated by foul insults.

The dark of evening fell fast as the shots and shouts continued. After several hours of conflict, the man suddenly and without warning kicked the screen door hard. It slammed open with a startling bang, and he marched out the door and down past the smoldering corpse of his pickup truck. He didn't even look at the results of his arson, but kept his face turned down as he headed right at me and his own demise.

Everything shifted into slow motion. I rose up and flopped onto the trunk of my police car. I stared into the oncoming spits of orange discharges from the barrel-end of his weapon. I aimed my shotgun at his chest, and a gun discharged from another cop on my right. At that same instant, my sweaty finger compressed the trigger of my weapon, and it recoiled hard into my shoulder. The blast rang in my ears as a blinding yellow ball of flame spewed from the barrel. I heard the sickening sound of air sucking from the man's gaping chest wounds as he flew back into the dark shadows of the bushes. I stood over the man a few steps later. He lay on his back, blood pooling around him. I stared into his startled eyes. He stared back at me for a few moments, and then the life faded from his face.

I knew right then that both of us would start our respective new journeys. His journey would end in an eternal destiny established by his personal life choices, and my life would be spent struggling to forget that moment.

NOAH'S ARK

CHAPTER 2

MOUNT ARARAT
AND JIM IRWIN

I left law enforcement at the end of the 70s, shortly after the shooting incident, and it threw me into a mid-life crisis. My wife and I moved away from southern California, and my new life in Colorado left me yearning for something to fill the void of lost excitement. I eased into the booming Colorado real estate market of the early 80s as a private developer, partnering with my brother Paul. Paul is one of the most honorable, hard working men I have ever known, and we got off to a fast start in business together. My days were busy and fulfilling, but I still felt a hollow place in my chest just below where my badge had been. I had *enjoyed* the sense of adventure and accomplishment all those years as a cop, and to this day I don't understand why I left the police force so soon after that shooting. In retrospect, maybe God had other plans for me.

FEBRUARY 1985

I first met astronaut Jim Irwin during this time. One of my friends asked me along to share lunch with the living legend, so I joined a small group of Jim Irwin's family and close friends at a restaurant.

Jim and I hit it off immediately. He was a humble guy, lacking the self-importance that his astounding resume of accomplishments might evoke. This was a man who had once been jammed into a small capsule 360 feet above a hissing

Saturn Five rocket. If it had exploded, the million gallons of propellant stored in its tanks would incinerate him to a small lump of charcoal. Jim had logged 295 hours in space as a lunar module pilot and had spent 18 hours and 35 minutes walking on the moon's surface. This was an extraordinary man who had done truly remarkable things, and I had the opportunity to sit and chat with him over a friendly lunch!

Jim and I had many conversations in the years after that day. On one occasion, he described for me the tension of his first space launch as the time dragged on before blastoff. When the countdown sequence finally hit…"Ten-nine-eight-seven-six-five-four-three-two-one-ignition" the events dashed by at a dizzying speed. A tremendous roar of the rockets erupted under Jim as that metal monster shuddered and then thundered to life. Bathed in a flaming cyclone of unimaginable fury, the rocket violently but slowly clawed its way upward. Soon the speed increased, with G-forces that plastered Jim and his two companions back against their seats. The rocket eventually reached the velocity of a bullet and, just minutes later, the blazing daylight morphed into indigo blue and then into consuming blackness that extended forever past the expanse of stars.

When the Apollo 15 space capsule splashed down 13 days later on August 7, 1971, a physically exhausted Jim Irwin emerged safely from the capsule. His boot prints had been left forever stamped in the moon's primordial dust. From that moment onward, Jim held a rare spot in the narrative of mankind's greatest accomplishments. He had walked on the moon! He was a world-wide hero for the ages.

Jim's space travels were not the only stories that interested me. Jim resigned from the Air Force and NASA in 1972 to form the High Flight Foundation, and Jim's excursions on Mount Ararat searching for Noah's ark intrigued me as well. Just thinking about Noah's ark made me dizzy. If the ark were found, it would be the greatest discovery of all time! Jim himself told me it would far surpass even his trip to the moon.

As we talked during first lunch in 1985, I imagined I might join Jim on a search for Noah's ark one day, but my enthusiasm dampened when I learned there was a long list of very qualified people clambering for a spot on Jim's team. There was also a serious danger-factor in hiking high up Mount Ararat, and Jim himself had a bad fall there in August of 1982.

NEAR-DEATH ON ARARAT

He explained to me that he'd been exasperated with himself, because a few hours earlier he had failed in his attempt to reach the icy summit of the nearly 17,000-foot-high Mount Ararat. For perspective, that's about a half-mile higher than Pike's Peak in Colorado. Jim seldom failed at anything, and in irritated frustration, and out of breath, he decided to leave the rest of the climb team and walk down alone to base camp. That was a huge mistake.

Jim told me that he had to stop above a treacherous northern chute high on the mountain. He needed to descend, but he'd reached a treacherous boulder field. The cumbersome metal crampons lashed to his boots had worked great up on the glacier, where their steel fangs bit clean into the slick slab of ice. The crampons were of no use on this boulder field, so he stopped to sit down on a spine of rock jutting out from the snow, and he reached down to undo the leather straps that secured the crampons to his boots.

As he sat laboring over his crampons, a rock above him pulled free. This stone had been nested in volcanic tuft for millennia, but now it bounced along, gaining speed in its decent until it clipped the base of Jim's skull. He was sent cartwheeling like a rag doll down the craggy slope, eventually sliding to a stop on an ice-crusted rock field far below. Jim lay limp, unconscious that his contorted body was a bloody mess. Four big gashes gouged his head, four teeth were knocked out, and his hands were cut so severely that they would swell to almost twice their normal size. His entire body was horribly busted, bludgeoned, bloody, cut, and bruised.

The embers of the sun had long since dissolved into the horizon when the rest of the climb team arrived at base camp. They looked around and asked each other, "Where is Jim?" The team set off to search for the missing Jim Irwin, but their echoes were answered by nothing but mute blackness and a rising icy wind. Their headlamps probed the shadowy crags, but the sheer drop-offs in the mountain proved to be far too deep. It was as if the mountain had swallowed Jim whole.

It became evident that finding Jim at night was impossible, so the team returned to camp. There, they huddled together in the numbing cold and prayed all through the long night. When the seemingly eternal darkness gave way to the glow of morning, they set out again to search for Jim. They knew the prospects were grim; many climbers had gone missing on Ararat and had never been seen again.

Jim's injuries were not his only concern that night. If Jim hadn't regained consciousness, he could have frozen to death. After the fall, though, Jim eventually woke up to brutal pain, and he carefully, agonizingly wriggled out of his back pack and removed his sleeping bag. He spread it out and then ever-so-slowly shimmied inside inch by inch. He then rolled a few feet to a protective spot behind a big boulder to keep himself safe from additional rock falls. Just then, another massive rock from above rumbled down the mountainside. With a thunderous impact, it collided against Jim's stone shield, and that crashing, shaking sound was the last thing Jim knew before lapsing into unconsciousness again.

The rescue team found him about eight o'clock in the morning, inside a sleeping bag stiff with frozen blood. The ice-encrusted fabric had to be peeled away from Jim's open wounds in order to treat them. The 53-year-old retired astronaut had survived the dangers of space, but Ararat had nearly killed him. The Turkish commandos that escorted the climbing group announced that if the team wanted Jim Irwin to survive, they needed to get him off that mountain fast.

The climbers attended to Jim's many injuries, and one of the commandos hiked to a nearby nomad village where shepherd Kurds lived in tents. The soldier frantically asked the Kurdish elder to provide a donkey to carry the injured astronaut down to a hospital. Dispassionately, the elder refused to help. The Kurds vehemently hate the Turks, and the old man was unwilling to cooperate in any way whatsoever. Finally, the Turkish soldier pulled out his pistol and pressed it into the Kurdish leader's forehead, and a donkey was made available.

Over the next several hours, Jim was transported down to a legitimate road, where a car was flagged down to drive him to a medical facility. As Jim told me the story, I studied a grayish scar above his eyebrow as an indelible souvenir from that expedition. It *should* have given me a sober sense of warning about the dangers of venturing out with him onto that mountain. Instead, an excited hope rose in me that one day I would be able to climb that beast called Ararat, and I would be the one to find Noah's ark.

HOW I GOT STARTED

A month later, and without warning, Jim Irwin asked me if I wanted to help with an ark expedition. I was instantly swept up in the exhilaration of going along with him, and my mind filled with grandiose visions. I fancied myself with an ice axe in hand, high upon an Ararat glacier, gazing through the distorted optics of ancient ice. In my mind, the rotting timbers of Noah's ark stared back at me. I would change history!

That moment of unbridled vanity soon dissolved into a puddle of realism. Jim wasn't asking me to *join* him on the actual journey; he only wanted my assistance to raise money for a High Flight expedition that others would take.

Still, I felt honored to be a part of the adventure in any capacity, and I accepted the opportunity. I recruited my brother Paul, and we brainstormed about efficient ways to produce funds. Since we were in real estate development, we came up with an idea to build a new house: "The Noah's Ark House" we called it. We would sell this house for a profit, then donate the proceeds to the High Flight Foundation. Paul and I lent the project money up front and used our contacts to get discounts on labor and materials. The house sold quickly, and it gave us a tidy profit.

The day after the property closed, Paul and I handed a sizable check to Jim. It must have impressed him, because the next day he invited me to join him on the expedition to

Turkey. I was excited about the prospect of going, but I also felt uncomfortable with the perceived pay-for-play. Jim eased my concern by explaining that he needed security in the hostile Turkey environs where terrorists were plentiful. I had law enforcement experience, and he said I would be a valuable asset.

That's how I got started exploring the historical locations of the Bible. I had left law enforcement behind, but God filled the resulting hole with a promise of new adventure, and it sprang from a "chance" encounter with a living legend.

CHAPTER 3

CLIMBING ARARAT

ARK PREPARATIONS

I had entered my 30s by the time Jim Irwin invited me to join him in Turkey. While I had received a full football scholarship in college, the following decade had added a slight paunch to my stomach, and it needed an exit strategy. Searching for Noah's ark required both physical and technical preparations, so I started jogging. I made daily lung-searing runs to the top of Cheyenne Canyon in Colorado Springs. I also solicited the help of local Colorado mountaineers to hone my limited climbing skills.

On one of my training climbs, I joined two younger climbers to tackle some high altitude cliffs above Leadville, Colorado. One of these tutors was a cocky young guy named Steve, and the lesson for the day was rappelling off of a sheer cliff. The other tutor and I watched from below as Steve tied off his rope on an egg-shaped boulder at the top of a small cliff and prepared to rappel down the rock face. It had rained the night before, and just as Steve dropped over the edge, the boulder rotated a few inches in its muddy socket. The rope slipped over the round crown of the boulder, and Steve fell the full distance to the rocky ground below. The impact was a sickening, lung grunting thud, and his leg snapped like a dry twig. He continued on in the momentum of his fall, careening down an angular slab of granite and finally sliding to a stop on a patch of dirty summer snow below us. He left a trailing smear of blood after him.

We rushed down to where Steve had landed. His foot and ankle dangled hideously, and a jagged shard of bloody bone protruding from his lower leg. Sickened disbelief washed across the other climber's face, and he just walked in circles mumbling incoherently. I had seen many things much more shocking than this during my years as a cop, so I took charge of tending to Steve. I stabilized and splinted Steve's leg using a nearby stick and some duct tape from Steve's backpack. (To this day, I always carry duct tape on all my trips.)

I asked Steve whether he wanted us to go for help or to try and carry him out. Could he handle the pain if we carried him? He wanted for us to get him down right away, and I saw his point because it would be dark by the time we'd have returned for him. We had no cell phones in those days, and our options were limited.

It was a torturous effort getting Steve off that mountain. We didn't carry him completely; we each took a side and supported him as he took one agonizing step after another on his good leg. His face twisted and tightened at the slightest jostle, but Steve was one tough guy as we covered the miles back to our car. It still amazes me how we got him down from there. I doubt few other men could have endured such constant pain without passing out. We finally reached the car about twilight, and in relief we zipped him away to a hospital. After that whole fiasco, I had a new respect for gravity and the urgent need to be in top shape.

TROUBLE IN TURKEY

I made my first expedition to seek Noah's ark in 1986, and I discovered it's not a simple thing to just go climb Mount Ararat. When we arrived in Turkey, we had to start the frustrating process of getting climbing permits from the Turkish government. In the end, Jim Irwin obtained permits that were especially amazing because they allowed us to actually fly an airplane around the mountain. That was fortuitous, because a plane could cover more ground in a minute than we might cover during weeks of laboriously searching by foot. If something that looked like the ark were sighted from our aircraft, then our climb team would hike up into the mountain to investigate the object. That was the idea.

Of course, our adventure didn't quite go as planned. Pilot Dick Bright and two Dutch photographers flew a rented Cessna 206 around Mount Ararat on the scouting mission. They made several passes around the mountain, capturing points of interest on film while the rest of us waited anxiously at the airport for their return. That's when the trouble started. As Bright made his approach to Erzurum Airport, the Turkish secret police radioed him and told him he couldn't land because the airport was "closed for the night."

"That's absurd," Bright erupted over the radio. "Do they expect us to stay in the air all night?"

After arguing with the control tower, Bright landed the plane with only vapors of fuel left. The Turks accused him, and by association all of us, of violating Russian and Iranian airspace. It was an infraction nearly impossible to monitor or prove, but the allegations earned us a rude escort back to our hotel, where we were placed under house arrest.

We were not incarcerated in dark cells or beaten. The hiccup didn't last long at all, considering. It had been a long day, but after pressure from the international press corps, the Turkish police released the famous Jim Irwin, along with his team.

There was something about the intrigue of it that I enjoyed, though. I loved the risk, the uncertainty of the hunt, the adventure of it all. We didn't get to climb Mount Ararat that year, but I left Turkey with a longing to return and try again to find the missing ark. It seems I had developed a bad case of *ark fever*.

I climbed Mount Ararat many times in the years that followed. In studying about Noah's ark, I discovered that a puzzling amount of mythology surrounds the ark's location. Various stories have the ark concealed in any number of ice-gorged, inaccessible or forbidden canyons and crevasses on Mount Ararat. Depending which account one reads, or which person one listens to, the ark survives as an angular, barge like structure jutting out of a glacier. Some searchers say they've seen the ark peering up at them—a murky, spectral shadow floating beneath the surface of an ice sheet—as they've flown over in a passing jet. Others feel certain they've spotted its rounded bow nestled among boulders of a sheer canyon wall. Yet, with all the alleged sightings—and, more recently, with the aid of modern satellite imagery—there remains no convincing photographic evidence of Noah's ark on Mount Ararat in Turkey.

THE AHORA GORGE

Of course, traditions tend to grip tightly on the popular mind, and most people still expect to find the ark on the mountain where Jim Irwin had his near-fatal tumble. One day, I received an urgent plea from my old friend Dick Bright the pilot. Bright called me up from Erzurum, Turkey, sounding breathless with what seemed like urgent and amazing news.

"*I think I found it!*" he repeated over and over in his gravelly voice.

"Found what?" I asked.

"The ark!" he barked.

"Where?"

"The Ahora Gorge," he said. "Low into the Abich II glacier, embedded in the cliff face." Then he added with a whimsical twist, "I've got a *picture*."

Turkey was completely off my list as a candidate site at this point, but Bright was a smart guy and his news demanded that I check it out. When Bright's package containing the "famous picture" of his ark appeared at my door, I ripped it open and scanned his discovery with curiosity. Indeterminately dark and grainy, awash in the canyon's bleak shadows, the photo framed a section of a fractured rock face that overlooked a ledge scattered with boulders. At the center, an angular, flint-edged object of uncertain size did look vaguely boat-shaped, but I'd seen hundreds of rocks just like it scattered across Ararat's face. Everyone mistakes rocks for boats on the mountain. A closer look revealed to my satisfaction that his structure was nothing more than a boxy, pointy-shaped boulder. The phone rang just as I decided to give the photo, and the trip to Turkey, an enthusiastic thumbs down.

Bright is a persuasive guy, however; and I did need to get some additional footage high on the mountain for a documenatry I was producing on the ark searches. So I begrudgingly agreed to go on the trip. A few weeks later, I was walking across the wide Anatolian plain towards Mount Ararat. It was a decision I would soon regret.

At the mountain's base we gathered the pack horses, which were rearing and snorting against their bits. Our Kurdish guides struggled to keep them from bolting, and I suspect the horses knew something we didn't.

The horses were not the only team participants in a nervous fit. Bright told me the Kurdish guides were fearful that the Turkisk military would discover our clandestine climb up the mountain. Bright supposedly had garnered assurances of safety from ranking Turkish authorities, but our guides seemed scared to death for some reason. They insisted that we needed to hike at night to avoid being seen.

To climb Ararat during the day takes every bit of courage and stamina one can muster, but to attempt the trek at night is plain absurdity. Added to that, we were told we would *not* have the use of our flashlights. Which made the venture beyond the realm of insanity. Lashing our packs haphazardly to the horses, we stumbled off into the darkness.

Perhaps the best climber in our party, Bob Stuplich, suddenly shouted, "Wait!" Stuplich had scaled the heights of Ararat numerous times in his life, yet he cried out in a panic, "I can't find my backpack!" He ran from horse to horse, fumbling feverishly in the dark for his pack. The Kurds tugged angrily at the horses, but Stuplich jerked back. "I'm not going up that mountain without my backpack!" He knew well the terrors of Mount Ararat, where summit temperatures can dip as low as 40 degrees below zero at times, and where winds can scream by at 150 miles-per-hour. As he frisked the horses, I reached for my flashlight, cupping my hand over the bulb so we could see a few inches in the dark.

"*No lights!*" the elder Kurd hissed. He bounded over and ripped the flashlight from my hand.

Stuplich finally found his pack strapped awkwardly to a horse. He relaxed, and at last we resumed our manic trek into the Anatolian steppe. I'd never seen such a chaotic, panicky start to an expedition.

"Why are the guides so petrified?" I asked Bright between breaths. "Haven't the Turks been compensated for our safe passage?"

He shrugged and said, "We've just got to keep going."

My traveling companions that night included Bob Stuplich, Dick Bright, photographer David Banks, Canadian fireman George Kralik (invited along as our medic), and the two skittish Kurds. We hiked fast, blind to all but the plain's most obvious shapes and forms. I navigated by sound, keeping pace and staying on track to the muffled clop of horse hooves. I'd regained a degree of composure, having momentarily forgotten about typical dangers like twisted ankles and venomous snakes. For long moments, I simply stared up at the outline of the dark mountain, now eerily silhouetted against a vast canopy of stars. It seemed so far away, so impossibly distant. It appeared almost unapproachable.

We trudged five miles across the plain at the base of the mountain, trekking through an endless, meandering network of rugged ravines that girdled the lower basin. It was only after several hours that we started a mild ascent. We walked on and on, climbing ever farther into the dense mantle of darkness. We crossed sharp, invisible draws and shuffled down into rocky washes and dead-end cul-de-sacs, and each step began to take a toll on our cramping legs and backs. For a few miles we stayed together, keeping a compact perimeter about the horses, but as the hours passed, each man found his own stride, and the team spread out across the slope. At times it felt like climbing alone, marching silently in the dark with a nervous wind as my only companion. I occasionally fell off pace and had to stop to listen for . . . yes, the faint sound of a hoof or boot kicking a stone or trampling the brush. All night, I stared up at the mountain, still so mystifyingly far away. At this snail's pace, I didn't see how we'd ever make it to the top.

At about 1:30 a.m., just as we began to enter the lower foothills, the moon came out and illuminated the entire plain. It seemed a miracle that this thin, glowing wafer could brighten the flats like daylight. To eyes dilated by hours of walking in darkness, the moon ignited the heavens like a supernova.

We walked nonstop for ten weary hours up Ararat's western haunch, stopping to rest only when the first threads of dawn glowed drowsily over the eastern plateau. By 5:30 a.m. our furious pace had paid off. We'd chopped a sizable chunk out of Ararat's interminable plain. What had, a few hours earlier, seemed insurmountable, in the cheering light of morning showed itself a doable climb. Standing exhausted on a flattened patch of meadow at nine thousand feet, we pulled off our boots and unfurled our sleeping bags. There we collapsed on the ground and slept as if drugged.

We didn't rest long. Soon we roused and continued on upward to Lake Kop on Ararat's northern flank. I'd seen the lake from the air, and I knew the glacier-fed pool acted as the traditional low base camp of veteran ark searchers. It also served as our crucial first water refill stop, and we felt we had arrived just in time. At our blistering pace, we'd literally burned through our water supplies, and we all looked forward to reaching the lake and enjoying its crisp, fresh water.

The moment the horses caught the scent, they charged toward the lake and started sucking like industrial Shop-Vacs. We arrived seconds later, ready to follow suit...and then stopped short. Instead of the crystalline blue, pristine mountain lake we'd expected, we stared in disbelief at a slime pit pocked with hundreds of sheep hoofprints and freckled with floating dollops of sheep dung. The sight alone, not to mention the smell, made me queasy. We felt dead on our feet with only a few swigs left in our bottles, but we had to turn away. There would be no refills at Lake Kop.

By 7:30 p.m., the sun slowly slunk into the plain behind us. We had arrived at twelve thousand feet, where a flat patch of wind-battered grass nestled in the shadow of a cold cliff wall. We'd been charging hard for twenty-two straight hours with only one short rest and one other water stop. Our bottles ran dry as dust, and we desperately needed liquid.

Too tired for words, we threw down a makeshift camp and dragged out our portable gas stove to heat a dinner of freeze-dried chicken casserole. As the others sprawled on the tundra, too exhausted to move, I climbed fifty yards over a small rise to a large slab of melting ice wedged into a stand of boulders. Below it, just as the Kurds promised, sat a drizzling pool of melt-off ice, ten-feet wide, but just like Lake Kop, it brimmed with hoofprints and floating sheep dung.

I had no choice. I didn't expect to find a water fountain up this high, and the guys below, cracked-lipped, cotton mouthed and dispirited, needed rehydration, and *fast*. Against my strongest impulses, I knelt down and stuck my filter into the turbid pool to keep out as many pollutants as possible. Returning to camp, I didn't have the heart to tell the others the condition of the water they so greedily guzzled. *Ignorance is bliss,* I thought. They didn't seem to mind the green bits of gunk swirling about in their bottles. Then, we pulled out our sleeping bags and settled down for a much-needed night of sleep.

We set out again the next morning, but it wasn't long before our hike was met with the WOMP, WOMP, WOMP of helicopter rotors speeding up over the rise.

"Get down! Get down!" Bright yelled, and like panicked deer we ditched our packs in the rocks and wedged ourselves under a granite overhang. I knew that if the Turkish military chopper—likely searching the peak for Kurdish rebels—saw us or mistook us for Kurdish freedom fighters, they'd blast us off the mountain.

"Pray them away," Bright whispered desperately under his breath. "Pray them away."

The chopper buzzed overhead for 90 minutes, skimming Parrot Glacier down to the fringe of the gorge before sweeping its way up towards the summit. When the whirl of rotors finally faded below us and disappeared, we couldn't believe our good fortune. The next day, our Kurdish organizer Micah contacted us on his cell phone and told us that the Turkish military had ambushed several Kurds near Lake Kop just hours after we left the area. The subsequent gun battle left seven Turks and four Kurds dead on the mountainside.

We were alive and unharmed, but we had suffered another painful delay. Every hour of daylight was precious.

We pulled our packs out of the rocks and hiked up a harrowing path through new vistas of sharp, rolling scree. The next two hours were spent hiking into the stratosphere, fighting against an unseasonably hot breeze that surprised Stuplich, who'd been blown off the peak by icy blasts at this height.

Figure 1: Cehennem Dere at the Ahora Gorge. Photo by Bob Stuplich.

Our team finally made it to the mighty ice cliffs known as the Cehennem Dere. We hiked on further until Bright called out, "This is the place!"

The others followed Stuplich and me as we walked over to look into the maw of the canyon.

"That's where I saw the ark," Bright pointed down into a breathtaking chasm two miles wide and two miles deep. We followed his pointing finger along the ice, peering over the edge into a rift far wider than the Grand Canyon.

We stood there for a long while, scanning the flinty cliffs and shadows. At long last Bright spotted his target: a large, angular object embedded in the opposite cliff face. It appeared sharp, with a nautical nose that angled down from the side of the gorge just like in the picture. We surveyed it from several angles with our binoculars. As expected, it proved to be nothing but ice-covered rock sticking out from the canyon wall.

I climbed all the way up here for this? I thought.

The next day at base-camp, I awoke to find Bright sitting by himself on a rock, looking gloomy. The Kurds had huddled off by themselves near the horses, and were shouting into their cell phone.

"They're talking with Micah," Bright said. "He called to warn us that the *gendarmes* are on the mountain." I looked back at the Kurds, fussing and fuming, looking more agitated than ever. "They're scared to death," Bright continued. "Micah, too. He says he's very afraid for us." Bright stared off into the distance, then added, "Micah says he won't be able to pick us up where he dropped us off. We'll have to go down the mountain a different way."

That grabbed my attention.

"A different way?" I said in disbelief. "What do you mean, Dick, a *different* way?"

"Remember the helicopter?" he asked. "There was a gun battle yesterday near Lake Kop. It stirred up the Turkish military, and now they're combing the mountain for rebels."

We were with Kurdish guides, and the Kurds were the mortal enemies of the Turkish military. That was the bottom line.

"We'll have to descend the southwest side of the mountain," Bright said.

The southwest slope? I'd never heard of anyone descending the southwest slope on Ararat. I doubted even Stuplich knew that terrain, but we had no time to debate the point. The Kurds had already packed the horses and were shouting at us, *"We go! We go!"* I hated to see the raw fear in their faces.

We descended all day long. The afternoon turned to dusk, and steep canyons changed into high foothills. Mild breezes transitioned into a sweltering heat. Traversing down the southwest side of the mountain, we entered a patchwork of smooth, wide pastures bleeding into long, lazy valleys. *Not bad,*

I thought. Until I peered over a wide ledge and stared down into a steep drop-off.

I suddenly understood why the Turks never patrolled these cliffs. No fool would attempt an ascent up this suicide precipice. With a moonless night fast upon us, we shimmied down off the ledge and found ourselves instantly slipping and clawing down a steep granite wall into a waking nightmare. The near-vertical pitch would have made for treacherous climbing during broad daylight. But at *night,* with *horses,* our prospects could only be described as insane. I have terrible night vision and, without even a trail, I had to feel and fumble my way down every foot of the slope, using my ski pole to probe the large, empty black spaces in front of me. Pulling the horse along, I'd take a hesitant step down into the rolling scree, probe the dark, take another baby step, then another, sometimes poking my pole where the next step should be and feeling nothing—anywhere.

The horses, who could see into the darkness, whimpered and whined with each step, making pitiful crying sounds as they wobbled and heaved under their heavy loads. Their hooves kicked up sparks on the granite as they skidded and clopped down the winding course. I found myself following the sparks of the horse in front of me, keeping a hand on its bony haunch, tapping my pole for a foothold, then nudging the horse along and feeling my way down through the crumbling rubble.

If the Kurds knew a way down, they didn't share it with us. I could hear them chattering frantically back and forth in the distance, clearly petrified themselves. They cursed the horses and refused to wait on any of us. In the interminable darkness, our team soon found itself spread across the cliff face. It was now every man for himself.

For years I climbed mountains and took risks, but this easily ranked as the most grueling, frightening seven hours of my life. As I inched blindly through the darkness, my pulse pounded in my temples and my tongue felt like wallpaper paste. Hour after agonizing hour passed as we made our way down into the valley, where we encountered another sea of rocks. I kept praying for the moon to come out, but it remained in pensive seclusion. We caught up with the Kurds in the valley and found them chattering on the cell phone with Micah our van driver. They gave us another shocking bit of bad news: Micah said the military had formed a noose around the base of the mountain, and he couldn't pick us up where we had planned. This meant walking another five miles across the plain to meet him at an alternate site.

My heart dropped, but I didn't have time to feel sorry for myself. In that instant, military flares exploded over our heads, shattering the blackness with petrifying hues of pink. Dogs started barking, and we could hear trucks grinding their gears in the distance. The panicked Kurds set off at a wild sprint across the valley floor, screaming back at us, "Go! Go! Go!" We raced after them, yanking our horses and straining to keep pace.

We avoided the patrols, but that final slog across the plain nearly ended us. Completely out of water, we had long lapsed into the advanced stages of dehydration. I hadn't sweated for hours. My contacts had dried up and fallen out, so I put on my glasses. I worried most about Banks, our photographer, who'd gone without water the longest. His parched and blistered throat made it almost impossible for him to speak. I could hear him breathing hard, silently counting his steps, and I sensed he was in anguish over having decided to make this journey—possibly never to return to his wife.

"Bob," he finally croaked through cracked lips, "I'll make it, but . . . my God, I'm so thirsty."

Up ahead, Bright haggled with Micah over the cell phone. "Tell him to bring water," I interrupted. "Whatever he does, don't let him forget to bring us water."

Flares exploded in the sky behind us as we trotted across the plain. Suddenly we all stopped and listened.

"Hear that?" I asked.

The faint groan of gunning engines had gotten louder. So had the barking. The dogs had caught our scent, which set us running again as we tried to stay out of range of the hounds, flares, and circling flashlights. I expected any second to hear the whop whop of the blades and feel the wind of a helicopter as it zoomed across the steppe and swooped down upon us.

I didn't know how much longer my body could hold out, but I kept pushing, trying to encourage Banks along. When we finally crested a small knoll and saw the flashing headlights of Micah's van, my watch said 2:00 a.m. The Kurds circled the horses to make sure no one followed us. Then, as we approached the van, the doors burst open and five Kurds jumped out and grabbed our mounts. Without a word, our guides vanished with them into the night.

We hopped in the van, and Micah sped off down the road. No one spoke until we were safely out of range of the flares. Finally Micah turned and gave us a broad grin.

"Welcome home, gentlemen."

"Where's the water?" I demanded.

"I'm sorry," he said with a frown, "but the military stopped me earlier at a checkpoint. I had to give them all my water to get through."

I could feel my throat closing up, and we still had more than an hour's drive to reach Dogubayazıt. I looked over at Banks, who was clearly drained by the news. I doubted he would remain conscious for another hour; his eyes looked like they were being sucked into his skull. Just then, Micah pointed at the floor of the van to a dusty six-pack of beer.

"Help yourself," he said. Like starving men, Stuplich, Bright, and Kralik grabbed cans and ripped off the pull tops, spewing warm sprays of fermented foam across the van's interior. As they guzzled, I grabbed two cans and handed one to Banks. I could have gulped down that warm, flat beer without even opening the can; I had never been that thirsty in my life. As I put the warm can to my lips, I noticed that Banks wasn't drinking.

"C'mon," I said relieved by the gift of liquid.

The others, already lost in the giddy postmortem of our adventure, gleefully swigged beer and replayed our close calls and outrageous exploits. Banks stared at me helplessly, eyes empty, his lips cracked and bleeding. With a voice reduced to a scratchy whisper, he said, "Bob . . . I . . . I . . . ." He paused to compose himself. "I'm a recovering alcoholic. I can't drink that."

I lowered my beer as he continued. "I haven't had a drink of alcohol in fourteen years, and I promised my wife I'd never drink again."

He stared at the can in his trembling hand, then slowly handed it to me. He closed his eyes and pushed his head back against the van's wall.

I just could not drink any of the beer, not in front of a suffering friend. It turned out to be a long, thirsty, dusty, bone-jarring ride back to Dogubayazıt.

Micah finally drove into the gravel driveway of our fleabag hotel, and weakly we climbed out. A case of water sat on a table inside the doorway of the rundown café. Ripping the caps off the plastic bottles, we drank the water so fast it draind from our lips and soaked our shirt fronts and the laps of our pants and dripped onto our boots. We drank and drank until our stomachs swelled out as hard as cast iron kettles.

That was it. I agreed with myself that I would never ever climb that mountain in Turkey. Ever!

That is, until I receive a phone call late in the summer of 2004.

CHAPTER 4

PAY DAY

I never required nor requested any fees for my services in searching for Noah's ark, but that didn't mean people weren't interested in hiring me. In 2004, I got the biggest payday of my life from a man named Dan out in Hawaii. Dan called me one day and said, "Just name your price, and I will pay it to you if you can climb Ararat and photograph the ark."

Dan had my attention as he went on to explain himself. He told me that he possessed satellite imagery showing beams from the ark's remains, and he was even able to see the inside cavity of the ark itself. I had heard similar claims before, but I was taken aback when he offered me a lot of money to go check it out. I had never considered myself a paid mercenary in all my explorations. I'd gone hunting for the ark and other lost artifacts because I'd wanted to find them. That was my simple motivation.

But my kids do like to eat. I decided to hear Dan out.

Dan told me he had located his object on the north side of the mountain at about 16,400 feet. He was utterly convinced he was looking at the remains of the ark through those satellite images. I had a speaking engagement in New Zealand within a few weeks, so I decided to arrange a stopover in Hawaii to meet with Dan and study his images.

Dan had retained a foremost expert in satellite imagery analysis, who was even more convinced than Dan that they had images of the corpse of Noah's ark. However, I was less optimistic when he showed me the pictures. Dan sensed my lack of interest in the project, and he said, "I will pay whatever you want, because there have been many who have tried to get to my object but have failed."

I told Dan that it was not just the climb itself that was the problem. Anybody hiking that mountain had to get past the Kurds who were in a civil war with the Turkish government. If we were to get to the object in question, we'd have to pay bribes all around. That would be one tricky part in all of this.

Dan almost pleaded with me, but I explained that besides the troubles between the Kurds and Turkish military, his object happened to be in a near-impossible location to reach. It was perched on the north face of the mountain, nestled in a steep glacier. If that was not enough, it was getting into a bad time of year. We were nearing October, and Ararat weather during the fall months can dump as much as six feet of snow at a time. If we were buried high on that mountain, our bodies would be brought down the following July.

None of my arguments dissuaded Dan, and he seemed even more determined. He could smell the greatest discovery of all time right in front of him, and he wasn't going to let go. So, I made him an informal proposal, thinking it would end the search for good. I told Dan that if he were to wire the ludicrous sum of $150,000 into my account by the close of business that coming Friday, I would do it.

I went home certain this huge sum would completely scare him off, but surprise surprise, all the money landed in my account the next Friday. That same day, I called my old climbing partner Bob Stuplich and told him that I would pay him very well if he would go with me to Turkey and photograph the object. Bob was the best climber I have ever climbed with, and he knew Ararat better than any westerner. I knew Bob would have gone if I'd just offered him an airline ticket and food, but this was a risky proposition, and I told him that. After I explained where the object was on the mountain, Bob expressed a rare moment of concern, but he still quickly accepted my offer as I'd anticipated he would. The trip was a go, but I knew there were a million things that could still spell disaster.

The day before I took off to Turkey, I spoke for a church men's group in the Shenandoah Valley of Virginia. Like a real airhead, I tore my calf muscle running up a hill playing paint ball with the guys. I tried walking, but I couldn't even take the smallest of steps. The next afternoon, I painfully inched my way onto the plane bound for Istanbul. Like I said, there were a million things that could go wrong, and this was the first of many that did.

My buddies Jon Arnold and Kim Orr also agreed to join us. They would set up at base camp in case of emergencies. After stops in Istanbul and Ankara, we arrived in Erzurum. From there, we took a four-hour cab ride to the mountain. Now came the tricky part. I would have to get permission to climb Ararat from both the Turkish military and the Kurdistan Worker's Party (PKK) guerilla fighters. Then, we still had a long and hazardous climb to the object high on the mountain.

We drove to the small village of Dogubayazıt at the base of Ararat, looking for our old savvy guide Micah. I still remembered the warm beer from the last time in his van. I hoped he would still be around when we arrived, but when we hunted down Micah's father, we learned Micah was in jail for killing a Turkish man in a drunken brawl at a wedding. Micah was out of the picture, paying his debt to Turkish society, which meant it was time for our backup plan. Unfortunately, I had no backup plan.

Sitting at an outdoor restaurant in the crisp night air, I stared at the looming mountain, thinking I had failed before I even got started. I tried to keep a game face for my team. I talked the situation over with them, when a man approached our table and introduced himself to us as Micah's younger brother Si. He was a well-dressed Kurd of about thirty, with short, coarse black hair almost the same color as his penetrating dark eyes. Si scooted up a chair and sat down, telling us that he had recently been on the mountain and had found over twenty skeletons of Kurds, their bones bleaching in the sun with their rusting rifles by their sides. He explained that the Turks were very hard to deal with because of all the fighting. Then, with a crooked smile and narrowing eyes he said, "I assume you are here to climb the mountain. I can help."

In short order, we asked Si if he could help us reach an object that we wanted to photograph on the Abich Glacier. Si immediately bragged that he had many contacts in the military

33

and that perhaps he could make a deal with them for safe transport up the mountain. Then I saw the glint of chrome from a 9mm pistol stuck into his waist band. "But," he added, "it will be very expensive." He clasped his hands behind his head as if to say, "You guys have no other choice but to use my services." He was right.

We had a situation. Some 11,000 military troops were stationed around the lower elevations of the mountain in an attempt to control about 2,000 PKK terrorists higher on the mountain. The factions were locked in brutal civil war, and we were supposed to pay off both the Turkish military and the Kurdish guerillas just to let us walk through their ongoing hostilities. We had to climb a monster mountain with ominous perils of its own and find our way to Dan's object. And our success in accomplishing these things seemed to be dropped into the hands of a shifty, unproven character we had just met, who was negotiating his services by flashing a handgun in front of me.

Any motivations of ego and adventure had long faded away inside me. I contemplated the shifting dynamics of my predicament in my mind. I had more than $30,000 taped under the insoles of my shoes in $100 bills for the needed bribes. I must have stood about a full inch taller with all that money stacked under me.

Si had no idea how much money I really had when he invited me to his home for dinner to continue negotiations. When I arrived, we sat down in his dining room, where women with scarves across their faces cooked food over the glowing coals of a smoky fire pit. Si took out his pistol and set it on the table in front of me and then coldly said, "Take off your shoes." I swallowed hard and asked, "Why?" He told me that it was a Muslim home and it is the custom that shoes are not worn. He then pointed to the front door and instructed me to leave my shoes outside on the front steps. His house fronted a narrow street where villagers milled all over the place, so after I left my shoes with 30,000 crisp Yankee dollars taped inside, I knew some lucky thief would be the wealthiest guy in the village. I was most relieved, however, when after dinner the shoes and money were both still there.

Our plan was soon set. I agreed to the steep fees imposed by Si for climbing approval, and I tried to be as hopeful as possible that my leg would get better in time to climb. The plan was simple: get up fast, get to the object, take a photo of whatever it was, and get the heck off that mountain. There was nothing cluttered about it, but then again, there were a million things that could go wrong.

We stayed in a small cement hovel at the edge of town to avoid notice by the locals—police or military. Two days later, at 4:00 a.m., Si kicked at our door and said, "We go." A Russian-made jeep-like contraption rolled up in the dark and we stacked our packs on top. Stuplich, Kim, Jon, Si, a Kurdish climber named Juma and I jammed ourselves inside a space made for no more than four men. We drove around the west side of the mountain on a paved highway that eventually turned toward Ahora village on Ararat's north slope. There we bounced along on a narrow dirt road that wound its way up the lower slopes, where three men armed with Kalashnikov automatic rifles met us. It was now early daylight. The men asked a few questions of Si, who glanced over at us and explained the situation.

The men waved us past with no problem. Si turned to me with unabashed arrogance, saying, "Those were Turkish military men. We are free to go up."

It appeared that our sizable payment of passage was working for now, but we still had the Kurdish PKK to worry about higher on the mountain.

The squatty little vehicle struggled up the rutted path. It churned through the dust mile after jarring mile, heading for the higher elevations. Fields of wheat, endless stacked rock walls, and children herding sheep and cattle surrounded us. The children were young, barely able to lift the big sticks they used to whack the bony rumps of cows and prod stubborn sheep along.

We continued to climb. Small clusters of black, wool nomad tents dotted the rolling hills, framed by sharply cut bluffs. Kurdish women carried large plastic water jugs lashed to their backs, their brightly colored dresses and flowing scarves billowing in the crisp mountain breeze. Men with bushy black mustaches on their leathery faces watched as we drove past, but did nothing.

At about 8,000 feet, we came to a nomad village on the side of a valley. Five wool tents framed a large flock of sheep. Several young children stopped their play and scampered over to greet us. Smoke swirled around an open fire tended by Kurdish women who quickly covered their faces with their multi-colored cotton scarves.

Figure 2: Kurdish villagers. Photo by Bob Stuplich.

"We stay here," Si said, unlatching the creaking door of the jeep and stepping out onto the hard ground. A stocky, unshaven Kurd of about forty-five, the elder of the camp, strode over and hugged Si. "These are friends," Si said. "We will be safe in his camp."

That was comforting, because I knew we were right in the middle of terrorist country. As I got out of the crammed jeep and stretched, I couldn't help noticing a peg-legged young man standing in the distance. He stared at us, standing with a wild-looking, dirty man who clutched a beat-up shotgun. The pair never took their eyes off of us as we unloaded our gear.

"Who are they?" I asked.

Si whispered, "The man with one leg is a rebel fighter with the PKK. His leg was recently cut off because of a bullet wound he received from a Turkish soldier. The other is famous."

"Famous? How?"

"He has killed 24 people. They call him the 'Young Assassin.'"

"Charming," I grumbled.

My sarcasm was wasted on Si. "The Turkish government pays poor Kurds who live below the mountain to be village guards. They provide information against the PKK guerilla freedom fighters, but anyone who helps the Turks is targeted for death by the Young Assassin. He slips into their homes at night and slits their throats while they sleep. He then stuffs money in their mouths as a warning for others not to provide information against the PKK."

The assassin glanced at me, his vacant black eyes mirroring his dark, vacuous soul. He knew that Si was talking about him, and he smiled at me with nicotine-stained teeth, cradling his shotgun.

Si's cell phone chirped from his pocket. After a loud and animated conversation, he hung up and explained that a Kurdish official higher on the mountain had instructed that only one member of our group would be allowed to climb up. He would have to go with one Kurdish climber and be escorted part way up the mountain by the assassin. The caller also demanded that we take a prescribed route up the mountain because the PKK was operating out of a nearby cave. Without hesitating, Stuplich said he would be the one to head up with the two Kurds. Si told me that Juma would go with Stuplich and the young assassin. It was a hastily arranged plan, and after another round of animated discussions between the Kurds, it was set. In a way, I was secretively glad I was not going up on the climb, as my leg was still hurting badly. I probably couldn't have made it up the mountain anyway. If all went well, Bob Stuplich would locate the object the next afternoon and snap away with his digital camera at whatever it turned out to be. The climbers were packed in ten minutes, and with game smiles, Stuplich and the two Kurds headed up into swirling clouds.

After the climbers left, a young boy from the nomad's village brought us each a steaming cup of tea thick with sugar. Si took a sip of the sweet brew and lowered himself onto a big rock. He rubbed his stubbled face and said, "Six days ago, three Russians went up the same route as your friend and the two Kurds. The Russians did not pay the PKK as we have done, and because of that, they were killed. Shot in the head. It was a most unfortunate

37

thing to have happen. I need to renegotiate some extra pay to avoid an unfortunate accident from happening to Bob."

"And how much will that cost?" I asked, knowing I was dealing with a pirate. He had maneuvered me to the end of the gangplank, and I had no choice but to pay him. As if his words were carried on the winds of total sincerity, he told me, "Any additional fees will be minimal, to be discussed later of course."

I set up camp with our remaining team members, praying for Stuplich and Juma to make it up and down the mountain alive. A majestic orange sun greeted us in the morning, and news from Stuplich via Juma's cell phone reported tough going. The assassin had retreated at about the 10,000-foot level the night before, leaving Stuplich and Juma on their own to make it to the ice cap. Stuplich told Si that loose rock scree and sheer cliffs had stalled their efforts, and they might not be able to go any farther. Massive rocks were crashing around them, and in order to traverse these treacherous boulder fields, Stuplich and Juma had to time the rate of the falling rocks, then scurry across the bare face of the mountainside before another loose boulder from above came hurtling down on them.

"There were so many rocks falling," Stuplich would later say, "that it was difficult to see how the mountain itself would be any more than a nub a hundred years from now."

It was treacherous climbing, and Stuplich became angry that Si had sent them up such a difficult route. At 10:00 a.m., Si got another call on his cell phone from Juma, who had badly twisted his knee when his boot slid off a rock. "Juma was in horrible pain," Stuplich later told me.

Si hung up, and with a concerned expression said, "We have to go find Juma. Bob cannot carry Juma's seventy-pound pack down with his own, and Juma says he will not leave his pack up there."

Stuplich told Juma he was going to head down and drop off his heavy load and return to get him, because he was the only one who could find Juma again. I thought it a poor plan because it would be too exhausting for Stuplich. I remember his telling me many times that you never leave someone alone on the mountain. Perhaps he thought that Juma was experienced and had enough food, water, and warm clothes to make it for the time being. I tried to talk to Stuplich on the phone to tell him to stay put, because we would climb up and help them, but we lost the connection and I couldn't re-connect.

I looked at my leg, which only six days earlier had been so bad I could hardly walk. Now I was thinking of going up the lip of the Ahora Gorge to assist an injured climber. My friend Kim couldn't go; he was lying in his tent after eating some unsanitary food, beyond sick with dysentery. Jon Arnold had no real mountaineering experience, so he wasn't an option in such dire circumstances. So that left it to me.

We hurled our packs onto the jeep's luggage rack and drove up a wisp of dirt road, trying to squeeze in a little more altitude before getting out and heading up on foot. We made it about a mile to a twenty-tent nomad camp bustling with people. Jon remained with the jeep to guard it while Si and I headed off on the rescue climb.

When we got out of the jeep, I hurriedly shouldered my pack. I took a quick look at Jon, who stood alone with fifty Kurds gawking at him as if he were from Mars. Most nomads have never seen a westerner. It was also strange for Jon, because it was his first time traveling overseas. It was a slight moment of levity, but my smile dissolved when I glanced up at the big mountain, crowned with testy clouds through which I caught intermittent glimpses of treacherous rock pinnacles encrusted with ice.

"What about the terrorists up there?" I asked Si. He said nothing, which told me a lot.

My leg was stiff as we started out the climb, and I struggled along. After a half hour of hiking, though, my leg began loosening up, and I was able to keep a slow but steady pace using my ski pole as a cane. We trekked a snaking ridgeline on the western edge of the enormous gorge. Boulders as large as automobiles hurtled down the slope, sending a guttural rumble through the ground and up my legs. Misty clouds exhaled from the ancient black glaciers on the floor of the gorge, like steam rising from a two-mile-wide cauldron. Si kept a constant vigil, looking up at the ridgeline, where he eventually spotted a small figure. It was Juma tucked among some boulders about a mile away. He was alone and not moving. When we reached Juma, Si hugged him and quickly hoisted his friend's big pack on his back. I assisted the injured climber all the way down, and when we made it to Jon and the jeep, Juma and I were limping in unison. We didn't see any sign of Stuplich hiking either up or down.

Later that day, I got news that Stuplich had simply gotten lost in the clouds and had wandered into a nomad village, where he crashed on the floor of a tent. He was beyond exhausted and lapsed into a deep sleep. The next day when we were finally all altogether again, Si suggested that we try again. This time, he said we should take a much easier path up the south side of the mountain. Two experienced Kurdish climbers with good horses could be arranged. "With some good weather it could be done," Si said, convinced it was a more prudent plan. The southern route would be a much longer hike, however, and we were running out of time.

At 4:30 the next morning, I was packed and ready to go. I was going to climb with Stuplich, and my adrenaline had kicked in. The jeep was about to show up at any minute to take us to the waiting pack-horses at Eli village. After that, we would push hard to make it to the object. My calf ached from the prior day's climb to get Juma, but I had succeeded then, and just possibly I could make it all the way up today. As Stuplich and I walked outside in the cold morning air, we looked toward the mountain but could not see it in the darkness. As I tried to conceal my limp, Stuplich clamped his hand tight on my shoulder, like a vice, and said, "Are you 100 percent?"

"I'm okay," I replied with a forced look of resolve.

Stuplich gripped even harder and said with more intensity, "Tell me, Bob, right here, right now. Are you 100 percent?"

"Almost," I admitted. "I'll be fine."

Bob Stuplich had seen me gut it out on other mountains before, and I was surprised when he chided, "You will be more of a problem than a help to me. You're not going." I started to protest, but I knew he was right. My injury could compromise the whole mission, as well as Stuplich's safety. If my leg caused me problems at high altitudes, there was no telling how bad things could get. The object we were hunting was embedded over a sheer drop-off, and it would take real alpine skill just to get to it. I would not go.

We reached Eli village as the sun spread across the Anatolian plain. The settlement was a rock-walled cluster of crude mud and rock dwellings on the lower flank of the southern side of the mountain. A young boy was saddling three well-fed, good-looking sorrel horses. Looking at the peak, I could see dark clouds forming with the taste of snow in the air. I worried that the snowfall might arrive in the next few hours, making real trouble for Stuplich and the Kurds. I glanced at Stuplich and saw a steeled expression. He had climbed high on Ararat's punishing slopes and had almost died there once because of a snow storm, but I sensed that he was going to climb no matter what he faced. I had seen so many others who had ark fever push themselves beyond reason, but never Stuplich. He was a cool customer; he possessed good sense and the climbing ability of a cat. He had been hiking up Ararat for over thirty years, establishing his impressive mountaineering resume by leading climbs for high-profile expeditions. He had often endured hardship and, frankly, physical agony beyond description, but had never been beat on the mountain the way he had the day before.

The young boy packed the horses, cinched the load, and brought the animals to the climbers. "Don't get caught in snow," I cautioned, as he hiked off with his Kurdish guides. I was talking like a nervous father who just has to offer some last minute advice, but Stuplich simply turned back without comment and flashed me his patented reassuring grin.

Si and I spent the next two hours at the local military base, where I shelled out a lot more money. Then we returned to our concrete hovel at the edge of Dogubayazıt and waited. The top of the mountain remained dark with menacing clouds throughout the day and into the night. I knew that it would be brutally cold and miserable up there.

Stuplich explained to me later that they made it to 12,000 feet by late afternoon and tied off the horses. Grass doesn't grow any higher, so they left the animals to graze throughout the night. The horses were probably in the most danger at those heights, because wolves prowl the slopes of Ararat. Si told me

41

that on his last trip up the mountain, wolves killed one of the pack horses during the night while he slept nearby. His words chilled me as he described how he found the remains in the morning, after the wolves had eaten its entrails and chewed off its snout. It was a mental picture I could have done without.

After leaving the horses, Stuplich and the two Kurds went on to 14,000 feet and stopped for a short sleep. At 2:00 a.m., they rose and advanced towards the ice. It was a bitter cold morning, inky black with a cutting wind. Stuplich wore a CamelBak with a plastic bladder and a drinking tube. The water in the camel froze solid, and to make the situation worse, someone at the nomad village had stolen Stuplich's gloves the previous day, which he didn't realize until he was high on the mountain. This could be a real problem in such frigid conditions. The block of ice on his back made Bob shiver, but he knew he needed body heat to thaw out enough water to squeeze out some drips for drinking.

After an hour or so, the three men stopped for a snack of goat butter and bread, but the stop made the cold seem worse, so they resumed walking. At 7:00 a.m., they finally made the 16,444-foot saddle that was beyond the early morning shadows and into the warming sun. Stuplich increased the pace but the Kurds couldn't keep up; they were suffering cerebral edema from the fast ascent and had debilitating headaches.

When Stuplich came upon the first deep ice crevasses that stretched across the huge glaciers, the Kurds stopped in protest. Apparently they did not have the confidence to walk over the crevasses, which were three to five feet wide. Ice crevasses are very long, deep cracks in the ice that drop down as much as 100 feet into the bowels of the glacier. The only way to cross one of these crevasses is to walk across a snow bridge over the gap— little more than drifting snow piles that melt in the afternoon sun and freeze at night. The process of melt and freeze, melt and freeze creates a crusted ice platform, but the brittle bridges are often unstable and very unpredictable. Climbers rope themselves together before crossing, with the idea that if one falls through, the other two can pull their fallen comrade out.

At this point, the Kurds refused to go any further. Stuplich thought the snow bridges looked good, but he also knew they can give way even when they look passable. Stuplich understood the dangers. If he went in alone and fell, he would be wedged like a human cork in a grave of eternal ice.

With spiked crampons on his feet and carrying a metal ice axe in each of his bare hands, Stuplich went on without the Kurds, who sat down on the big glacier and shouted "Crazy man!" as he disappeared over the vast ridge. When Stuplich finally made it to the gorge, he peered into the rocky abyss.

I remember the first time I saw that gorge. It was five years earlier with Stuplich himself. My knees went limp, and my heart crawled up my throat. Stuplich was going to walk alone down its sixty degree ice slope to the object in Dan's satellite images. If Stuplich slipped, he would hurtle over the lip of the gorge and freefall for 4,000 feet before his abrupt stop on a slab of rock.

Stuplich stopped 150 feet above the object, but he could not climb down the steep wall of ice any farther. He had pushed the boundaries of extreme, but controlled risk, and he now entered into the realm of insanity. He twisted a five-inch ice screw deep into the ice. He then strung a nylon rope through the carabiner on his waist harness and attached it to the ice screw. He grabbed the frozen 150-foot rope with bare hands and lowered himself inch by inch. Clouds that crawled out of the gorge enveloped him in blinding snow. Rocks were avalanching below him and the wind seared his bare hands as he gripped the icy rope. In a few minutes, he had reached his goal and stood on Dan's ark object.

It was only rock and ice.

It was one of the most daring, courageous, and perhaps insane feats I have ever known of, and Bob Stuplich did it. When Bob finally made it back, I had the job of calling Dan at his home in Hawaii. He had paid us well to get the job done, and I deeply respected his motives for the search. Like so many others, he felt sure that he had seen the ghost ship of Noah, and he was convinced that this discovery would change the world and introduce lost people to God. We returned to the States, saying nothing to the press. Dan told us, "I want no publicity for now."

CHAPTER 5

THE ED DAVIS OBJECT

An old man named Ed Davis would change the trajectory of the ark search for me. I first met Ed in the winter of 1986 while attending an odd gathering of ark searchers in Farmington, New Mexico. He walked up to the lectern, hunched and slow, and he began to speak in a folksy cowboy drawl. Unruffled, and with a trace of dry humor, he led us on the incredible journey he'd taken fifty years earlier as an army sergeant serving in Iran during World War II. He claimed to have seen the ark, and while his story was hard to believe, he did make a convincing case that he'd seen something interesting. He described the ark as an enormous, dark and timbered boat-like object high on a mountain. "It *looked* an awful lot like Noah's ark," he said in words so spare and unvarnished that he disarmed even his worst critics.

Two years and two more frustrating trips to Turkey passed after I heard Ed Davis speak in New Mexico. During that time, I conducted two pioneering airborne reconnaissances of Mount Ararat, once by plane and once by helicopter. They ended up being two essentially fruitless trips that left me increasingly dubious about whether the ark had even survived. I kept saying to myself, "Ed Davis, where is your old boat?"

We had a millionaire investor named Larry Williams who wanted to know if Ed was a lying old fool after all. Larry told me, "I want to find out if this guy is for real." So he asked me to go down to New Mexico and supervise a lie detector test on Ed.

Ed Davis never stumbled a bit, and the polygraph needle never spiked. His answers indicated he told the truth when he said he saw Noah's ark. A guy named Pierangel administered the test, and he seemed shocked and disbelieving as he asked Ed questions. He re-administered the test to see if he'd get different results, and Ed passed again. Pierangel told me flat-out, "I don't know *what* he saw, but he definitely *believes* he saw a huge boat on top of a mountain during World War II."

I walked to a phone and called Larry. When he answered, I didn't even say hello. "Larry," I stammered out, "I don't know if Davis saw the boat, but he definitely *thinks* he saw it. He passed the lie detector test."

Thus started my long quest to find the Ed Davis object. In time, I came to realize that Ed had not seen the old boat on Mount Ararat or even in Turkey. Others had told Ed that Ararat was the mountain of the ark, so I guess he always just assumed he was on Ararat. But, Ararat was simply too far away from where he was based in Iran during World War II. After untold hours of listening and relistening to his voice recordings, I began to hear clues that other ark researchers had ignored or missed. Ed was never on Mount Ararat in Turkey, no matter how much others desperately wanted to stretch the distances to fit their pre-packaged theories.

I decided that Ed had to have been somewhere in Iran when he saw his ark-like object. I realized that I needed to head farther east for the Ed Davis mountain, so I jumped headlong into the second stanza of my ark ballad. Over time, I made five trips to the land of ancient Persia and I climbed several high mountains. I discovered that Iran has a slough of ancient legends about the ark landing there. I also realized that Iran fit the wording of Genesis 11:2, in which Noah's descendants migrated "from the east" to the land of Shinar—which worked if the ark had landed in Iran, but not at all with a landing in Turkey.

No more searches in Turkey for me anymore. I decided that Ed Davis was the best chance at finding clues. In 1943, during the height of World War II, Ed had worked for the Army Corps of Engineers building roads in Persia (Iran). The local Lurs took him to a certain location and showed him timbers, which they said were from the ark. Ed worked as an engineer, and he created a map of the location where he believed he had seen the ark.

My big break in finding Ed's boat came in November when a professor named Ed Holroyd contacted me by phone. Holroyd was a remote sensing scientist at the University of Denver who had examined Ed Davis' map and noted that it included a variety of detailed landmarks. Based on those landmarks, the good professor said he knew right where the object was. It was a mountain named Takht-e-Soleiman, the "Throne of Soloman," a peak and a sub-range in the Central Alborz Mountains of northern Iran.

I took Doug Scherling, Steve Crampton, and Mike Morrison along with me to Iran, and we climbed Takht-e-Soleiman. Amazingly, we found an object at 13,300 feet that matched what Ed had described.

After we returned to the U.S., there were a lot of people excited by our photos. I was talked into taking a larger team back to the object, so Steve Crampton and Doug Scherling returned to Iran with me, along with some notable participants like Josh McDowell, Dr. Frank Turek, geologist Reg Lyle, Boone Powell, former President of Avis Rental Car, Barry Rand, and attorney Jim Stock. We climbed back to the object high on Takht-e-Soleiman and we took samples of the object. To my complete surprise, some of those samples were later determined to be petrified wood. Several on the trip wanted to make the stunning claim we had actually found the real ark. But even though the object had beam-like features and looked freakishly like what one might envision as the ark, I could not make any such dogmatic pronouncement. I felt confident we had found the Ed Davis object, and I was more than satisfied with just that.

Over the years, I made five separate expeditions to research ark legends in Iran, and they were jammed with wild adventures. Twice in that country I faced armed guards and was placed under arrest. They were two very unpleasant experiences that I don't have space to relate here, but I will close out this chapter with one last story. I didn't necessarily find the ark of Noah, but I did find awe.

COLUMBINE AND THE LAMB

On April 20, 1999, the heart of a nation broke when two gunmen entered a Littleton, Colorado, high school and made its name infamous as the tragic site of what was at that time the deadliest school shooting in American history. Ever after, the name of a beautiful woodland flower, the columbine, has been associated with massacre and tragedy. Besides the shooters themselves, 12 students and one teacher lost their lives that day, and 23 others were either maimed or injured. I lived in Colorado Springs, just fifty miles from Columbine High School, and I watched the news stories, read the articles, and learned something about the lives of those slain and wounded.

Rachel Scott was among the first to die in a hail of bullets on the school lawn. John Tomlin lost his life in the school library, while doing his homework. Darrell Scott and John Tomlin Sr.—the fathers of Rachel and John—were my friends.

About a year after the Columbine shootings, these two grieving fathers heard about my plans of venturing back into Iran on another research trip. John and Darrell had spent much of the previous year immersed in the horror of Columbine, doing interview after interview. They wanted to join me on the adventure, so I called them both with a message: "If you want to go, mail me your passports for the visa applications!"

We traveled to Iran without any real trouble. I had friends in key positions to make it all happen. We had several days of bone jarring travel down bad roads in Land Rovers full of smelly men and supplies. When I say bad roads, I mean these roads had deep ruts inside even deeper ruts. We eventually made it to our research area, where a promising satellite image encouraged us that our target object was at least worth investigating. We hiked to the object's location, though, and we found nothing.

There was a bigger problem. We ran out of food. Our guide Ali had given the last crumb of our supplies to starving villagers as we made the three-day journey up the high mountain. To solve the problem, I had Ali stop at another village and buy a sheep—with the provision that the villagers would cook it. Ali negotiated a price of $35 for the animal, minus the pelt.

The temperature dropped dramatically as the sun ducked behind the mountains, and the chilly breeze sent us to our packs for jackets and sweaters. The shepherd boys called us over to a tripod of lashed logs where they had stacked wood for a fire and tethered the sheep we had purchased for our dinner. They hobbled its front legs with leather straps so that it knelt involuntarily as if in prayer, head bowed to one side. I imagined that its eyes had a sad cast to them, as if it knew what was coming. It knelt before us, not struggling or fighting, but silent. It was the meekest creature I had ever seen.

The sight of the poor animal hobbled before us quelled the frivolity of our campout, and the mood turned somber. Everyone was quiet. The boy walked back over and, in one smooth motion, reached down and made a deep slit across the sheep's throat. A violent spurt of blood shot ten feet across the meadow. The animal dropped to its stomach, supported by the boy's steadying hands. David and my brother Paul turned away and walked up the slope to the tents, unable to watch. The rest of us remained, jaws clenched, watching a life bleed out before our eyes.

"It's the nomad way. It's how they live and survive," I kept telling myself, thinking that normalizing the ritual might lessen its sting. Killing a sheep this way seems as normal for them as buying cellophane-wrapped hamburger at the grocery store is for us. Every day, thousands of animals are killed to feed hungry humans. It is normal—nothing new or unique.

Then why did it move me so?

I had seen the same ritual acted out time and again in my travels, but always as a sideline observer. Before, I had watched someone else's exotic customs; I'd never seen a lamb slaughtered because I was the needy, hungry recipient seeking food for survival. Yet here I stood, out of my element and in need. The lamb was heaving its last quivering breaths.

As I watched it dying, I thought of Jesus. He had stood silent before His jury, quietly endured His beatings, and refused to defend himself. Finally, He suffered an agonizing death on a cross. I glanced about the circle; did the others catch this piercing allegory?

The sheep's body went slack, its breathing ended. It died quietly, but the agony and desperation of its final moments had been painfully real, just as Jesus' agony erupted in a final, desperate cry, "My God, why have you forsaken me?"

The boy cut off the animal's head, then began massaging the carcass to drain the rest of the blood. About five feet from the spreading crimson pool, the villagers skinned and butchered the sheep as if they were peeling a potato.

The silence in our group was palpable. Darrell Scott and John Tomlin stood side by side, transfixed by the rustic passion play. One could only imagine what was going through their minds. Their children had been brutally slain just the year before, and the death of that lamb was personal.

I hadn't fully seen it until that moment. I hadn't fully understood that I'd lost something over the years. I had travelled the world, giving all my efforts to point others to the Savior. I had hurried along on my ministry treadmill, sharply disciplined, focused on who Jesus was and why He had come to the earth and died. I knew the details of Christ's birth, death, and resurrection. Amid the clamor, I could "Jesus talk" with the best. But slowly, steadily, I had lost something. Over the years, I had visited so many churches that they all looked alike, and I had heard so many messages that the simple, unadorned truth of Christ had become blurred and diluted. Somewhere along the line, the Bible got wrapped in cellophane and the church packaged in Styrofoam. It had all become so tidy, so clean.

Even as I had globe-trotted, searching for emblems that should have kept my heart fixed and fervent, the pain, the anguish, the miracle, and the ecstasy of the Gospel had become a slice of dry curriculum. It had lost its immediacy, its power. But here, on a chilly, windswept mountain in northwest Iran, I watched a blade make its deadly cut. I saw and smelled the blood, and I was given a vivid reminder of the enormous sacrifice my Savior had made 2000 years ago on a windswept hill in Jerusalem, the one the Greeks called "Calvary."

50

MOUNT SINAI

CHAPTER 6

SHARM EL-SHEIKH

It was 1988, and the bus belched diesel smoke into a cloudy Egyptian sky as it rumbled down the road across the Nile Delta. We bounced and jolted our way south through a lush landscape that painted a colorful contrast to the arid sand that stretched from the edges of the world-famous river delta. Channels of life-giving water snaked through miles of lush farmland. Vast fields of cotton, maize and rice carpeted the terrain. Water buffalo worked the plows or turned wheels for grinding grain or otherwise grazed in lazy indifference to us.

Once again I found myself traveling with Jim Irwin into the middle of nowhere. This time, *nowhere* was the Egyptian Sinai Peninsula. This time, Jim was bent on discovering the route that the ancient Israelites took out of Egypt during the Exodus on their way to crossing the Red Sea. He also wanted to find the mysterious "mountain of God" on which, according to the Bible, God appeared to Moses and gave him the Ten Commandments. The ancient texts said Moses had this encounter with God on a remote desert mountain called Mount Sinai. Could the Scriptures be believed… literally? Jim and the others with us certainly believed they could.

In preparation for the trip, I read and reread the biblical account of Moses and the Israelites. I was familiar with the story of Moses in Exodus 3, and how he was drawn to a burning bush on the "backside of the desert." There at the Mount of God, the LORD spoke to Moses and sent him back to Egypt to lead the entire nation of Hebrew slaves out of bondage to worship God on that same mountain. The Israelites camped near the foot of Mount Sinai, while Moses climbed up on the mountain to receive the Ten Commandments from God. It is a place where the Lord revealed Himself and His laws, and great miracles were presented to the Israelites in Exodus in a way never duplicated at any other time in all the Old Testament.

The exact route taken by Moses and the people of Israel is unknown. No one has ever pulled evidence from the sands of Egypt or connected artifacts to the Exodus event. No trace of evidence has been unearthed to suggest that the traditional Mount Sinai on the Sinai Peninsula—a major tourist destination—is the holy mountain spoken of in the Bible.

It is traditionally held that Queen Helena, the mother of fourth century Emperor Constantine of Rome, first christened Mount Sinai on the Sinai Peninsula. She was a mystic, and after she designated that particular mountain, it quickly became a pilgrimage site. "Mount Sinai" became cemented on maps, and few people over the centuries have questioned the tradition she started. Saint Catherine's Monastery, officially "Sacred Monastery of the God-Trodden Mount Sinai" was built in the sixth century at the traditional site of Mount Sinai, but biblical and archeological support for this site is murky at best. The fact is, there isn't any evidence that the people of Israel stopped on

Figure 3: St. Catherine's Monastery on the Sinai Peninsula. Photo by Berthold Werner (2010).

the Sinai Peninsula at all. Not a scrap of archeological evidence suggests that millions of people camped out in the Sinai for 40 years, and this lack of evidence has led scholars to doubt that the Exodus actually took place as the Bible describes.

Most people who visit the traditional site on the Sinai Peninsula are totally unaware that the mountain they see is only one of several proposed sites for the real Mount Sinai. Tour buses rumble there in an endless stream, and Jim Irwin had gotten me onto one of them.

I sat on the tour bus, watching one mile dissolve into another. My mind walked back through the years to that most singularly intriguing event in history—the LORD's giving the Law to Moses. I was now driving across sand where the entire nation of Hebrew slaves had rushed to escape Pharaoh 3,500 years earlier. I was looking at the same horizon that Moses had once trudged toward.

According to Exodus 13:20-22, God led the children of Israel with a pillar of cloud by day and a pillar of fire by night. In Exodus 16:1, one month after they left Egypt, they reached Mount Sinai. The Red Sea has two arms that frame the Sinai Peninsula, and it's been long assumed that the Israelites crossed the western Red Sea arm, the Gulf of Suez. Our fellow team mate Dr. Roy Knuteson proposed that the real Mount Sinai was located on the other side of the Red Sea's other arm, the Gulf of Aqaba, in the country of present day Saudi Arabia. He quoted the words of the Apostle Paul in Galatians 4:25, "*And now Jerusalem is just like Mount Sinai in Arabia, because she and her children live in slavery.*"[1]

Dr. Knuteson was not the first to make this proposal. In 1936, a man named Stephen L. Caiger commented in his book on biblical archaeology, "A very reasonable conjecture would place the Holy Mount of Sinai, or Horeb, not in the peninsula, but east of the Gulf of Aqaba in the volcanic region of northern Arabia."[2]

These men—Jim Irwin, Dr. Knuteson, and Stephen Caiger—

---

1 New Living Translation
2 Stephen L. Caiger. *Bible and Spade: An Introduction to Biblical Archaeology* (Oxford University Press, 1936), 79.

had me thinking. They took the Bible as a literal, not mythical, representation of history. They believed, as many others do, that the Bible can be trusted as a reliable source of information on past events.

We visited the traditional Mount Sinai in the Sinai Peninsula, and we all left with a sense that nothing pointed to it as the real Mountain of God. We drove onward to the tip of the Sinai Peninsula to a place called Sharm El-Sheikh, where Jim and Dr. Knuteson believed Moses and thousands of former slaves had actually crossed through the parted Red Sea while fleeing Pharaoh.

Then Moses stretched out his hand over the sea; and the LORD caused the sea to go back by a strong east wind all that night, and made the sea into dry land, and the waters were divided. So the children of Israel went into the midst of the sea on the dry ground, and the waters were a wall to them on their right hand and on their left. And the Egyptians pursued and went after them into the midst of the sea, all Pharaoh's horses, his chariots, and his horsemen.

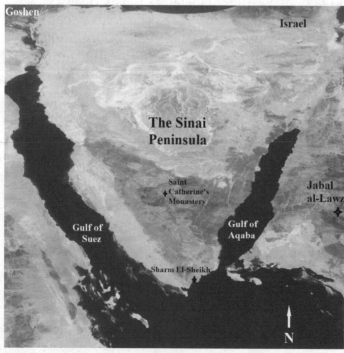

Figure 4: A view of the Sinai Peninsula from space, courtesy of NASA Johnson Space Center. Modified to note the traditional Mount Sinai location at St. Catherine's Monastery and the alternate site at Jabal al-Lawz,

Exodus 14:21-23 (NKJV)

The Bible tells us that during the time of Joseph,[3] the people of Israel settled in the land of Goshen, and they still dwelt there during the time of the Exodus. Goshen is northeast of present-day Cairo, east of the Nile Delta. When the Israelites fled Egypt, they headed southeast from Goshen onto the Sinai Peninsula. The Bible tells us that God did not lead them along the easy route to Israel directly east and up to Gaza, but instead He led them into the desert along the Red Sea:

Then it came to pass, when Pharaoh had let the people go, that God did not lead them by way of the land of the Philistines, although that was near; for God said, "Lest perhaps the people change their minds when they see war, and return to Egypt." So God led the people around by way of the wilderness of the Red Sea. And the children of Israel went up in orderly ranks out of the land of Egypt.

Exodus 13:17-18

The escaping Hebrew slaves lacked the military skills to fight the occupants of the northern areas of the Sinai Peninsula, so God led them south. Dr. Knuteson and others reasoned that the route went down the western edge of the peninsula's wide, hard-packed beach, which extends all the way from the Nile Delta in the north to the southern tip of the Sinai Peninsula. There was no Suez Canal in those days, and the marshy areas

Figure 5: The approximate location of Jabal al-Lawz northwest of Tabuk.

---

3   Genesis 47:1-6, 27;
    Exodus 8:22.

from Goshen to the Sinai would hardly have hemmed in and trapped the Israelites as they were pursued by the Philistines. At the tip of the Sinai, though, the road turns up the eastern flank of the Sinai and abruptly stops at an imposing mountain range whose tall, sheer peaks jut vertically from the shoreline. When we finally arrived at the seaside town of Sharm El Sheikh, we could all see for ourselves that the terrain there matched the Bible's description.

> *"For Pharaoh will say of the children of Israel, 'They are bewildered by the land; the wilderness has closed them in.'"*
>
> Exodus 14:3

Larry Williams joined-up with our team at this point. Larry was the wealthy benefactor who had funded our entire expedition. The goal was to use a dive boat to explore the ocean bottom and hunt for any existing chariot wheels. As a former investigator, I doubted that any chariots would still exist after 3,500 years, but … nothing ventured, nothing gained.

Another issue with the traditional view is that the Egyptians were drowned when the sea collapsed on them after the Israelites had passed through. The marshy, shallow waters south of Goshen were hardly capable of drowning Pharaoh's men. The deep waters of the Gulf of Aqaba, however, had the power to destroy the Egyptians as the walls of water crashed back into place. There was a possible land bridge at the narrowest part of the channel between the Sinai and Saudi Arabia, which we see as a series of reefs about 4-5 miles long to Tiran Island. These are known as the Gordon, the Thomas, the Woodhouse, and the Jackson reefs. They would have provided a path through the sea possible to cross in one night's journey as the Bible says.

> *And Moses stretched out his hand over the sea; and when the morning appeared, the sea returned to its full depth, while the Egyptians were fleeing into it. So the LORD overthrew the Egyptians in the midst of the sea. Then the waters returned and covered the chariots, the horsemen, and all the army of Pharaoh that came into the sea after them. Not so much as one of them*

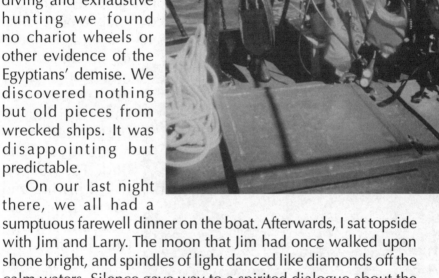

Figure 6: Bob Cornuke after diving in the search for Pharaoh's chariots opposite Sharm El Sheikh at the tip of the Sinai Peninsula.

remained.

Exodus 14:27-28

Our initial research into the Sea of Aqaba proved disappointing. After a few days of diving and exhaustive hunting we found no chariot wheels or other evidence of the Egyptians' demise. We discovered nothing but old pieces from wrecked ships. It was disappointing but predictable.

On our last night there, we all had a sumptuous farewell dinner on the boat. Afterwards, I sat topside with Jim and Larry. The moon that Jim had once walked upon shone bright, and spindles of light danced like diamonds off the calm waters. Silence gave way to a spirited dialogue about the week's events and the meaning of the reef.

As if talking to himself, Jim said, "If that's where they passed through the sea, then Mount Sinai has to be ... over there." He pointed to a distant ribbon of shadowy land awash in purple, nearly invisible in the darkening mottled sky. It was the west coast of Saudi Arabia. Until then, the legendary mountain where Moses received the Ten Commandments had remained in the background of our daily discourse. "Bob, do you see it?" Jim said. "Mount Sinai has to be in Saudi Arabia. The Bible says in Galatians that Mount Sinai is in Arabia."

As the evening wore on, Jim pulled Larry and me aside. Reaching into his shirt pocket, he removed a crumpled letter he had received shortly before the trip from a fellow named David Fasold. The note detailed a journey Fasold had taken into Saudi Arabia some years earlier, when he eventually found and scouted a peak called Jabal al-Lawz. According to his descriptions, the mountain had the marks of the real Mount Sinai. Jim read from the letter, describing features on the mountain that told us Fasold had at least found something incredibly interesting.

Unfortunately, as he left the mountain, Fasold and his companion Wyatt were arrested by Saudi police. They spent a terrifying week in jail, charged by the king's prosecutor with "robbing Saudi Arabia of its wealth from antiquities." This is a capital offense that could have resulted in public beheading. Saudi officials finally released the pair, badly shaken and stripped

of all film, video, and notes. They no longer had the evidence they needed to authenticate the find. Fasold had risked his life and come up empty-handed, though the harsh Saudi response suggested that he had found a significant archaeological site. Fasold told Jim that he would never

Figure 7: Larry Williams left and Bob Cornuke right searching for Pharaoh's charities in the Red Sea.

return to Saudi Arabia because it was far too dangerous. He had written hoping that the famous astronaut would have the stature and the clout to gain official Saudi clearance and mount a legitimate excavation of the peak. Fasold had given it a historic try; he now wanted to pass the torch to someone else who might be able to get in (and *out*) with the goods.

In essence, his note said, "Here is a fascinating place. Its features make us believe it is Mount Sinai, but we don't have anything to prove it. My photos, maps, and notebooks were confiscated. The mountain is called Jabal al-Lawz. It sits in the middle of a vast military reservation."

After what we had just been through, the letter lent stunning force to Knuteson's theory; practically every piece of evidence from Fasold's trip advanced the notion that Mount Sinai was in Saudi Arabia. Dangling the letter between thumb and forefinger, Jim smiled and raised a hand toward the eastern Saudi shoreline.

"What did I tell you?" Jim's voice was edgy with expectancy. "That's where we need to go." Jim handed the letter to Larry, who tucked it carefully back in his shirt.

We spoke no more of it that night. But as we returned to the party, my eyes caught Larry's. In his deadpan expression, I thought I saw the faintest glint of acknowledgement—that kindred spark of wonder—needed to launch two incurable thrill seekers into the misty unknown. *We were going.* I was certain we'd make our way into Saudi Arabia and find that mountain, one way or another.

Larry called me some months later. Not given to pleasantries, he got right to the point. "I'm thinking of going to Saudi Arabia to check out the Mount Sinai site." He paused and then said, "Are you interested in going with me?"

That caught me off guard. "Am I interested? Of course I'm interested," I told him. The question stunned me, and my mind raced to keep up with my heart as I considered the possibilities.

Larry made it clear I wouldn't have to put up any of my own money. "I'll pay for everything," he said. Not much to think about there.

"Count me in." I said. Then I hung up the phone.

I thought of the letter that Jim Irwin had given Larry in Egypt. It wasn't just a wrinkled piece of paper. It was a map, a guide that pointed to a treasure more valuable than Ali Baba's troves of gold. That crumpled note had the potential to lead us to a discovery that would rock the world of archaeology. Larry and I both knew that we had been given clues that offered a singular chance to find one of the most important sites in all of history. I also knew that Larry had just offered to make it possible for me to follow that dream halfway around the world. I reminded myself that two men had been arrested and jailed while exploring the mountain, and that their photographs had been confiscated. They left with no evidence. Could we do what they could not? There's an old saying, "It's the second mouse that gets the cheese."

Days later, I spoke with Larry again and began with a pointed question. "How are we going to get into one of the most closed countries in the world? The only Americans getting into that country are employed by international oil companies, or assigned as military personnel."

Larry said, "Don't worry. We'll get in." This ambiguous answer meant that he didn't have a clue how we would do it, but he was determined to figure it out. In the days ahead, he spent a pile of money traveling and making countless telephone calls to find a way into the forbidden kingdom of Saudi Arabia.

CHAPTER 7

FROM LONDON TO THE DESERT

We got a flash of hope when a friend of Larry's in London said he could get us a visa for Saudi Arabia. Jack Trimonti was a smooth-talking commodities broker who boasted that he knew a Saudi prince who happened to be in London. He assured us that he could get us a sponsorship into Arabia! This totally fell flat. The prince had flown to Scandinavia to see the northern lights or something, and we had no idea when he would return. Once again, Saudi Arabia seemed out of reach.

Jack had not given up, though. He told Larry to come to London, where he had another friend who knew people in the Saudi embassy. *This* man could get us visas. The promise was good enough for Larry. He called me to say, "It's a go," and there wasn't a hint of hesitation in his voice, not a single waver. We cleared our calendars and flew out to London.

Jack met us at the airport—a dapper and sophisticated looking man. He introduced us to his friend Dimitri, a flamboyant Greek who chain-smoked and spoke in rapid, broken English. Dimitri was heavy set; the buttons strained on his shirt and looked as if they would give way at any moment. He struck me as a shifty sort of man, one who constantly used the phrase, "I assure you there will be no problem." Every time he smiled, I got nervous. With rock-solid conviction, Dimitri promised that we would have our visas the next day. The next day came and Dimitri met us with, "Surprising news. No visas."

The announcement didn't sit well with Larry, and his displeasure brought on a wave of defensiveness from Dimitri. In an effort to save face, Dimitri rushed us across town to his office. The rain poured down in silver sheets, and the day seemed as gloomy as the gray skies.

Dimitri had an idea. From his files, he pulled out an old letter that the Saudi prince had faxed him about an oil deal gone sour. The letter had been printed on royal letterhead and bore the prince's official signature. The top of it displayed a logo of the Kingdom of Saudi Arabia. Dimitri programmed his fax machine to match the identification number at the top of the prince's letter and then programmed it to display the correct time in Saudi Arabia. He did a test fax to a friend. When the friend called to say that the test fax looked like it had come from the royal palace in Saudi Arabia, Dimitri beamed with pride.

"This isn't what I bargained for," I told Larry. I could see what was happening, and I didn't like it. In a matter of days, we had gone from entering the country legally to concocting a wild scheme with a forged royal signature. This was foolish, and I knew we were risking our lives going through Dimitri. He seemed determined to push us into a grossly illegal intrigue that could get us imprisoned and possibly killed.

The acid churned in my stomach as I watched Dimitri make a copy of the letterhead and signature and affix it to the fabricated sponsorship letter. He managed to make it look like the prince had written it himself, but when it came off the copier; the signature was blotchy and blurred. It honestly looked like the fake that it was, and none of us knew how to fix it.

"I'm very uncomfortable with this," I told Larry. "We could get in tremendous trouble." The room went silent except for the splat of raindrops pelting a large window.

"Are you bailing out on me, Bob?" Larry said. "I've spent a lot of money on this. If you can think of another way, say so now. But I need to know, are you in?"

There was no other way to get into Saudi Arabia, and I knew it. At that moment, with those words in my ear, I crossed over. Thousands of miles from home, neck deep in international intrigue, I felt that my very manhood was in question. I bent to the pressure of the moment.

"Yes, I'm in."

Christians are persecuted in Saudi Arabia, and more terrorists—including the 9/11 hijackers—have come out of that country than any other. Some might say that gave Larry and me ample justification to maneuver around their laws. Others would say that it was dishonest of us to fake our way into the kingdom, and with good reason. At the time, it seemed to be the only choice we had, a sliver of opportunity dangling in front of us. We went for it. As the gray clouds turned black, ushering in a dark London evening, I made the fateful choice that I would later regret.

I turned to Dimitri, who sensed my disgust with the whole matter. I demanded that he give me the letter with the prince's signature.

"If we're going to do this, let's do it so we don't get caught," I said.

I took the prince's signature and enlarged it on the copier to several times its normal size. I then took a pen and carefully retraced it, coloring in the gaps and imperfections. I then returned to the copier and reduced the text to normal size. It looked perfect—bold and official. We re-copied the letter, transposed it over the prince's signature and letterhead, and then faxed it to the Saudi embassy with the pre-programmed Saudi time and country code.

It worked. The embassy faxed us back at a number we had put in the letter, telling us to come down with our papers and passports. A bit more finagling was required at the Saudi embassy, but we were able to make a flight the next day.

When they closed the door on that Saudi airliner, I knew that was it. We were on our way, and there was no turning back. We were exchanging a world of green verdant fields for a world of choking dust storms and unimaginable heat. We were on our way to hunt down the remote stone sentinel Jabal al-Lawz, known to the local Bedouins as Jabal Musa—the Mountain of Moses. I felt uneasy about what we had done, but I also knew we had come too far to turn back. The adrenaline that had propelled me this far was now waning. The insanity of what we were doing settled in my soul.

Henry Ward Beecher once said, "In things pertaining to enthusiasm, no man is sane who does not know how to be insane on proper occasions." I wondered if this was a proper occasion to be insane, and I hoped that something good would come of it all.

JEDDAH

Larry and I landed in Jeddah, Saudi Arabia, and worked our way through customs without much trouble. We both exhaled with relief and wove our way through the crowded terminal to our connecting flight to the city of Tabuk. We could almost taste the dust of Jabal al-Lawz.

On our night flight to Tabuk, noise from yammering men rattled down the interior of the plane. They wore pressed white robes, complete with headdresses held to their heads by the traditional black *agal* that was standard attire among Saudis. The *agal* is a black cord usually made of goat hair, but it always reminded me of a car's fan belt.

I tried to doze on the plane, but it was impossible. I was still too amped. My heart hadn't settled down from the excitement of entering the country and clearing customs knowing full well we were doing so under the shadiest of circumstances. Uneasiness clung to me like sweat, a foreboding that any moment I would feel a tap on my shoulder and hear the words "You are under arrest. Come with me."

Larry sat next to me. He pulled out a compass and stared at its wobbling needle. I leaned over and watched the compass slowly rotate to the right. Larry frowned when the dial made a second revolution.

"We are flying in circles," he whispered. I looked out the window and saw nothing but the black velvet desert below. It seemed we had flown far enough to reach Tabuk. Shouldn't we be landing?

After a few minutes, the distant cluster of lights of Tabuk came into view, but we hadn't stopped circling. The lights passed slowly by the plane's window, once for each revolution of the teetering compass needle. It was well over an hour after our scheduled landing, and anxiety tightened the muscles in my stomach.

Larry tapped the face of the compass. "Something must be wrong."

We continued circling, but the other passengers seemed oblivious to the fact that we were still airborne. Suddenly the airplane jerked, then pitched as if seized by a giant hand. I heard the roar of the engines as the pilots increased power. There was a surge forward, then the power dropped and the plane began to plunge. Overhead bins popped opened, disgorging bags of fruit, carry-on sacks, and luggage. A cascade of personal belongings fell into the aisle and onto stunned passengers.

Someone screamed.

The aircraft went into freefall, but recovered moments later. It heaved to the left, then back again to the right, snapping us back and forth in our seats like a rollercoaster. One engine roared, then the other. I guessed that the pilot had lost intermittent control of the flaps. If I was right, we were in a lot of trouble.

Panic spread. I looked at Larry. He shrugged and gave an unconvincing smile.

"This does *not* look good." He got no argument from me.

I looked out of the window. I was surprised and disturbed to see buildings. We were much closer to the ground than I had realized. Just below, the runway and beacon lights came at us fast. An eternity of seconds later, the landing gear slammed onto the tarmac. The plane bounced and shuddered, and its engines moaned painfully as the pilot reversed thrust. We hit so hard that the front tires exploded on impact. A hideous screech pierced through the plane as the big jet's bare wheel hubs gouged a groove in the runway. Sparks flew past my window.

The impact shook me, compressing my spine and driving the air from my lungs. Stunned, I waited for the inevitable, whatever that might be. Finally, the plane shuddered and lurched to a stop at the end of the runway. My heart began to beat again.

Chaos filled the cabin. People struggled, desperate to get off the plane. I assumed they expected the fuselage to erupt in a ball of fire any moment, so they pushed and shoved and cried out in fear as they crowded the aisles. A mass of arms and legs and bodies pressed against the exit door. Larry and I waited for the stampede to subside. There was nothing else we could do. Fire trucks arrived, their twirling crimson lights splashing the runway and the airplane. Firemen in silver fire-protective suits unfurled hoses and bathed the plane with white foam.

"Welcome to Tabuk," I said.

We stepped down to the tarmac safely as the last ones off the plane. In the terminal, we overheard talk of a hydraulic problem on the plane. The outcome had been very fortunate.

Around 3:30 a.m., we finally checked into our hotel rooms. I collapsed into bed and did not wake until mid-morning. It was Friday, a weekend day for the Saudis. Our first order of business was to rent a truck and collect supplies and provisions enough to last us a week as we ventured off into no-man's land. A cab took us into the business district of Tabuk, a drab, antiseptic town of gray and white cement buildings. We stopped at a truck rental company. Larry spent twenty minutes signing papers, and soon we were presented with a small, white Datsun pickup truck.

When we drove off to purchase our supplies, though, we found that all shop owners had closed their doors for prayer time. The Muslim culture in Saudi Arabia requires compliance to prayer time. Most attendees are sincere in their faith, but there is also severe social pressure for shop owners to attend. Their patrons would frown on absence from prayers, and that might affect business. We simply had to wait until prayers were over, at which point the streets once again filled and commerce resumed.

We foraged from shop to shop to supply our trek into the Saudi frontier. We filled the back of our pick-up with canned meat, fruit, and cases of bottled water. We bought shovels, ropes, flashlights, batteries, and several empty twenty-gallon jerry cans for storing reserves of gasoline. We even bought Arab outfits, robes, scarves, and agals, foolishly thinking that we could fit in among the desert Bedouins. Larry had the bright idea of buying instant suntan lotion to darken our skin and perhaps allow us to blend in better. Unfortunately, the cream only gave our skin a sickly orange color.

After we finished our shopping, we retired to the hotel to cool off in the pool. There we quizzed each other, trying to think of everything that could go wrong. We came up with countless scenarios and what-ifs. However many times we rehearsed our plans, though, I couldn't stop imagining two sets of bleached bones perched on some sand dune in the middle of nowhere. In my mind, I saw Larry clutching an empty canteen with his bony fingers and me holding a hand-scrawled note that said, "Obviously we didn't think of everything that could go wrong."

The evening wind unleashed a sandstorm. Powerful wind hurtled across the flat desert, sucking up grains of sand. There was nothing to blunt its advance. Outside our hotel, sand pinged off our window and the howling wind seeped through the rattling panes of glass.

CHAPTER 8

ON THE ROAD TO JABAL AL-LAWZ

S leep was sporadic, but the winds finally subsided, and I rested solidly for a few hours. Larry awoke with enthusiasm, eager to get onward to the mountain. We checked out of the hotel by 6:00 a.m. and headed into the predawn gloom. Soon the sun's orange disk spilled over the desert horizon, casting long shadows from dramatic, furrowed rock formations.

We crossed the ancient land of Midian, where the Bible says Moses met God at the burning bush on the slopes of Mount Sinai. Forty years prior to the burning bush experience, Moses had gone to the rescue of a Hebrew slave and had killed the Egyptian beating him. Exodus 2:15 tells us that Pharaoh sought to kill Moses when he heard about this, but Moses fled the wrath of Pharaoh and found refuge in Midian.

Moses would not have ran down to the Sinai Peninsula for asylum, because it was controlled by Egypt. Archaeology shows that Pharaoh had multiple mining interests and military outposts in the Sinai, and Moses would have sought refuge in a land far from Egyptian patrols. The Bible makes clear that Moses left Egypt altogether, escaping to the land of Midian. Later, he had to leave this other land to return to Egypt. It is believed that ancient Midian lay south of present-day Jordan in northwestern Saudi Arabia.

So Moses went and returned to Jethro his father-in-law, and said to him, "Please let me go and return to my brethren who are in Egypt, and see whether they are

still alive." And Jethro said to Moses, "Go in peace."
Now the LORD said to Moses in Midian, "Go, return to
Egypt; for all the men who sought your life are dead."

Exodus 4:18-19

Figure 8: Bob Cornuke left and fellow explorer Larry Williams right.

We followed the snaking highway for two hours looking for
our first landmark, the remote Al Kan gas station. According to
David Fasold's letter, we had to turn off into the wilderness four
miles beyond that point. When we drove the required four miles,
however, we found no exit, no turn off, and nothing that even
resembled a road. David Fasold's map showed a road at Al Kan,
but all we saw in reality was a wisp of a trail that stretched into
the dunes and jagged mountains, barely discernible among the
scattered rocks of the desert floor.

We took it anyway.

With the benefit of today's technology, we would have been
able to pull out our cell phones and—connecting by satellite
if necessary—give Fasold a call to clarify which route we were

supposed to take. This was 1988, though, still a few years before common cell-phone use. So, we just jumped into the adventure. Within minutes, I negotiated our little Datsun along the floor of an immense desert valley that split into scores of narrow forks and wadis. Each one of these subdivided the desert into clusters of winding ravines and stone-filled ditches. We encountered huge rocks every 50 yards or so, and sand drifts and sagebrush blocked the hardly discernible trail before us.

Maps were useless. We soon decided that we had followed the wrong path. We bounced and crunched through bruising ruts and scrub-filled ravines, bottoming out every few yards and fearing that we'd crack the oil pan and end our expedition miles from any form of civilization.

The heat had grown unbearable. Our small thermometer read 117 degrees, and it was only late morning. Within two hours, that thermometer climbed to 128 degrees, and our small truck had no air conditioning. Even if it had, the extreme temperature and the toiling exertion would have quickly overheated the already-strained engine. In fact, we rolled *up* our widows, because the heat blowing off the desert sand was unbearably hot. It was like looking down the barrel of a hair dryer. Larry and I sucked down prodigious amounts of water and pushed across mile after mile of rough terrain. Occasionally, we poured the warm liquid over our heads, but this soaking only helped for a few minutes. Dust seeped through the air vents, caking our sweaty skin in layers of gray, gritty film.

We weren't alone in that wretched oven. Occasionally, we passed small Bedouin encampments, where pickup trucks hauling sheep, cases of supplies, and large tanks of water were engaged in the difficult work of desert commerce.

Our little Datsun lumbered deeper into sheep country. At dozens of points, we passed what looked like huge beach umbrellas raised several feet off the ground and tethered by ropes to tall poles. Tightly bunched herds of sheep huddled under each of these, standing on tiny patches of shade to escape the sun's brutal rays.

We were lost. We had initially seen the desert as a scattering of safe landmarks on a small map. In reality, it had opened its vast mouth as a foe that would easily consume us if we ventured any farther into the sandy expanse. I finally turned the truck around, hoping we could hobble our way back to the asphalt highway. At least, that's what I tried to do. As I made the U-turn, the wheels of the truck strayed off the two grooves of hard-packed sand and sank into the soft shoulder. I tried gunning the engine, but the wheels merely spun in place, spewing hot sand like a geyser. In a moment, the truck had sunk up to its axles in the soft sand. Without a word, Larry swung open the creaking door to see how badly we were stuck. I joined him outside to survey the situation.

We were absolutely, undeniably trapped. The image of bleached bones returned to my mind.

It got worse. In desperation, I grabbed the rear bumper, planted my boots on the ground and told Larry to gun the engine. I lifted and pushed, giving it all I had. As I did this, something snapped in my lower back, and a piercing, surging pain shot up my spine. I couldn't even breathe during the next few seconds. I clenched my teeth, stifling a scream, then dropped to my knees as though I'd been shot.

Larry killed the engine and strode around to the back where I kneeled in the searing sand. I looked up and nodded, wanting to assure him that I would be okay. Larry wasn't fooled even a little. He saw the agony on my face, and he leaned over to say something to me. Just then, a pickup truck pulled near— seemingly from nowhere. Neither of us had heard it coming, yet there it appeared over those blistering sands.

It was a sun-faded olive green Jeep with a makeshift pickup bed bolted onto the back. This was crammed full of gawking human children. The driver stared at us for a moment in disbelief. His expression said it all: *What in the world are two white guys doing out here?* The robes and instant suntan cream hadn't fooled him. The man cautiously approached us, his head covered with a red checkered *kufiya,* the traditional headdress worn by men in that region.

I imagine we made an unusual sight. I struggled to stand as Larry helped me to my feet. The Bedouin could see my pain and our immovable truck. He looked at me, and then he looked at the truck again. With a wave, he called some of the older boys from the Jeep, and they scampered over. Within a few seconds they had rocked the Datsun side to side and freed our truck from the sand.

Larry thanked the man and boys profusely, bowing and shaking their hands.

Then Larry asked, "Can you take us to Jabal al-Lawz?"

The smiles of celebration vanished. The Bedouin's countenance darkened, and his gracious manner evaporated. A look of fear swept across his face as he talked quietly with the boys. One produced a pencil and paper and jotted down the license number of our truck. Clearly, something forbidden was associated with that mountain. I feared we had just crossed a line of demarcation, and our expedition had just gone from insane to impossible.

Larry was not easily put off. After long and tense negotiations, Larry persuaded the man to show us where the mountain was located among the chaotic jumble of peaks that surrounded us. Our rescuer finally gave in and returned to his Jeep, by which he led us down a gentle slope and up a high narrow ridge. Five minutes later, we were parked at the foot of a wide, sloping wall of granite. Our reluctant guide stepped from his truck and, crouching like an Indian scout in an old Western movie, began crawling up the rock face. Larry and I followed, keeping low as our guide maneuvered to a rocky crest overlooking a low, yawning plain. There, the Bedouin knelt beneath the silhouette of a huge boulder and pointed toward something in the distance.

"Jabal al-Lawz," he whispered as if unfriendly ears were nearby.

We peered over the valley. There it was, the mountain we had traveled so far to see. Rising majestically from the desert floor, it displayed two sharp, distinctively blackened summits. Were we finally looking at the real Mount Sinai?

The short trip had clearly agitated the Bedouin. He moved closer to me and pointed again toward the mountain, "Jabal al-Lawz." The man then turned and vanished, leaving us alone overlooking the boiling expanse. We gazed back out at Jabal al-Lawz and realized we were staring at a chain-link fence. In this land of open spaces stood a fifteen-foot high fence topped with barbed-wire, complete with a warning sign that effectively communicated to us that trespassing was not allowed. Of course, we spent the next hour poking along the perimeter of that chain-link barrier.

Before we left the States, Fasold had told Larry to look for a series of petroglyphs, ancient rock etchings of bulls or cows, on a pile of boulders. He had said the boulders appeared to be a purposeful construction, not a random accumulation of stones. That construction was supposed to be in the valley we were exploring. Fasold thought it was a religious site, perhaps the altar where Aaron placed a pagan deity in the form of a golden calf. The altar and the golden calf had been made by a frightened, impatient people.

> So all the people broke off the golden earrings which
> were in their ears, and brought them to Aaron. And he
> received the gold from their hand, and he fashioned
> it with an engraving tool, and made a molded calf.
> Then they said, "This is your god, O Israel, that
> brought you out of the land of Egypt!" So when Aaron
> saw it, he built an altar before it. And Aaron made a
> proclamation and said, "Tomorrow is a feast to the
> LORD."

Exodus 32:3-5

Larry and I split up to search for the altar, and in a short time I had found a pile of large stones surrounded by another fence. I called out to Larry, who had gone searching over the rise. The huge pile of granite had clearly been stacked by men. Near it, another sign was posted in Arabic and English warning trespassers to stay out.

The Book of Exodus opens by explaining how the Egyptians enslaved the Hebrews in the centuries after Joseph died. Over time, the descendants of Jacob were forced into bitter back-breaking labor by their Egyptian masters, and they even built cities for the Pharaoh. If these people were able to build cities, then they certainly were capable of constructing a giant stone altar.

Figure 9: Alleged golden calf stone altar at the base of Jabal Al lawz.

Larry joined me and began studying the pile of stones with me. There had clearly been an arrangement several boulders high, but some of the stones had tumbled down. As we studied the structure, we noticed ancient-looking engravings in the flat rock face of the altar. The form of a bull and another of a calf shone out at us from the granite. The most striking petroglyph shook me with excitement. It showed a man holding a calf over his head, its spiraling horns replicating those of the ancient Egyptian *Apis* and *Hathor* bull gods.

This wasn't cattle country. This was sheep country and *had* been for as long as I knew men had walked these plains. It was a strange thing to see pictures of bulls etched onto the stone faces of granite boulders all piled up.

Our search had just begun, but the presence of these engraved cattle offered us something beyond mere coincidence. It was important to be objective, but I couldn't help thinking that I was looking at the very altar mentioned in Exodus 32:3-5.

77

Figure 10: Bovine inscriptions on the alleged Golden Calf altar.

We searched around some more before we decided to set up camp for the night. We planned to wait until morning, and then—if my back allowed—climb up the back side of the mountain, away from the guard house. I tried walking, taking easy steps in hope that I could limber up my back muscles, but they only cramped tighter with intermittent shooting pain. I felt humiliated. My whole life I'd dealt with pain, and I'd been able to just make due. I'd played football in college and had learned how to put my dislocated shoulder back in joint to keep playing. As a policeman, I'd been banged around and beaten bloody, but I'd always just kept going. Now, standing where Moses himself had (in all likelihood) once walked, I was struggling to hobble along a fence perimeter. I had to question whether I'd even be able to rise to my feet in the morning.

Dawn breaks fast in the desert. The heat slaps you like an open hand before the sun's rays even have a chance to stretch across the desert floor. There's no soft transition from the predawn chill, but an instant, prickly discomfort, a rude warning that another day of relentless, withering heat is on its way. On our first morning at the foot of Jabal al-Lawz, the sun crawled from behind the jagged outline of the eastern mountains and blazed fast.

I had spent the night in restless, uncomfortable sleep, my back refusing to forgive me for the previous day. I have a phobia about snakes, so I had spent the night in the pickup, squeezing my bulk onto its narrow bench seat. I stretched my legs out one door and rested my feet on three boxes of water stacked beside the truck. Sleep was intermittent and made worse when headlights from a rattling truck glared into our camp sometime after midnight. I heard some quick Arabic chatter, and then the truck backed off and left. I was glad for that, but the event had ratcheted up my senses. I woke at every noise from the desert. My brain viewed every sound as a threat. Even the crinkles and crackles from Larry's high-tech, silver-foil Mylar space blanket sounded ominous in the breeze.

In the morning, I stood and tested my back, taking short, tentative steps. It still throbbed painfully, but it was a little better. Despite the poor sleeping conditions, the muscles had loosened, and at least I could stand, walk, and bend. I gazed up at the black mountain peak above me. I was going to climb Jabal al-Lawz. It wouldn't be easy, but the pain of staying would be worse than the pain of going. After a quick breakfast of dehydrated fruit and bread, Larry and I filled our packs with water bottles, cameras, film, and protein bars. I found a six-foot cane pole left from a disbanded Bedouin camp and used it as a hiking staff to help me climb.

We shuffled across a thin stretch of valley to the base of the mountain. Unlike the east side of the peak, the mountain's backside had no fence. We planned to climb up the back and come down the barricaded front where most of our archeological interest lay – actively guarded by the Saudis. We wore khaki clothing as camouflage against the sandy terrain. We figured that sooner or later the Bedouin patrols would spot us, but there was no reason to make it easy for them.

A web of thin trails fanned out before us like strands of a spider web. We chose a path up the hillside, then set a brisk pace up the surprisingly tame gradient. Jabal al-Lawz isn't a big mountain, rising just 8,465 feet above sea level, and the climb from the land below is just over 5300 feet. Larry and I had both done a fair amount of technical climbing, so in spite of an occasional sharp spasm from my back, it was an easy ascent. I pictured Moses, eighty-years-old when he first climbed the peak, marching stoically to the top without undue difficulty. The most intimidating obstacles we faced were the jagged rocks and stinging briers that made me glad we'd worn leather gloves. The other issue were the cactus needles that seemed to be everywhere, and the gloves didn't help against those. Every few feet yet another needle gouged me. Tiny spots of blood peppered my socks, pants, and shirt.

Only once did we have to backtrack when we encountered impassable cliffs. We quickly found our way back on course, scrambling up an alluvial fan of loose gravel. It ascended into a twisting, upward-sloping ravine, through compact fields of huge boulders and unstable scree, but my back had loosened considerably, and I managed it better than I'd expected. The trail dissolved near the top, so we clambered up the final pitch as best we could, forcing one foot in front of the other. At times we had to hand-over-hand it, skirting flimsy rows of narrow ledges and stretching our bodies past sharp spires and fat outcroppings. There were some tricky moments. We shinned along a slick granite wall that angled over a sheer 40-foot drop. We kept moving, our excitement overwhelming caution and common sense.

Two hours into our climb, we reached the summit. The twin snub-nosed peaks were separated in the middle by a broad, rock-strewn bowl. It pitched down like a huge, open-air amphitheater. I thought, "This is where Moses himself might have walked!" With each footstep, I wondered if I was crossing the stage on which the most extraordinary drama in human history had unfolded. We strained over the last, flinty hogback, and we gazed down on the stunning panorama that stretched out on the desert below. As the tallest peak in the area, Jabal al-

Lawz offers a spectacular view of yellow-tinted hills and taupe plains fixed in shapes and textures sculpted by wind and sand. The morning was clear, and we could see for miles in all directions. To the west lay the faint, slate-tinted coast of the Red Sea. To the north and south, majestic, rugged mountain ranges were bounded by broad desert.

We crested a final stair-step of crumbling sandstone terraces, and Larry asked, "Do you think we're the first people—the first *westerners*—to reach this summit since the time of Moses?"

We were standing near the very place where we believed Moses had received the Ten Commandments. This was a unique location in all of history, the spot where God met with man in a singular season of unprecedented intimacy and fearsome power.

Larry produced a piece of paper, and we both wrote a note to future travelers, extending our greetings and giving the time and date of our arrival. He then placed the note in an empty plastic water bottle and buried it under some rocks. I thought it an excessive gesture, but for Larry it sealed the deal as a time capsule for posterity.

Glancing around, I noticed that the entire summit bore an unusually black hue. The rocks—and even the dirt—had a shiny black appearance, like polished obsidian. The effect was startling, and we were genuinely baffled. We had hiked through acres of sagebrush and beige sandy ridges to reach the top. We had walked over typical desert terrain until this point, but here at the summit, we stood on what appeared to be burnt rock.

The sun was rising. The Bedouins below were probably awake and steeping their breakfast tea. The early morning was slipping quickly away, so we scurried about collecting as many loose rocks as our packs would hold for future laboratory analysis.

Larry seemed utterly mystified. "This has *got* to be a volcanic peak."

I could think of only one way to find out. "If it's volcanic," I said, "then the rock inside will be black, too. Right?"

Larry nodded. "Makes sense."

I picked up a watermelon-sized piece of charred rock, lifted it over my head and slammed it down hard on the sharp edge of a boulder. My back had protested, but we needed to know. As the rock made contact, it cracked open, and Larry and I both leaned in to look. The slick black exterior encased a reddish-tan core of ordinary brown granite.

Larry broke the silence. "Well, I guess that answers that question." But it didn't add up. What type of heat could melt the surface of a rock to black marble, glazed and smooth to the touch like buffed opal, yet leave the underlying granite intact? Clearly, something intensely hot had torched the mountaintop. What heat source could be potent enough to create a black rock rind while leaving a natural, tan marrow?

Larry picked up several rocks and examined them as though they were fine china.

"There's something in the Bible about this," I said.

I pulled my Bible out of my pack and flipped the pages to Exodus 19. "Here it is," I said, and I read out loud:

> Then it came to pass on the third day, in the morning, that there were thunderings and lightnings, and a thick cloud on the mountain; and the sound of the trumpet was very loud, so that all the people who were in the camp trembled. And Moses brought the people out of the camp to meet with God, and they stood at the foot of the mountain. Now Mount Sinai was completely in smoke, because the LORD descended upon it in fire. Its smoke ascended like the smoke of a furnace, and the whole mountain quaked greatly.
>
> Exodus 19:16-18

Those few words said it all.

Seeing the rock and holding it, I could understand why the Israelites had been so frightened that they begged Moses to speak with God while they retreated to a safer distance. A holy, omnipotent God would have been terrifying—an unbearable reality to an unruly people. It was unbearable to me as I stood on that mountain.

I thought of the forgery to which I had been a party. I thought of the deceit and self-seeking stubbornness that had brought Larry and me this far—how we had bullied aside any restraint and decorum to enter the Saudi kingdom—how we had strong-armed our way to this sacred spot. I stood there on God's holy mountain because I had committed illegal acts. It was a location so holy that in Exodus 19:12, God told the Israelites not to touch even the base of the mountain, or they would die.

Shaken and unthinking, I turned to Larry and urged, "Let's go. Now! We've got to get off this mountain." I grabbed my pack.

We stumbled and slipped our way back down the mountain, and from a height we were able to see another set of evidence that we had found the right place. We looked down on large stone markers set up around the mountain's base. They were stands of rock, and Larry and I could see them set in orderly distances at the bottom of the mountain. Again I thought of Exodus 19:12:

"You shall set bounds for the people all around, saying,
'Take heed to yourselves that you do not go up to
the mountain or touch its base. Whoever touches the
mountain shall surely be put to death.'"

Those physical barriers were erected to spare humans and livestock the fallout of God's wrath, and sure enough, we found stands of rock that would have worked as sacred markers set up at intervals. A collage of evidence was revealing itself to us as Larry and I surveyed the bottom of the mountain.

From a distance, we saw another altar. Near the mouth of the ravine, nestled against the bluff, somebody had assembled an angular altar of stones. It was clearly a manmade structure assembled in a V-shape. The tip of one arm pressed into the fold of the ridge, and its companion slanted away at a 45 degree angle. I estimated its length to be about 120 feet. It was badly weathered and crumbling in spots, but it looked like something on which animals could be sacrificed. It stood five feet high and about twenty feet across. The remains of a center support wall ran the length of both arms of the V. Right beside the altar, in an almost straight line, we found what looked like the hewn stumps of stone pillars. Time and the elements had toppled them, and they lay in broken sections near and away from the altar.

I flipped through pages of the Bible again, pummeling through my memory and seeking references to explain what we had found. Exodus 24:4-5 gave a thrilling explanation for what Larry and I were looking at.

And Moses wrote all the words of the LORD. And he rose early in the morning, and built an altar at the foot of the mountain, and twelve pillars according to the twelve tribes of Israel. Then he sent young men of the children of Israel, who offered burnt offerings and sacrificed peace offerings of oxen to the LORD.

Exodus 24:4-5

This must be it. We had found an altar sitting precisely at the foot of the mountain, and the remnants of pillars remained there. What we found matched the description of the altar that Moses had built in preparation for Israelite worship. It appeared that Dr. Knuteson was right after all, and Paul meant it in Galatians 4:25 when he said that Mount Sinai was in Arabia.

As we left the mountain, we imagined goldsmiths overlaying the Ark of the Covenant with gold, there in the shadow of that black-burned peak. The rich fabric for the tabernacle was woven and its luxurious walls were erected over these very sands. Thousands of tents surrounded that holy place where God spoke to Moses from between the cherubim on the Mercy Seat above of the Ark of the Covenant. Inside the Ark's holy darkness rested the Ten Commandments received by Moses on top of the mountain.

We had probably over-stayed our time, and we worried that government officials would appear at any moment to haul us off to a Saudi prison. We had seen a lot that morning, so we packed up. We wanted to head for the coast to seek out the other landmarks described in the Exodus account. We had to find the Bitter Springs of Marah described in Exodus 15:23-25 and the seventy palms of Elim mentioned in Exodus 15:27.

However, we had battered the Datsun quite a bit to that point, and it was starting to fall apart. Larry and I weren't in much better shape, and every time we hit a rut or a bump, I winced. My back had still not forgiven me, and sunburn had broiled my skin like a salmon. Larry stoically nursed his own collection of cuts, scrapes and contusions. All I really wanted to do was get back to our Tabuk hotel and order a nice room service dinner, then fall asleep in the full blast of the air conditioner. I longed to book our flight back to the good old USA. We decided to call off any further exploration and head for home. It was a long, bumpy, dusty ride back to the glorious asphalt, and when we reached our hotel I was ready to wash the desert grime out of every wrinkle.

Of course, we wouldn't be able to stay away forever. The desert would call us back to finish the job.

CHAPTER 9

BACK TO THE DESERT

We returned to the States, and I was grateful to plant my boots once again on American soil. A few days later, however, Larry called me to complain that the photos he'd taken were unconvincing.

"Listen Bob," Larry groaned. "I can barely convince my friends and family with these shots, and if we can't convince *them*, then…" He trailed off. He didn't need to finish the sentence. Larry was gracious, and he didn't criticize me for refusing to go one more round, but sometimes kindness hurts more than blunt speech. Larry hadn't given up, and curiosity had obviously been chewing at him.

Finally, he presented a challenge. "What's behind that fence, Bob? I want to know what they're hiding." There was a pause on the other side of the phone. Then Larry spit it out. "Let's go see what's back there. If we believe—I mean really believe—that Jabal al-Lawz is Mount Sinai, then we must get behind that fence. If we don't do it now, it will eat at us the rest of our lives. If this is the real Mount Sinai, then we will be making history."

Larry's passionate plea was unnecessary. I agreed we needed to do it right.

We spent a very short time in the safety of American civilization before returning to the Saudi kingdom. This time, I wanted nothing to do with faked letters and shady faxes. I poured myself into a whirlwind schedule of preparation and planning, and this time we procured legitimate visas. The Saudi prince had returned and promptly provided a letter of sponsorship. Using his London contacts, Larry fast-tracked our paperwork through the Saudi embassy. We had barely returned home when we were back on a plane to Jeddah. Shortly after sunrise a mere two weeks after our first trip, we touched down again in Tabuk.

This time we didn't bother with a hotel. We rented another truck, bought our supplies, and drove straight to the mountain. We felt much better prepared on this trip. There were no miscues, no getting stuck in the sand. We knew the way, knew what we needed and knew what to expect. We faced the same dust and the same miserable desert oven, but we cruised past the pit where I had injured my back and arrived at the mountain by late afternoon. Rather than approach the mountain's exposed backside as before, we drove straight to its east face, to the portion protected by the chain link fence. We stayed low and out of sight by driving slowly into the ravine left by a dry wadi, until we reached a crescent-shaped stand of rocks. About a quarter-mile across the valley from the golden calf altar, we hunkered down in the protection of the gully, just out of sight of the guardhouse, waiting for dark.

To minimize the risk of guards spotting us, we planned a nighttime incursion into the fenced-off area. We had invested in a pair of infrared night-vision binoculars in London and had brought them tucked into our supplies. We cooked a quick dinner on the truck's radiator and lay down in the sand to rest. We'd traveled halfway across the world and hadn't even bothered to sleep. We were exhausted, and we hoped for a few hours of shut-eye before climbing through the Arabian rocks.

The buzzing in my mind made sleep impossible, however. We knew what lay ahead. We were embarking on a rigorous, high-risk operation. Climbing the craggy, scree-covered slope at night would prove much more difficult than a daytime venture, and I lay awake, thinking of the challenges we faced.

First, half a dozen Bedouin camps were scattered at the base of the mountain. We could see the campfires flickering across the valley floor, and we heard bleating sheep and barking dogs. What's more, at least two armed sentries guarded the base of the peak. We couldn't figure out why the peak had become such a popular gathering place in the two short weeks we'd been gone, but these guards significantly raised the stakes. I lay wide awake, listening to the breeze rustling in the scant vegetation and staring at the black-crested mountain. It rose above us, both beautiful and menacing under its lunar spotlight.

At 10:30 p.m., we gave up on trying to sleep. Larry shook his head and sat up. "Let's just do it," he said.

Our plan was simple. We would use our night-vision binoculars to pick a path across the quarter-mile of exposed plain, and then we would bee-line it to the fence. If all went well, we'd dig under the chain link and dash to the safety of the rocks. That would put us within a hundred yards of the archaeological site, with its array of pillars and the altar we'd seen from a distance on our last trip. We counted it a mixed blessing that the moon was now bright enough to read a book by. It would light our way, but it could also betray us to our adversaries.

Moving as cautiously as possible, we crossed the valley in spurts. Larry would lead for fifty yards, then I'd take over. We could hear every footstep we made in the sand. When we were approximately 200 yards into the plain—and fully exposed on the flats—the dogs started barking again. First one dog, then two began yapping, and soon there were yelps bouncing up from everywhere. The quiet night erupted into an ear-splitting cacophony of demonic howls echoing their alarm that something was out there walking around.

"Oh my God," Larry whispered. "Do they smell us? Can they see us?"

The uproar grew so loud and intense that the dogs seemed to be right on top of us. I pulled out my knife, fully expecting to see dog shadows racing at us from across the plain. Larry scrounged up a stick to use as a club. I thought about a recent encounter we'd had with a snarling behemoth of a dog on the road from Tabuk. The beast charged from nowhere and attacked our truck. It actually tried to rip a tire off its wheel with its fangs! I had little doubt that these dogs could smell us, and our only hope was that the Bedouins would assume we were rabbits or other animals and would keep their packs tethered.

We continued moving toward the fence, trying to block out the noise. We even dropped down and shuffled on our hands and knees to avoid the sound of footfalls. We were less than forty yards from the fence when Larry's arm shot up.

"Wait!" he whispered, pointing. "There's someone there."

Larry handed me the night-vision binoculars, and through them I saw the green-white dot of a lighted cigarette dancing in the dark behind the fence. A guard or a shepherd was smoking there, which meant that digging our way under the fence was out of the question.

This means we'd have to fall back on Plan B, the alternative we had hoped to avoid. It involved soft-stepping another mile north along the exposed plain, dodging those sheep dogs and Bedouins in the dark, until we reached the end of the fence. From there, we'd have to climb halfway up the peak and descend down into the archaeological site without alerting the guards to our presence. Plan A would have allowed us to quickly penetrate the area from ground level, snap a few pictures, and hastily retreat to the hidden safety of our truck. We did not relish the idea of Plan B, which meant a demoralizing all-nighter on the precarious slopes of the mountain.

We walked a long way until we were able to dig-out a sandy place to crawl under the fence. It was well after midnight when we finally began our climb. While Jabal al-Lawz is not a steep mountain, the hike onward was arduous and exhausting. Larry kept the night vision binoculars glued to his eyes to keep us from tromping through a slumbering shepherds' camp, and I worried about stepping on an ill-tempered snake or scorpion. We picked our way through the darkness, always unsure whether the next shadow would prove to be a shallow chuckhole or a deep crevice with sharp rocks at the bottom. I found each step suspenseful and unsettling. Even in the cool of the desert night, we chugged water and gushed sweat.

We ran out of water much quicker than we'd anticipated, and it wasn't long before a ferocious thirst afflicted us. We climbed hand over foot, debating every move and painstakingly traversing a diagonal path up the steep mountain flank.

It took us another two hours to reach a point where we could look down on the big V-shaped altar. The moon had changed hues, and it now suffused the mountain in surreal aquamarine sparkles. In that light, the valley floor looked like a bluish snowfield. A wind rose, and we shivered in our sweat-soaked shirts. Soon it gusted across the rock face with a menacing howl, throwing dust and biting sand into our faces. We teetered on a narrow ledge, feeling exposed and vulnerable. I could just make out the shape of the guardhouse below. Further south we saw the ghostly white outlines of the pillar stumps and the vague, arrowhead-shaped altar.

Shielding my eyes from the stinging sand, I asked Larry, "What are we doing here?"

I could see the moon reflecting in his eyes, the sheen of sweat on his brow. With a widening grin, he replied, "We're making history, Bob."

We started down. What had appeared to be a straight shot from above turned into a maze of ridges and trenches. Descending from our rocky perch, we made two false starts toward the pillars. Scrabbling around in the dark on all fours, we had to climb back up the slope, make a new sighting to re-calibrate our position, then return down over rocks and through prickly bushes to the bottom. We communicated with whispers and hand signals, ducking in and out of the moon-shadows between boulders. We tiptoed past the guardhouse, only to come upon a series of odd stone circles that neither of us had expected.

"Remember David Fasold's letter?" Larry asked. "These must be the stone pillars he found inside the fence." These structures measured eighteen feet in diameter, and the twelve of them were spaced five feet apart. Each one had three large rings that formed exterior walls two-and-a-half feet thick. Buried at ground level, each circle was filled with dirt. First Fasold, and now Larry, had called them pillars, but they looked more like ceremonial platforms, or possibly large cisterns. They lay at the bottom of the ancient riverbed we had seen before, so perhaps they were once water storage reservoirs for the Hebrew tribes.

91

Fasold had explained in his letter that he had partially excavated one, thinking he would find Hebrew gold or treasure buried inside. Larry and I saw where his crew had dug, but we didn't have the time or tools to investigate further. We took a few pictures, shielding the flash with our hands, and we started looking for the V-shaped altar.

THE PILLARS AND THE ALTAR

As Larry and I walked along, Bible verses percolated in my mind.

And Moses wrote all the words of the LORD. And he rose early in the morning, and built an altar at the foot of the mountain, and twelve pillars according to the twelve tribes of Israel. Then he sent young men of the children of Israel, who offered burnt offerings and sacrificed peace offerings of oxen to the LORD.

Exodus 24:4-5

We took our time, moving methodically across the rocky terrain and using the shadows for cover whenever we could. We tried to avoid open, moonlit areas. We finally located the pillar stones, or column fragments, along a makeshift road some thirty yards from the V-shaped altar. We counted exactly twelve of the columns, or what was left of them. The pillars were smooth to the touch, and hand-chiseled, like polished marble. They were close to the altar at the foot of the mountain, just like the Bible described. If these weren't the pillars that Moses had erected, then I didn't know what they were.

"It's like finding fine marble pillars in the Mojave Desert," Larry said. "Something like this doesn't get here by accident."

I agreed. There was always a specific reason that humans built structures like those pillars. Their size alone, eighteen inches in diameter, made them a find of some consequence. Whether these were the bases for taller columns or the columns themselves, the rounded stones we found were twenty-two inches tall. With growing excitement, we took several close-up photos and moved on toward the altar.

When seen from above, the altar was impressive. Up close it was breathtaking. It had been built at the exact foot of the mountain, and I felt as though I were standing next to an airliner with spread wings, ready for take-off. We walked the entire length of the structure, marveling at this hand-constructed stone formation. It was an anomaly, erected there at the base of a mountain in the middle of the desert. Standing next to it cemented our impression that we were examining an ancient foundation.

What was it for?

The Bible states that Moses and the people built the altar for "burnt offerings." It was a place where young bulls were sacrificed "as peace offerings" to the LORD.

When we'd first seen the altar from an elevated vantage point two weeks earlier, we noticed that its outer stone walls sandwiched an interior wall that ran the length of the V and was parallel to the exterior ramparts. It looked like a corral for penning animals. After we had thoroughly inspected and filmed it, we agreed that it could be the altar described in Exodus.

Figure 11: The alleged twelve stone pillars of Moses located at the base of Jabal Al Jawz.

ELIJAH'S CAVE

It was 3:30 a.m. and the moon filled the sky. Excitement and wonder had fueled our efforts. We pressed on, hiking and climbing. We were dangerously dehydrated, and the physical exertions and lack of sleep had deeply fatigued us. My body said that it was time to quit, time to make our way back to camp to sip much-needed water and rest over-tired muscles. We'd made it this far, though, and the urge to continue won out over the physical need to rest.

"There's still time to reach Elijah's Cave," I said, looking up. I could see it clearly several hundred yards above us. A moonlit hollow gouged into the craggy slope beckoned me, and we worked our way upward toward a spot that offered good potential to be the cave described in 1 Kings 19:

> So he arose, and ate and drank; and he went in the strength of that food forty days and forty nights as far as Horeb, the mountain of God. And there he went into a cave, and spent the night in that place; and behold, the word of the LORD came to him, and He said to him, "What are you doing here, Elijah?"
>
> 1 Kings 19:8-9

We began one of the most dangerous climbs of our lives. The slope was already treacherous enough because of its distorted angle and the sometimes confusing moon-shadows on the rocks. Dehydrated and on the brink of exhaustion, the climb straight up through loose rock and talus was madness. Step-by-step we proceeded, placing one foot after the other. The night-vision binoculars were for distance vision and offered no help. There was no clear path, so we had to muscle our way up through the scree and around jagged overhangs. We struggled on; after nearly an hour, we had hiked to within seventy yards of the cave, and victory was in sight.

The next few moments were nearly my last on Earth. I began to worm my way around a sheer rock face when the ground gave way beneath me. I clawed frantically for a handhold, but only seized handfuls of loose gravel. I slid faster and faster toward a blind drop-off that I had avoided earlier. I grabbed and kicked, trying to sink the toes of my boots into the ground, but I couldn't stop! At the last possible second, as the earth turned to air and nothing else remained but a bone breaking death, Larry reached out and clutched my vest. His grip held firm as my legs dangled over the edge. Carefully, I scratched my way back and regained my footing. Safe again, I gazed in terrified disbelief at the black maw of the ravine that had almost become my grave.

We sat for several minutes gasping air. We both knew that I had almost died, and I was feeling especially mortal and frail. It made me stop and think about what we were doing. The sun was now creeping over the horizon. Soon we'd be climbing in broad daylight for all to see. Our legs felt like wet bags of concrete. We had nothing to drink, and there were still 100 yards of dangerous cliff above us. I looked at Larry, and we both knew it was over. We weren't going to make it to the cave. We dusted ourselves off and started back down.

We had accomplished what we had set out to do. We were satisfied with the photos we had taken. I shook off my regret and privately began to celebrate a successful mission.

It felt good to be working with gravity again. We made good time to the bottom and found a hidden draw near the fence that provided a safe exit point. When we reached the truck, I unlatched the tailgate, ripped open a box of water, and started gulping. It tasted better than anything I had ever experienced. We didn't pause long. Within minutes, we had dropped into our seats and started off.

Unfortunately, our zigzagging over and around the dunes had confused us, and within half an hour it was clear we were completely lost. I drove up a small hill to get our bearing, but the truck spun its tires in protest. I slammed my boot on the gas pedal, as if stomping harder would make a difference. The rundown truck agonized, but its threadbare tires spun and refused to bite into the loose rock. I offered Larry a weak smile. His face was caked in grimy sweat, and I could only imagine what I looked like. Larry said nothing. He simply stared up at the ridge, knowing it would not yield to our desperate efforts.

Finally, I leaned forward and shut off the engine. The Saudi Arabian desert offered no mercy to novices like us. We left the truck and stood on the loose desert soil.

"The truck will never make it up," Larry said as he began to trudge up the sandy draw. There was nothing for me to do but follow. We crested the ridge together and surveyed the horizon. In every direction we saw desolate stretches of sand, bleak rocky bluffs and high, barren mountains.

Far across the vast plain to the east, I saw the movement of wild camels. Just beyond them, a billowing dust spout rose from the desert floor as it followed a small truck.

"There!" I shouted, my voice raspy and parched. Larry gazed out to the east and saw the welcome apparition approaching us. We trotted down the sloping wadi and hopped into our truck. I started the vehicle and jammed the gears in reverse. The battered vehicle bounced off rocks as it careened downward to the wisp of a road, recognizable only by two thin, rutted trails. Cranking the wheel and gunning the engine, I bounced the truck along in the general direction of that rising dust.

THE OUTPOST

We soon met the approaching truck, which slowed immediately. Pulling alongside, we encountered a nervous Bedouin. He peered suspiciously into our truck and then sat back with his arm resting on the ledge of the window. He waited for us to speak. I leaned out the window and blurted, "Asphalt" which was my way of asking directions to a paved road.

The Bedouin nodded and then drove ahead of us, leading us across mile after mile of wasteland and through a broad canyon to an outpost in the middle of nowhere. We rolled into a collection of nothing more than a few black wool Bedouin tents and three mud hovels plugged into the side of the chalky cliffs. Two large, rusted tanks were supported by a leaning wooden platform. Some words were painted in block print on one of the weathered wood planks, but sandblasting windstorms had long rendered the lettering illegible.

A gust of hot wind greeted me as I stepped from the truck, sweeping a swirl of sand in my face and pelting my sunglasses with grit. Staring at me from the meager shade of the two tanks, a group of squatting Bedouin men sat wrapped in drab robes. They seemed uninterested in our arrival.

The whole village had an otherworldly feel about it. Apparently, it was a place where people came from miles around to fill their tanks with gas, get some water, and conduct their desert trade. I turned to see six men walking toward us, brandishing old, battered rifles. Standing statue-stiff and afraid to even blink, I was shaken by the unmistakable anger in their eyes. These desert dwellers wore flowing Bedouin robes soured yellow by the harsh sun. As best as I could tell, they were some of the frontier forces I had heard about, a kind of desert police that handled feuds or disputes between remote Bedouin clans. They now faced two Americans caught wandering in the desert near a fenced-in military facility.

Larry and I were quickly encircled and escorted to a mud-walled structure with patches of whitewash peeling from crumbling daub walls. A rifle butt prodded us along until we stood before its darkened doorway. I instinctively stopped short, but a foot against my lower back propelled me inside. Turning in anger, I could only make out the shape of a man standing in the entryway, his robed frame eclipsing the blinding rays of the sun. As my eyes adjusted to the darkness, I heard the word *Jew* and felt warm spit trickle down my cheek.

Larry and I were pushed to the ground inside the hut, and there we waited for the worst. Outside, a whipping wind whistled against the mud walls, blowing sand through the cracks and under the door. The air in the room was nauseating. The odor of putrefied mutton oozed from the floor and walls and clung to my skin, invading my nose, and mixing with my sweat-saturated hair. From, the moment they shoved Larry and me into this wretched place, I had to fight my stomach. I kept my breath shallow and rhythmic, battling against the urge to retch.

Soon a stocky man in frayed military fatigues pushed his way past the other guards and tossed a camel's saddle on the floor. Dirt rose in the stifling air of the dim room. With an exaggerated huff, the man lowered himself onto the saddle and glared at me. He had a brutish, sun-scarred face, like blistered leather, and his stare unnerved me. He appraised us with only one eye. His other eye was a blood-red, puffy orb, swelled nearly shut.

Larry and I sat on hard dirt, our backs now pressed against a wall stained with gun grease and sweat. Our captors had confiscated our socks, shoes, keys, wallets, passports, and other papers, and piled them on a Persian carpet in the middle of the room. Overhead, the rusted tin roof radiated triple-digit heat, and pencil-wide beams of sunlight pierced through holes in the tin, further searing my already burnt skin. I felt like a hapless ant at the mercy of a half-dozen school boys with magnifying glasses. I lowered my head and waited for the questioning to begin. When the man began speaking, he shouted angry words in a language I didn't understand. The questions were incomprehensible to us, and my answers—and Larry's—were equally incomprehensible to our captors.

The commander was constantly rubbing his red eye. He obviously had a chunk of desert grit lodged under the lid. He was dressed in military fatigues and wore boots, which indicated that he was a member of the frontier forces assigned to police the vast Saudi desert. I suspected that his first goal was to discover what we were doing in his domain, and keeping us alive was not so important to him.

It was frankly terrifying that his men had spit on us and called us Jews. From childhood, it is pounded into the Arabs to loathe Jews, and many of them think the more dead Jews, the better. If they thought we were Jewish spies sneaking into territory with military radar tracking stations on nearby mountain tops, then we were in the worst kind of trouble.

The commander parked himself on the camel saddle in front of us. He reached into his shirt pocket, pulled out a date, and rolled it in his fingers. He stared at us through his good eye and popped the whole date into his mouth, gnawing at its brown rind. It was summer, when dates in Saudi Arabia are considered best as they begin to turn from a dark brown to a buttery yellow. The man then stood and lifted a brown camel-stomach bag, the desert version of a canteen, from a peg. The commander snapped a quick order, and one of the boys hopped up to get him a small glass. Untying a shriveled intestine that dangled from the dried stomach, the commander poured a cloudy liquid into the glass. He handed me the drink. I raised it to the fading light that dribbled in through the doorway. The milky substance had several long camel-colored hairs floating in it. My tongue felt like a piece of tar from a Texas highway, so I held my breath and slogged it down. I had to pluck some hair out of my mouth.

As the sun slipped low on the horizon, something stung my leg. I reached down to slap it, and I saw that biting ants had begun to swarm the Persian carpet. The small reddish insects avoided the midday heat, but they were now marching out in rank and file as the sun dropped down. In a moment they were crawling all over us. I raised my hand to swat one, but a guard sprinted forward and pressed his rifle barrel against my forehead. My sun-scarred captor shook his head and a gaped-toothed, venomous smile split his face. We had to endure those fierce little brutes as they crept under our shirt collars and up our pant legs. I could only squirm and scratch when the guards momentarily looked away.

After hours of watching us, the guards became edgy and began bickering among themselves. To pass the time, they slid shells into their vintage rifles and put the muzzles to our heads. I held my breath as one captor after another pulled the trigger. I tried not to wince when the hammers fell, because I saw that they were loading empty shells. Still, I tightened every time metal struck metal. When the guards had finished their game of Terrorize the Prisoners, I leaned back against the wall, feeling lightheaded, as if my heart were pumping syrup to my brain. I started succumbing to thoughts of some very possible grim realities.

We had endured a grueling day of heat, abuse, threats, taunts, foul tasting tea, and carnivorous ants. It was time to do something, but no clear plan presented itself. I had churned over a variety of ideas, and all of them seemed destined to have unpleasant, maybe deadly, ends. Then, I glanced at Larry and saw it: the look. Without exchanging words, I knew Larry had an idea. I just didn't know whether it was a good idea.

Larry had just received another verbal assault, but this time the guards seemed to be gearing up for something far more physical. Larry leaned his head in my direction and whispered, "I think they're going to kill us. We need to do something and we need to do it soon." He paused, studied me, and glanced at the guard. From the corner of his mouth, he said, "Pretend you're a doctor."

"What? How am I supposed to do that?"

Larry raised a hand, pointed at me, and said loudly, "Doctor. He's a doctor."

I don't know what shocked me most; his willingness to plunge into the plan or his ability to fabricate with a straight face. The room went silent. Every guard stopped and looked at me. Across the room, the surly, red-eyed commander stood and walked my way. "Dooktar?" he mumbled, holstering his pistol as he pressed his scowling bearded face close to mine. He raised his hand and I steeled myself for a blow. Instead, he pointed to his puffy, irritated eye. He pried his lids apart. It was blood-red and watery. Apparently a grain of sand was embedded under his eyelid and had inflamed the normally white sclera of his eyeball. The guards, now engrossed in the drama, put down their rifles.

Everyone, including Larry, waited to see what the doctor would do. I sat frozen for a moment. The commander kept his finger pointing at his eye, slowly saying, "Dooktar," so I would be sure to understand him.

I turned to Larry, who sat expressionless. "What do I do?"

Larry was matter-of-fact. "I don't know; you're the doctor."

I had to play along, but that meant I needed my shave kit. I was escorted out to our truck by a fellow who waved a pistol around, and a minute later I returned to the dreary cell. There the commander stood, waiting for the doctor to perform his skills. I dug around in my bag while the commander fidgeted like an anxious child. I pulled out a plastic bottle of Visine and then gestured for the commander to tilt his head back. He complied and I squirted a thin stream of liquid into his eye. He blinked and pulled back out of reaction to the drops, then stood there smiling broadly. The Visine had soothed his tender eye.

Within minutes, the other guards began jabbering and pointing to their commander's face. The red of the eye was turning white. I was an instant hit.

Then, I remembered that a physician friend from home had given me medicine before we left for Saudi Arabia. He had donated some prescription drugs to us, for use in unforeseen circumstances that might require treatment for pain, infection, etc. He'd even included sleeping pills. When the next guard walked up to see the good doctor, I decided to give the guy five sleeping pills—one for each guard. My new patient bowed an appreciative thank you, then threw all five pills in his mouth, chewing the sour tablets like bits of hard-candy.

Larry raised his eyebrows and smiled. "Good plan!"

All the guards, including the commander, were soon crunching away on their sleeping pills. Within 20 minutes, the pills kicked in. Some of the Bedouins started to fidget, then to nod. Some yawned, while others searched for a cozy spot to nap in the stifling hot afternoon. The commander covered his camel's saddle with a wool blanket to use as a pillow. Two others leaned against the wall.

Then they all slept. All, that is, except for the young man standing guard just outside. We watched closely as he began murmuring to himself, pacing nervously and trying to shake his comrades awake. No one moved, which heightened his alarm. He started waving his pistol threateningly in our direction.

Pistol or not, Larry and I realized that this was probably our only chance to escape. We knew that if we waited around, the others would wake up and we would be in worse shape than ever. We'd never get out alive. With the guard agitated and distracted by his friends, we quietly put on our shoes and socks. Then, smiling and offering a few friendly nods, we walked from the cellblock toward the truck. The young guard stopped what he was doing and followed us, waving his pistol in our direction. We remained as calm as possible and then bowed politely. I noticed in his manner a youthful indecision and a reluctance to use the gun. With his companions all snoring away, he seemed lost.

We continued walking to the truck. I opened the door, took my seat, turned the key, and gave the engine a couple pumps of gas. Larry took the other seat. We were about to drive off when the young sentry flew into a red-faced rage. He screamed at the top of his lungs and ran in front of our truck, pointing his pistol at Larry's head. He motioned with his pistol for us to stay put. The frontier guard got into his own truck and, with a wave of his arm and a loud shout in Arabic, he ordered us to follow him. He popped the clutch and sped away into the wilderness. We raced across the desert floor, close behind our livid young jailer, heading straight towards the town of Tabuk.

While buying supplies in Tabuk prior to our foray into the desert, I had heard from a Muslim merchant that two Americans were being held in the Tabuk prison for preaching from the Bible. I also heard that they had beheaded an 18-year-old American who had smuggled cocaine into Saudi Arabia. Being a cop myself, I had some pretty sobering scenarios as to what might happen to us.

The whirring tires of the truck ahead of us whipped up a cloud of dust so thick I could hardly make out the road. I slowed down to get a little distance and the young guard slammed on his brakes, fish-tailing to a stop so that I almost rear-ended him. He leapt from the truck, ran back and pointed his gun at my temple. Then after some wild shouts and threatening gestures, he leaned into our truck cab and rapped his pistol barrel on the speedometer as if to say, "Hurry it up!"

After that, we bounced over land without a path or trail, at out-of-control speeds. We rammed into fat dunes, clattered across rock-strewn gullies, and bottomed-out over brush-covered ridges, before finally leveling out into a vast valley with a long smooth plain of red-hued powder. The reddish dirt covered Larry's face and hair. Even his teeth were brown from inhaling the choking dust. I was sure I looked the same.

Larry looked over at me and shouted, "We need to get rid of the stuff in the back of the pickup. It's evidence we don't want with us."

"How?"

"Slow down, only this time, easy does it. Slow down gradually."

"Got it."

Over the next ten miles, I gradually reduced my speed until there was a little more distance between us and truck in front. I kept the pickup in the dust cloud, hoping it would hide our actions.

"I don't think he can see what we're doing," I shouted. "Go! Quick! We don't have much time."

We speedily bounced along on the dirt-packed road. Larry pulled himself out the window, then slid his leg over onto the rear railing. Like a hero in an action film, he managed to climb into the bed of the pickup. He wasted no time in tossing out the incriminating evidence—film, infrared binoculars, satellite photos, topographical maps of Jabal al-Lawz, area maps, shovels, and even our compass and thermometer. The thought of all that amazing photographic evidence smashed and buried in the sand really sickened me.

Larry emptied almost everything from the bed of the battered pickup. I leaned over and opened the door and, in perfect form, Larry grabbed it and swung his legs and torso back inside the cab, absorbing several punishing body shots from the lurching chassis.

"You have another job to do," I said to Larry. "Take the grill off the air vent in the dashboard and hide a roll of film in there."

"What?" Larry frowned. "Why?"

"Just do it. Trust me on this." I closed the distance between the trucks, hoping to avoid another outburst from the pistol-wielding guard. Larry managed to remove the air vent.

"Open your duffle bag," I told him. "Take out a pair of socks—black socks, if you have them."

He did what I said, but not until he had given me a look that told me he was questioning my sanity.

"Now what?" he asked.

"Put the film in the sock and the sock in the vent, then replace the cover."

Again, he did as I instructed. Once the vent cover was snapped back into place, he leaned back amazed. "I can barely see the sock. If I didn't know it was there…"

"You wouldn't see it," I said, finishing his sentence. "It's an old drug smuggler's trick. I came across it a few times when I was a cop."

That trick gave me one thing to feel good about. One roll of film. I still felt heartsick about what we had left behind in the dust. All that effort, all those pictures, and nobody would ever see the results. With a little more time and better circumstances, we might have hidden more film away, but at that moment it was enough to get one roll. We still had to concern ourselves with getting out of this mess alive.

We pulled into Tabuk, and the young guard stopped at a T-intersection in front of a high-walled cement prison complete with curls of barbed wire and guard towers. My stomach dropped like an elevator with severed cables. As the truck idled at the stop sign, I swallowed hard, forcing down the wad of choking dust that had lodged in my throat.

"You don't think…" I began.

"I hope not," Larry said, looking at the barbed wire on the wall. Then the guard drove on, and Larry said, "He's moving."

I breathed with relief when the guard steered away from the prison and drove down the main street. He led us first to one police station and then to another. They were both closed; the police were probably sleeping or at prayers. Our young guard kept trying, but at every police station it was the same. The young man would knock, and nobody would answer. It would have been comical if I hadn't felt relatively terrified.

Finally, there was life at one station. A boy of about 14 answered the door as if he were the chief of police. He spoke with the guard and then scowled and led us to a holding cell. This cell had a few throw pillows and a wobbling ceiling fan that creaked at each revolution. There was no air-conditioning, and the heat was just as bad as in the desert cell. We were provided with liquid, but the foul drink still stank.

Several other officers arrived and listened to our captor's impassioned story, as he occasionally cast dark glances our way with sneers and snarls for effect. After some time and frequent requests by Larry, the desert guard allowed him to use the phone. Larry called the car rental place and told them what was happening. He also called our hotel. We hadn't checked in, but we were scheduled to, and the manager must have remembered Larry as a big tipper. Larry always tips well, and he certainly left enough of an impression that the manager wanted to bring him back safe and sound. In the end, the hotel manager invited everyone over to the hotel to sort it all out and have some cool drinks. Thank God.

Without knowing the details of the phone discussions between the police and the manager, it was difficult to unscramble what was happening. However, we were soon standing in the hotel manager's office at the Sahara Tabuk. It was there that Larry ran out of patience. We had been up for three nights; we were hungry and growing testy, and the constant stress had pushed Larry to the breaking point. He blew up. He pulled out the forged letter we had used to get our visas for our first trip and slammed it face up on the table.

I couldn't believe my eyes. Why would he bring that incriminating piece of evidence with him? It was a gutsy and dangerous move that could get our heads lopped off. Larry was hoping that it would get us out.

That false letter sat on the wooden table with the forged signature staring up at everyone. My stomach had clinched into a knot, yet Larry didn't even blink. He demanded that they release us and that they do so immediately. After all, we were honored guests of the royal family. The hotel manager read the letter aloud in Arabic. With an abruptness that startled everybody, the policeman placed our passports, cameras and keys on the table, then announced in Arabic, "We will check out your story."

The hotel manager cringed as he translated for us. He ordered us to stay put in the hotel until the police released us, because we were under house arrest. The officers left.

Then, we left!

A few hours later we were boarding a flight to King Kahlid International Airport, and after a gut-twisting layover in Riyadh without incident, we finally stepped onto a jet heading for New York City.

After all these years, hardly a day goes by that I do not think of that incredible trip. Had we actually stood (or trespassed) upon holy ground? Mount Sinai is the only patch of earth where the Bible tells us God actually came down and touched the earth. It was a place so holy that Moses was told to take off his sandals as he approached it. For me, it was a place of cathartic revelation. I had climbed up that mountain full of adventure and full of myself, but under the control of Saudi guards and behind bars, all of that evaporated into nothing but the realization that I had absolutely no control. It was a time of desperate prayers and promises to God, in which I pled for His forgiveness and deliverance. To this day, I am working to fulfill the promises

I made that day by telling people all over the world that the Bible is real. I believe it all, and I believe that God left His fiery fingerprints upon a lonely, scorched mountaintop in the desert of Saudi Arabia for all who were willing to believe.

ETHIOPIA AND THE LOST ARK OF THE COVENANT

CHAPTER 10

THE MYSTERY
OF THE ARK

In the winter of 1993, I read *The Sign and the Seal*, Graham Hancock's bestselling book that placed the Ark of the Covenant in Ethiopia. Indiana Jones might have found the Ark of the Covenant in a snake-filled cavern under the sands of Egypt, but Hancock offered convincing arguments that the Ark was actually safe and sound in eastern Africa. Hancock was far from a Bible scholar, but he was a notable journalist and tenacious investigator. His book presented a fascinating theory outside traditional paradigms, and many people were stunned by his suggestions.

I was dubious at first myself, but now after twenty-two trips to Ethiopia, I believe he may have gotten it right.

I love solving "whodunits." It was one of the reasons I became a police investigator in the first place. The quintessential question surrounding the Ark of the Covenant has long been, "Who did it?" Which ancient king of Israel allowed the Ark to go missing on his watch? Someone, somewhere in time, obviously permitted the most holy object in all of recorded history to vanish. It was either a blunder of incalculable magnitude, or a misdirection of great protective wisdom.

For starters, it is impossible to know the exact date the Ark was removed from the Temple. Only one person each year, one single day of the year, the Day of Atonement, was even allowed to see the Ark. On that most holy day, the Jewish high priest would enter the Holy of Holies with animal blood used to symbolically atone for the sins of the people. He would sprinkle the blood on the Ark and in front of the Ark. No one else joined him as he entered that inner sanctuary of the Holy of Holies, so nobody would know if the Ark was in there except for the high priest himself.

Hancock had come up with a pretty creative, yet basically logical theory. The last known reference to the Ark in the Temple was during the reign of Judah's King Hezekiah about 701 B.C. The Bible doesn't specifically tell us that the Ark was in the Temple, but logical induction suggests that it was, because Hezekiah went into the Temple and prayed before the Lord, saying in 2 Kings 19:15, *"O Lord God of Israel, the One who dwells between the cherubim..."* The cherubim in question were the gold-wrought angelic beings whose wings stretched across the Mercy Seat on the Ark of the Covenant, as described in Exodus 25:

> *"And you shall make two cherubim of gold; of hammered work you shall make them at the two ends of the mercy seat. Make one cherub at one end, and the other cherub at the other end; you shall make the cherubim at the two ends of it of one piece with the mercy seat. And the cherubim shall stretch out their wings above, covering the mercy seat with their wings, and they shall face one another; the faces of the cherubim shall be toward the mercy seat. You shall put the mercy seat on top of the ark, and in the ark you shall put the Testimony that I will give you. And there I will meet with you, and I will speak with you from above the mercy seat, from between the two cherubim which are on the ark of the Testimony, about everything which I will give you in commandment to the children of Israel."*

Exodus 25:18-22

Since the LORD promised to meet with Moses from between the cherubim, and Hezekiah was praying to the LORD, Hancock made the reasonable conclusion that the Ark remained in the Temple toward the end of Hezekiah's reign. We also know from

2 Kings 18:4 that the bronze serpent that Moses had made still existed, until Hezekiah had it destroyed because the people had started to worship it. It appears the Israelites had preserved the ancient holy items from the time of Moses through the years of Hezekiah.

However, after Hezekiah died, his son Manasseh took charge and ruled for fifty-five long years, during which time the king behaved like a completely vile madman. Manasseh was a veritable monster. He worshipped false gods and set up idols in the Temple of the LORD. We learn from 2 Kings 21:16 that he filled Jerusalem with innocent blood. He engaged sorcerers and those who consulted with demons, and he sacrificed his own children in the fire. The Bible describes Manasseh in the worst terms, declaring him to be worse even than the pagans whom God had driven out before the Israelites:

> And he built altars for all the host of heaven in the two courts of the house of the LORD. Also he caused his sons to pass through the fire in the Valley of the Son of Hinnom; he practiced soothsaying, used witchcraft and sorcery, and consulted mediums and spiritists. He did much evil in the sight of the LORD, to provoke Him to anger. He even set a carved image, the idol which he had made, in the house of God, of which God had said to David and to Solomon his son, "In this house and in Jerusalem, which I have chosen out of all the tribes of Israel, I will put My name forever;"
>
> 2 Chronicles 33:5-7

After Manasseh died, his son Amon only ruled for two years, and then the righteous King Josiah took the throne and began to try to undo the damage done by his grandfather. In 2 Kings 22:3-7 we read about how Josiah paid to have Temple repaired. During those repairs, the Book of the Law was found and read to Josiah, who grieved at Israel's failure to obey the Law. This young king did all he could to destroy the idols and their altars in the land of Judah.

Hancock found a verse that implies the Ark had been removed from the Temple during the reign of Josiah. This is unmistakable, because Josiah speaks to the priests of the LORD in 2 Chronicles 35 and tells them:

"Put the holy ark in the house which Solomon the son of David, king of Israel, built. It shall no longer be a burden on your shoulders. Now serve the LORD your God and His people Israel.

2 Chronicles 35:3

This verse indicates that the Ark had been removed from the Temple at one point. The sentence, "It shall no longer be a burden on your shoulders," indicates that the Ark was being carried in Levitical fashion, according to God's instructions in Exodus 37:5 and Numbers 7:9; but we don't know where it had been taken. The Levites carried the Ark on their shoulders only when transporting it from one location to another. In other words, the Ark had been moved out of the Temple and probably out of Jerusalem at one point. It might have been moved during the time that Josiah was having the Temple repaired, but it was more likely transported out during the evil years of Manasseh, when righteous priests of the Lord may have moved the Ark to protect it.

Manasseh had flagrantly mocked God and defiled His holy Temple. He had performed such unspeakable acts that any God-fearing Levitical priests would have been completely repulsed by his very rule and the evil he had done. It was unlikely that the Ark of the Covenant, holy to the priests and all Israel, would have been left inside the Holy of Holies while pagan idols were placed alongside it, corrupting the entire Temple. The priests would have assuredly taken the Ark far away from such wicked pollution, and they would have no doubt been willing to give up their lives in protecting it.

When Josiah consulted the LORD in the 18th year of his reign, he was told that God planned to bring all the destruction on the land that He had promised in His Word, but He would spare Josiah and bring him to his grave in peace. As a result of Manasseh's despicable actions, God pronounced a grave sentence on Israel. After Josiah's death, the hand of God was removed from Israel and it is safe to assume that Ark was removed from there as well.

*Behold, I am bringing such calamity upon Jerusalem
and Judah, that whoever hears of it, both his ears will
tingle. And I will stretch over Jerusalem the measuring
line of Samaria and the plummet of the house of Ahab;
I will wipe Jerusalem as one wipes a dish, wiping it and
turning it upside down*

2 Kings 21:12-13

Jeremiah offers the last instance in the Old Testament when
the Ark is mentioned, but even then there's no clear indication
that the Ark is still in Jerusalem. Jeremiah merely speaks of
a future time when the Ark will no longer be visited or even
remembered.

*And it shall come to pass, when ye be multiplied and
increased in the land, in those days, saith the LORD,
they shall say no more, The ark of the covenant of the
LORD: neither shall it come to mind: neither shall they
remember it; neither shall they visit it; neither shall that
be done any more.*

Jeremiah 3:16 (KJV)

Let's recap our clues from the Bible:

a. The Ark was in the Temple during the reign of
    Hezekiah, who prayed to God *"who dwells between
    the cherubim."* This even took place about 701 BC.

b. The Ark was absent from the Temple during the early
    reign of Josiah, and the Levites had carried it on their
    shoulders to an unknown location.

c. It appears that Josiah knew where the Ark was, and
    there's no reason to believe that the Ark wasn't
    returned to the Temple as ordered, but it is clear that
    the Levites were willing to move the Ark in extreme
    situations. Hancock believed the Ark disappeared
    during the reign of Manasseh, during which time it had
    been carried away.

d. Not long before the Babylonian destruction of
    Jerusalem in 586 BC, Jeremiah alludes to a future time
    when the Ark is not visited or remembered. There is no

113

mention of the Ark in the Old Testament after the exile to Babylon.

Once Hancock felt satisfied he had assembled a likely historical sequence behind the Ark's disappearance, there remained yet another question: where did it go?

Ethiopia is the only country that exists today that claims to have the Ark, and the Jews in Ethiopia have maintained this claim for over two thousand years. Falasha Jews from Ethiopia were airlifted to Jerusalem during Operation Moses in 1984, and Hancock interviewed a number of Falasha elders living in Israel. In Jerusalem, Hancock found a patriarch named Raphael Hadane who related the tradition that his ancestors had lived in Egypt's southern Nile region before migrating to Ethiopia.

Hancock discovered that a colony of Hebrews had indeed settled in that region, on Elephantine Island in the Nile, during the reign of wicked King Manasseh. Papyrus scrolls found by archaeologists on Elephantine Island indicate that a substantial Hebrew settlement existed there between the seventh and fifth centuries BC, and according to their tradition, the Ark of the Covenant arrived in Ethiopia in 470 BC. Even more significant, the refugees constructed a temple, complete with exterior pillars, gateways of stone, and a roof of cedar wood. Its dimensions and appearance were modeled precisely on Solomon's Temple. Papyrus records also describe the Hebrew performance of ritual animal sacrifices at the Elephantine temple, just as in Jerusalem, including the all-important sacrifice of a lamb during Passover. Other papyri describe the temple as God's dwelling place. Hancock concluded (as did I) that the Elephantine Hebrews believed Yahweh resided literally in their temple.

Unfortunately, the Elephantine temple of Yahweh was destroyed in 410 BC, within sixty years of the date that legends say the Ark arrived in Ethiopia. According to Ethiopian tradition, the Ark migrated south from Elephantine Island to a huge lake called Lake T'ana in the highlands of Ethiopia. There it is said to have been hidden for nearly eight hundred years on the remote island of T'ana Kirkos. That island is still considered a holy place to this day.

There is a prominent cultural myth that the Ark was brought to Ethiopia by Menelik, the illegitimate son of Solomon and the Queen of Sheba, shortly after the time of Solomon. This Ethiopian tradition is widespread and provocative, but it doesn't match up with research that places the Ark in the Temple in Jerusalem long after Solomon's day. The legend of Menelik has no basis in historical fact.

Hancock concluded that the Ark had indeed reached Ethiopia, traveling to T'ana Kirkos Island by way of Elephantine Island.

Following this historical trail of crumbs, Hancock decided to travel to Lake T'ana. There, he chartered a boat and docked at T'ana Kirkos Island. T'ana Kirkos is surrounded by high cliffs and dense jungle, and it rises up out of the lake like a haunted castle. It boasts a number of ancient artifacts, altars, and stone pillars that all seem to spring from the pages of the Old Testament. There, in the jungles of Ethiopia, we find the whisperings of an ancient Hebrew culture.

On T'ana Kirkos Island, the monks showed Hancock a slab of stone high on a ledge, where they told him that blood sacrifices had once been performed. They said that those sacrifices were made next to a portable tabernacle (tent) under which the Ark had been kept for eight hundred years. The chief monk explained that in AD 330, when Ethiopia converted to Christianity, King Ezana's troops removed the Ark from T'ana Kirkos and installed it in a great church in Axum, where it remains today.

CHAPTER 11

OFF TO ETHIOPIA

I knew that curiosity would drive me crazy unless I went to Ethiopia myself and followed the trail that Hancock had taken. Hollywood had offered its version of the Ark of the Covenant in the Indiana Jones film, but I hoped beyond all odds that I might be able to find the real deal. After much thought and prayer, I set about planning my first trip to Ethiopia.

In March of 1998, I flew out to Addis Ababa with my friend Joby Book. Joby was a good old boy born in Louisiana and reared in Houston. At that time he lived in Arkansas, and he managed to insert his favorite expression, "Hey Bubba!" into every third or fourth sentence.

From Addis Ababa, we then flew a twin prop Fokker 50 across the brown, deeply furrowed Ethiopian countryside into endless miles of gritty hills and desolate canyons. As the town of Axum eventually came into view, our pilot throttled back on the engines and began a steep, banking descent. Swooping out of the sky at a nearly vertical pitch, our plane leveled just in time to buzz by scores of shepherds, sending their flocks scurrying for cover. We arced skyward, and I looked down as several men in filthy white robes shooed grazing cows and camels out of the way with long sticks. I realized that the pasture below was our landing strip, and the animals had to move in order for us to land.

I held my breath as the pilot took a second pass at the runway, this time dropping down and making contact. As we bounced across the hard ground, rocks and debris jumped up onto the wings and pelted the plane's undercarriage. The plane shuddered down a washboard runway and braked to a stop in a swirl of dust only a few yards from a barbed wire fence.

I turned to see Joby's white face. I smiled and tried to make light of it for him as I hid my own perspiring neck and forehead. Touching down on primitive surfaces like this seemed suicidal, but those gutsy Ethiopian pilots did it every day.

Joby and I gathered our bags and stepped into the blinding sunshine. A few locals lugged bulky canvas bundles onto their shoulders and clambered out of the plane. We followed them down the steps to the most primitive, ramshackle airport I had ever encountered. Several burned-out, bullet-riddled military planes, trucks and assorted chunks of battlefield refuse were strewn about. Mangy sheep nibbled at stocks of grass growing through shrapnel holes in the rusted metal carcasses. Since the early 1990s, Axum had been locked in a bloody guerilla war. The conflict decimated the countryside, and graves peppered the surrounding hills.

The airport terminal was a knobby frame of wooden poles lashed together by wire; sheets of corrugated tin had been nailed to poles and rafters to form crude walls and a roof. Beams of sunlight bled through yawning gaps in the ill-fitting panels. A little hand-painted sign hung on a rusty nail, telling us we'd reached the Axum terminal, a leaky structure no larger than 30x20 feet. As we crossed the pasture to retrieve our luggage, we passed a bearded old man in a ratty robe sitting on a stool by the front door.

"Look at that," Joby mumbled.

He pointed to a spot behind the old man. There, quivering in the shadows, swarmed thousands of bees, flowing in and out of a large hive perched high on a wall inside the dilapidated terminal. The drone of rushing wings unsettled the otherwise quiet noontime air. The bees crawled over the man, head to foot, covering his ears, neck and beard. Amazingly, the old fellow paid the bees no mind, seemingly unconcerned with the buzzing necklace about his throat.

I heard the roar of an engine and turned to see our plane clatter off, its prop wash blowing Joby's hat from his head and sending it cartwheeling down the rutted dirt path. Down the runway, two men chased some straggling goats out of the way, just in time as the plane lifted off.

Joby broke the silence. "Welcome to the end of the world, Bubba."

For Joby, it was the end of the world. For me, it was the beginning of an adventure right in the rugged heart of Africa.

A young man in his early twenties strode up out of nowhere. "Hello," he said in clear English. "I am Ecuba. I would be honored to serve as your guide." Ecuba had a big, toothy grin in his shiny, dark face. He wore a t-shirt, sandals, and faded Levis. "If you come with me," he continued, "I will take you to get food, water and a hotel."

Joby and I stared at the abject poverty around us. It was hard to imagine that Axum had once been the center of a lavish, powerful kingdom that rivaled the mightiest nations of the ancient past. As we walked into the town, we found little more than a dusty village decaying into obscurity. Yet, at the center of Axum sits a simple thick-walled chapel known as Saint Mary of Zion Church, where the Ethiopians claim that the greatest secret in history is held. From the lowliest peasant to the highest public official, all Ethiopians insist that the Ark of the Covenant rests securely within St. Mary of Zion's fortified inner sanctum. No other location on earth makes such a bold claim.

Ethiopians also maintain that no one will ever see the Ark of the Covenant except for one man, the Guardian of the Ark. The Guardian is a spiritual man selected from the priests and assigned to spend his entire life in worshipful solitude as the Ark's sole caretaker. He will never leave the small, fenced chapel of Saint Mary of Zion Church until he is carried away for his funeral.

Joby and I took our bags to our new digs, a hotel called the Yeha. It had been recently built, but it still looked fifty years old. There, I was introduced to a very old man with a gray beard covering his mahogany face. His name was Birani, and he told us that the original Saint Mary of Zion Church was built by King Ezana in the fourth century, and it was there the Ark had been brought to rest. He told me, "It is the most sacred place in Ethiopia." That original church was now just a big rectangular pit filled with ancient foundation stones and choked with weeds and trash. The crumbling remains are those of the earliest Christian church on the sub-Saharan continent. The newer Saint Mary of

119

Zion that Joby and I saw had been built in the 1960's by Emperor Halle Salasee as a newer resting place for the Ark. This church looks more like a bunker than a holy building.

I turned my eyes to the small chapel silhouetted by the descending sun. Somewhere within its thick cinderblock walls sat what all Ethiopia believed to be the original Ark of the Covenant. I made a naive request to see the Ark, and Birani's response was instant and harsh.

"No one ever sees the Ark," he growled. "And the Guardian will not meet with you or anyone else."

I knew from Hancock that the Ark might have stayed on T'ana Kirkos Island on Lake T'ana after all, and I thought we might have better luck getting information there. I asked Birani about it, and he assured us that we would hit a brick wall there as well.

Ecuba offered us a different tone, however, and told us that a guide named Misgana would be able to take us to the island. So

we made the hasty arrangements and once again boarded a plane on that goat field of an airstrip. We flew out to Bahir Dar to meet with this mystery fellow Misgana.

Figure 12: Saint Mary of Zion Church, Axum Ethiopia. Said the be the resting place of the Ark of the Covenant by many Ethiopians.

CHAPTER 12

T'ANA KIRKOS ISLAND

W hen we stepped from the plane in Bahir Dar, the first thing that hit us was a suffocating curtain of humidity, one that reeked of burning rubbish. After we retrieved our bags in the terminal, we found ourselves face-to-face with a handsome, lanky young man in his early twenties.

"Hello, Mr. Bob. I am Misgana" he said. He had a pleasant face and a comfortable smile that set us at ease immediately. He informed us he had made the arrangements for a trip to Lake T'ana, and we would be headed there shortly.

Misgana was the son of a peasant coffee merchant, and he now worked as an up-and-coming entrepreneur in an impoverished land strangled by years of civil war. I didn't know it that day, but Misgana would become my close friend in the years ahead, and he would guide me on twenty-two more of my trips to Ethiopia. The stories of my adventures with Misgana could fill ten more books, but that first trip to Ethiopia with Joby provides a significant example of our times together.

En route to our hotel, Misgana, filled us in on what was to come. His said his good friend Gebeyehu Wogawehu, who worked for the Tourism and Information Department in Bahir Dar, had granted us very rare permission to visit T'ana Kirkos Island. Misgana then informed us that Gebeyehu must accompany us and oversee our journey.

"No problem," I answered immediately.

The next day we made a three-hour boat trip across the magnificent Lake T'ana, and soon the island came into view. It revealed little more than a rocky scab covered with leafy trees, where the surf lapped at the shore. The closer we sailed, however, the more impressive it grew. Tall cliffs hunkered near the shore, their thick foliage crowned by primeval trees and strange, towering cacti. As we drew near the shore, I spied a small hut on one of the cliffs. Overhead, three kingfishers circled, scouting for a meal of Nile perch.

The captain slid the boat into a lagoon shaded by a thick canopy of foliage. As he pulled close to the jutting orange rocks, I saw a thin flight of granite steps chiseled into the cliff. The captain tied off the boat, and Misgana ushered Joby, Gebeyehu, and me onto the rocks and up the precariously steep, jagged steps. Joby and I had brought camping gear along, but we left it in the boat for the moment. If the monks consented, we hoped to spend the night, but both Misgana and Gebeyehu cautioned us that, as far as they knew, no westerners, no outsiders, had ever slept overnight on the island.

Within minutes of our arrival, my optimism crumbled. The chief priest of T'ana Kirkos marched down the trail to meet us in his loose, flowing white robe and turban. He stopped us in our path by striding up to Misgana and Gebeyehu and peppering them with questions. His filthy prayer shawl had been thrown backward over his shoulders, and he seemed none too pleased to see us. After a few moments of heated discourse, Misgana backed away and whispered, "The village elder will not let you on the island if you are not an Orthodox Christian."

"What?" I said.

Misgana shrugged. "He wants to know if you are Orthodox. He will not allow us to go any further unless we are professed Orthodox Christians."

I wasn't certain what he meant by "Orthodox Christian," so I was unsure how to respond. I hadn't come this far to be turned away in the first minutes of my arrival. I stepped up to the priest and asked Misgana to translate.

"I am Bob Cornuke of the United States and I am a Christian. I would like to come onto your island and learn more about your culture."

Misgana relayed my message to the dispassionate monk, who answered in Amharic, staring straight into my eyes.

Figure 13: Monk on remote Tana Kirkos Island, Ethiopia.

"He wants to know if you are an Orthodox Christian," Misgana repeated.

I sensed this was the moment when everything could implode. "Ask him this: When he says his prayers, does he pray in the name of the Orthodox Christian Church or does he pray to Jesus?"

Misgana translated and gave me a reply. "He says, 'to Jesus.'"

"Then tell him that we pray to the same God." I pointed to the priest. "We are Christian brothers; we are followers of Jesus."

I held out my hand. The priest hesitated, and then smiled wryly as if conceding the mental chess match. After a moment, Misgana turned and said, "Abba says you are welcome."

Abba is a word that means "father." Abba bowed slightly and approached me with an outstretched hand, shaking mine with his right hand while holding my wrist with his left—a gesture of honor and respect. A lengthy greeting ensued, after which the priest led us up the overgrown path through a stone archway and into a grassy clearing. There we saw a couple of dilapidated

123

shacks and a few raggedly dressed monks. The holy men were stunned to see us.

After a brief round of introductions, they led us higher up the path toward their hillside village, which was choked with shrub but alive with hummingbirds and starlings. We walked under a canopy of vines. Along the path, I looked up and had a sudden shock. Concealed among the thick, green mantle of trees hung a curtain of spider webs packed with dozens of fat-bellied, long-legged spiders, some larger than my fully outstretched hand.

"Are they poisonous?" I asked Misgana.

"Yes, they are poisonous," Misgana replied. "But they are not aggressive. I have seen the monks let them crawl up their arms. They rarely bite."

I wasn't going to test the truth of that statement. I ducked under the webs, glancing up to watch the spiders scramble in all directions.

When we reached the village, the compound struck me as depressingly glum; it was little more than a small circle of dirty thatched huts. There were no creature comforts.

"Where are the monks?" I asked.

"Most of the monks are still at work on the other side of the island," Misgana explained. "They tend the monastery's fields of teff, coffee, and vegetables."

I peered west and saw a marshy finger of land stretching away from the main island, connected to another half-submerged sliver of peninsula. From a distance, I could just make out the bobbing white robes of monks toiling in the heat.

On the ground about us lay dusty piles of unshucked coffee berries. A few young boys gathered around us, staring. They were dressed in tattered prayer shawls that looked as if they had never been washed.

I didn't immediately ask about the Ark. Instead, I spent that first afternoon and evening watching the monks' routine. Over the course of those hours, I gained a feel for the rhythms of the village and sensed that the chief priest was warming to me.

Shortly before the evening meal, we met the rest of the order as a sweaty, dirty band of monks straggled into camp. One of them walked with the aid of a staff. Even at a distance, I could see that his foot was injured, and as he drew closer I could see that a deep, angry-looking wound oozed from his instep. They told me that he had injured himself while swinging an axe; the blade had missed the log and found his foot. He had been living with this nasty gash for several weeks, and I could even see the gray of exposed foot bone.

"Such injuries are common on the islands," Misgana explained.

I believed him. I looked around and saw a variety of discolored, swollen, deeply scarred limbs. The poor fellow's foot had swollen to twice its normal size, and with no medicine or antiseptic to fight the infection, the prognosis wasn't good.

I couldn't sit by and do nothing. "Ask Abba if he would allow us to help the monk."

Misgana did so. "He says it is permitted."

Joby and I took the monk aside, cleansed and bandaged the wound, then gave him a heavy dose of antibiotics. We also handed him a month's supply of capsules, which we hoped was enough to help.

The monks asked us to join them in their evening meal, and we followed them to a smoke-filled grass hut. It took several seconds to adjust to the darkness inside, but I soon made out an old man stooped over a black pot. It rested on a pile of coals, and he stirred the contents with a flat, broken stick. The lumpy brown concoction in the pot smelled horrible.

The man looked up and gave a toothless smile, then he dug out a paddle full of the stuff and slopped it in one of the wooden bowls stacked beside him. I bowed and took the steaming bowl of whatever-it-was and stood waiting for the group of monks to join us. One by one the monks filed in, got their bowl, and left.

"Where are they going," I asked Misgana.

"To eat," he said.

Unsure if I should follow, I walked behind the group of men. They scattered about the village and entered small thatched huts. These huts were little more than thatched boxes, hardly larger than a filing cabinet tipped on its side. They were made of tightly woven palm branches that harbored nests of leggy spiders and other insects. There were no windows. They were the most austere living quarters I had ever seen.

When asked to join the group in their evening meal, I had assumed that it would be a communal gathering. I was wrong. The monks got their food and left to eat it alone. I couldn't imagine living in those bleak, woven palm cubicles, but that's all they had in the world. They slept, prayed, ate their meals, and endured their monastic lives here from childhood to death. The island was their home, their universe.

After the meal (I had covertly dumped my whatever-it was and eaten a granola bar in private), the monks brought out another suffering soul. The old man sprawled on a mat of palm fronds, groaning with every movement. He had contracted a severe infection in his groin, and the pain had become so intense that for days he had been unable to walk. I snatched a pair of rubber gloves and some topical antibiotic cream from my pack.

I handed the items to Joby and said, "Put some of this on the infection."

Joby shot me a look as if I'd skinned his favorite hunting dog. "What?" he whispered, glancing down at the pus-filled ulceration.

"Here," I insisted.

With a long sigh, Joby pulled on the rubber gloves and began smearing on the cream. He acted as if he were handling rusty razor blades as he carefully daubed away. We left the man still wincing, yet thanking us with great sincerity.

"You owe me, Bubba! You owe me big!" Joby repeated as we left the monk's village.

As I had hoped, Abba decided to let us spend the night on the island. Joby and I could set up our tents on the cliff above the village. Misgana told us that the privilege, "should be regarded as a rare honor."

As their predecessors had done for the last 1,000 years, the monks turned in at dusk. They would rise, as always, at 4:00 a.m. for prayers. Joby and I gathered our gear and hiked to the highest point of the island, pitching our camp on a spine of ridge barely wide enough to support our tent. In those compact quarters, merely rolling over in our sleep might have sent us tumbling off the cliff onto the rocks of the lagoon, so we cleared the area of leaves and placed a ring of large stones around our tent to stop us if we should begin to slide.

A fresh breeze blew in off the lake, and a bank of thin clouds draped the moon. The dark skies dazzled with stars and Lake T'ana—black, sullen, and immense—seemed to mingle with the heavenly expanse.

Then I noticed the buzzing. By making a tent site and brushing away the leaves on this ancient cliff, we had stirred up thousands of creeping and winged insects from their nests. The mosquitoes came on. To counter the attack, Joby and I slathered ourselves with an entire bottle of mosquito repellent, fully aware that malaria was rampant on these islands. I started a fire and stoked it with rotting tree branches. The billowing smoke cloud and the repellent kept the insects at bay.

At last we were able to sit down and relax. I nudged the fire with a stick, prodding the embers to release a little more heat. Through the grey smoke, I noticed a row of white eyes staring at us from the dense palm leaves behind Joby. Curious monks, no doubt, had come up to spy on the crazy Americans.

I waved them in, but there was no movement for a few moments. Then, one of the bolder ones tiptoed to the edge of our makeshift camp. He was a boy, no more than fourteen years old and probably an apprentice from a nearby island. I stood up, and he jumped back into the security of the green foliage, startled by my sudden movement.

"Joby, hand me a candy bar," I whispered.

Joby rummaged in his pack and pulled out a chocolate bar. I handed it to the boy, motioning for him to take a bite. The monk chomped down on the Snickers, wrapper and all. Not only had these island dwellers never seen a candy bar, they had no idea what to make of a wrapper. In slow motion, I walked over and unwrapped the candy. The young man took a nibble, then a bite. After he swallowed, a smile crossed his face. Suddenly six other boys between 14 and 18-years-old leaped out from the darkness. They all wanted Snickers bars.

The older monks had gone to bed; the night belonged to the young. After endless nights of prayer, eating alone, and candles out by 7:30, they acted as if the circus had come to town. Joby and I handed out more candy and watched, amused, as the boys gobbled it up. After a strict diet of vegetables and sour injera, that first bite of chocolate must have exploded like ambrosia in their mouths. Unfortunately, their pure young bodies were unaccustomed to sugar and chocolate; they soon began bounding about the ridge like ferrets on a double latte.

Joby took out our two-way radios and turned them on. We gave a short demonstration, and two boys started shouting at each other through the radios, scurrying about the ridge. I took out my night vision binoculars and showed the young men how to see in the dark. Seconds later, they had commandeered the binoculars and taken them over to the cliff, where they peered down into the village. They began giggling uncontrollably. I walked over to see that they had undertaken a bit of island espionage, watching the older monks coming and going from the village outhouse. This was simply a woven palm mat with a hole in it situated at the edge of the lake, and soon the boys began laughing out loud. They fought each other for the binoculars and viewed with hilarity proceedings that had, until that very moment, been private. "Joby," I said, "what have we done?"

We had introduced chaos, and the boys were now running amok. Prior to our arrival, T'ana Kirkos had experienced 2,500 years of uninterrupted solitude. Now, laughing boys buzzing from sugar and bewitched by fancy gadgets ran through the jungle as if drunk on moonshine. In one brief interchange, I feared, we had unraveled centuries of religious tradition. I turned to Joby, who was watching the youthful antics with a mixture of delight and concern.

"Joby," I whispered, ducking sparks as one boy tripped over the fire pit while jabbering into a radio. "Joby, it took them 2,500 years to build this unique island culture of repose and solitude, and we've wrecked it in just 20 minutes."

Bong! Bong! Bong!

Prying my eyes open, I squinted at my watch. It was just after 4:00 AM under a black sky. A few fireflies circled in front of the tent flap. I crawled from our tent, shuffled over to the cliff and looked down to see a young monk clobbering a spent .50 caliber artillery shell with a fat stick. Someone had hung a rusty Russian casing by a string to use as a dinner/wake-up bell. Aside from the sooty cooking pot down by the village, it was the first refined metal I had seen on the island. A soldier, one who'd perhaps grown up on these islands, had dropped it off from the mainland.

I shook Joby awake. The night before, we had been invited to attend the monks' morning prayer service, and we needed to move quickly if we were to make it on time. I inspected our camp and found a few wadded up candy wrappers stuck in the bushes, the only evidence of the previous night's chaos. Our two-way radios, slightly worse for wear, lay intact on opposite sides of the camp. The night-vision binoculars, smudged with soot, had been abandoned next to the campfire pit.

The evening's riotous events had come to a swift halt not twenty minutes after they began, when an elder monk appeared on the ridge. Framed in moonlight, the older man regarded with astonishment a scene he likely had never even imagined. He barked an order in Amharic and the young monks immediately scrambled off the ridge into the village and shut themselves in their Spartan sleeping hutches. In seconds, the island was silent. Joby and I both groaned, relieved that no disaster had occurred as a result of our meddling. I prayed that we had violated no sacred customs.

The morning echoed with the soothing jungle sounds of island birds, kingfishers, and brisk lake breezes rustling the trees. The wind drafting off the vast lake reminded me of the Rocky Mountains after a morning rain, and I fought off a pang of homesickness.

Although I hadn't slept soundly, I felt energized and excited about what the day might bring. Joby and I shook the bugs off our damp boots and pulled them on, then padded our way down to the village. The monks had already begun to file into a small mud hut. Misgana strolled into camp, sleepy-eyed from his night on the boat. I told him what had happened on the ridge and he just laughed.

Gebeyehu Wogawehu stood nearby in his green jacket, smiling. "Did you enjoy your campout, gentlemen?" I nodded, thinking that for a government-appointed chaperone, Gebeyehu had been all but invisible.

One of the boys from the previous evening stood smartly at the door, grinning shyly as he ushered us into the room. Inside, the unventilated hut reeked of centuries of sweating monks, dirty feet, moldering candle wax, and musky incense. A conical depression in the middle of the floor, at least a foot deep, spoke of untold generations of monks shuffling their feet during morning prayers.

We took our place in the back, and a young lad with a shaved head handed us prayer sticks. These sessions can last a long time and I appreciated the prop.

Joby and I tried to join in, but within minutes, my calves and shins had begun to itch, then sting. I reached down to scratch and realized that the hutch was infested with fleas—not typical American fleas, but the feral African strain. My legs must have tasted like aged tenderloin compared to the monks' psoriasis and wound-scarred limbs. For the next three hours, the carnivorous little beasts feasted inside my pant legs until I wanted to sprint from the hut, duck behind a tree, and strip down to my skivvies. I waited it out though. After our rough introduction and the young monks' revelry the night before, I didn't dare risk offending Abba by snubbing his prayer meeting. I had no sense of the island's protocol, so I suffered in silence, praying for relief and longing for the vigil to end. Misgana told me later that I could have left at any moment without the slightest offense, but I imagined my quiet torment as a sort of penance, one that might earn me access to the island's secrets.

The sun began to rise over the lake as the monks finally broke for breakfast. I rushed into the sunlight and pulled up the cuff of my pants to examine my sweaty and inflamed leg, sheathed in a crimson rash that would not subside until I returned to the States. Raking the inside of my calves with my fingernails, I turned to Abba and—as casually as I could—I mentioned that I'd read Graham Hancock's book *The Sign and the Seal*. He nodded, unmoved. Next, I asked about the Hebrew stone altar on the island's cliffs. He nodded again, this time mumbling a few words to Misgana.

Misgana leaned near and said, "Abba says he would be happy to show you."

Abba led us up a narrow path bordered by prickly, overgrown bushes. A series of rough stone steps emptied out onto a narrow plateau at the island's summit.

"This is where the ritual blood sacrifices were made centuries ago by the Jewish caretakers of the Ark," Abba said, with Misgana translating.

Near the ledge stood a lichen-covered block of granite with a six-inch square hole carved in its top. Based on the thick layer of encrusted moss on it, I guessed that the stone was hundreds, possibly thousands of years old. The remains of stone columns protruded from the flat surface.

Abba walked over and demonstrated how the holes in the columns had been used to collect blood during the ritual sacrifice of the lamb. Abba held up an imaginary basin to illustrate how the ancient priests scattered blood over the stones, and he pretended to pour the remaining blood into the hollows in the pillars. In both size and shape, the columns resembled the stone *masseboth* set up on high places in the earliest phases of the Hebrew religion. These ritual altars had served for sacrificial offering ceremonies much as Abba described.

Abba showed us how the high priest dipped his right forefinger into a basin containing the blood, then scattered it over the stones and tent in an up-and-down, whip-like motion. He made a tipping movement, as if pouring blood from the imaginary basin into the cup-shaped hollows of the pillars. The manner in which he reenacted the sacrament seemed to mimic purification rites prescribed in chapters four and five of the Old Testament book of Leviticus.

The granite altar did seem appropriate for the ancient Hebrew ritual, but where did the Ark fit in? Where did it sit beneath the tabernacle? I knew the monks had never revealed to any outsider precisely where the Ark had rested on the island. The best they could offer Graham Hancock was that it lay "somewhere near" the cliffs where we now stood.

With nothing to lose, I decided to ask, "Abba, where did the Ark sit?" My heart skipped when he casually pointed to the smooth granite beneath my feet.

"The Ark sat right here?" I asked, looking down.

"Yes," he nodded.

Abba explained, and Misgana relayed to me the words in English. "The Ark sat here, on this ledge, so that the blood could also be sprinkled on the tabernacle at the time of the sacrifice. This tradition has been passed down through the centuries." This confused me since the Bible makes no mention of sprinkling blood on the tabernacle.

I stared at the smooth rock, perched high above the lagoon and surrounded on all sides by sheer cliff drop-offs. As a formidable watchtower from which to repel invaders, the ledge made perfect sense. I bent down to inspect the granite surface, an unremarkable table of stone covered in decaying leaves and layers of thatch.

I turned to Joby. "If the tabernacle sat here… how could a tent be secured over it? The winds whipping up this high would blow any free-standing structure into the lagoon." I looked around for socket holes where tent poles might have once been secured. I got down on my knees and began poking around, pushing leaves and thatch aside and feeling for something—I wasn't sure what. I took out my knife and slid it down through the thick mesh of grass and leaves and twigs, poking and prodding, sticking it into rocks and cracks, searching for a spot where the granite might yield to emptiness. After a few minutes of searching, my knife found a hollow indentation in the rock!

After some more digging, I managed to clean out a clearly-defined socket hole, hidden beneath centuries of decayed organic matter. This was a place where workers could anchor a tent pole. It sat approximately 25 feet from what Abba had called the altar of pillars, precisely where the tabernacle of the Ark once stood. I began clearing the rest of the ledge, probing the leaves and debris with my knife. After some minor excavating, I found a second hole under six inches of rotting palm fronds, roughly the same circumference as the first. This socket was not quite as pronounced as the first socket; it sat closer to the ledge and appeared to have been eroded by time.

I looked around, and then I noticed a pile of rocks stacked next to the altar, like a makeshift shrine. Among the chunks sat a sizeable piece of granite with a tent pole-sized hole carved into the top. It might have been a third socket hole, long since broken off from the ledge. Who knew? Abba didn't.

After two hours on the ledge, we walked back to the village. As we trudged down the trail, my mind swirled with provocative scenarios. Had we just stood on the *shetiyyah* of T'ana Kirkos, the foundation stone of an ancient Ethiopian Holy of Holies? Had I hollowed out the contours where tent holes were positioned to support the tabernacle of the Ark? I couldn't help think about those holes and their significance in determining where the holy Ark was once sheltered.

On our way back down to the village, Abba stopped and pointed to a long, narrow fissure in a huge boulder. The crack was filled with rocks that were said to conceal the skeleton of one of the original Hebrews who brought the Ark to the island more than two thousand years ago. The Hebrew had been entombed in that huge V-shaped crack in the granite and then covered over with a pile of stones.[1]

Back at the village, Abba led us to a thick-walled hut, where he unlocked heavy wooden doors. He disappeared inside the darkened room for a moment while Joby and I waited outside. "I believe the elder has something else to show you," Misgana said.

Emerging a few minutes later, Abba placed a small mat on the ground for us to sit on. He laid another mat a few feet in front of us, and then he instructed someone to help him carry over a large basin. The basin was broad and shallow, approximately two feet wide and no more than a couple of inches deep. A green patina covered its surface from many years of oxidation, which made it difficult for me to identify the metal. I guessed that the basin was bronze—and very old.

---

1   Years later, in the early morning hours while being drenched by a violent jungle storm, I went all alone to that alleged grave-site. I removed several rocks blocking the grave, and after some effort I eventually entered a cavity about six feet long. There I found small chips of brown bone and scattered pottery shards.

Abba explained, "The ancient Hebrews who brought the Ark to Lake T'ana called it a *gomer*. They used it up on the cliffs to collect the blood from ritual sacrifices. The priest would stir the blood in the basin to keep it from getting thick."

Abba reentered the storage hut and returned, balancing a heavy, bulky tangle of metal in his hands. It was a single stand of what appeared to be iron rods fused to a ring at the top and bottom. Abba told us that it had once been a sturdy stand to hold the bronze bowl, but it had long since collapsed from metal fatigue and extreme age. Its edges were mottled and encrusted with the same bluish pits and corrosion as the basin, but this object bore a deep, red-brown crust of oxidation rather than the green of the basin. The opening at the top of the stand seemed to be about the same dimensions as the bronze basin, so it made sense that this was its stand.

Cradling the basin like a newborn baby, Abba again described how his predecessors had used it to scatter blood in the ancient Hebrew fashion. Yet, the more I looked, the more the basin and stand seemed to reflect passages like Exodus 30:17-19 or 40:7-11 that describe the bronze "laver," the basin and stand, as an integrated unit for ritual washing. The laver could have also held the sacred anointing oil used to consecrate the Tent of Meeting in Exodus 30:28-29. The basin and its stand are mentioned several times, and they are anointed and sanctified in Leviticus 8:10-11, but Abba and his predecessors interpreted the basin as an instrument for blood sacrifice. It didn't really matter. The monks on T'ana Kirkos had neither the resources nor the technology to forge metal. Someone had obviously brought the items to the island, and the tradition that these were Jewish vessels correlated with items described in the biblical text.

At the Axum chapel we had seen silver trumpets, as described in Numbers 10:2. Silver trumpets are not a common item, and they are certainly not the first thing people think of when they think of the Temple. Yet, the chapel in Axum, Ethiopia had protected these silver trumpets from time immemorial. As I studied the items that Abba brought out to us, I thought back to those trumpets. I wondered if this basin and stand had been among the original vessels that were forged in Moses' time and placed in Solomon's Temple for service before the Ark. The original stand was described in Leviticus as bronze—a copper alloy—and this one seemed to have been made of iron, based on its oxidation. Had these instruments actually come to T'ana Kirkos with the Ark? The Monks insisted that they had.

"Mr. Bob!" Misgana whispered, nudging me. Abba had just reemerged from the hut holding a long, two-pronged instrument that looked like two long thin spears fastened together. I quickly identified it and recognized that it matched yet another Hebrew sacrificial implement—a meat fork used to burn sacrifices over ritual fires. "Abba says it is a meat fork," Misgana said. "It was left on the island by those who brought the Ark."

Heavily rusted, and showing signs of wear similar to the stand and basin, the implement's long double prongs met at a horizontal bridge at the top, crowned by what I took to be an old Axumite cross.

Abba corrected me, "It is not a cross, but the image of a budding almond flower."

An almond flower? My mind drifted back to Saudi Arabia and the mountain called Jabal al-Lawz, a name that means "mountain of the almond flower."

We find that the budding almond ranked high in Israel's sacred iconography. In Numbers 17:8, Aaron's staff miraculously buds overnight and produces blossoms and even almonds. That same staff, regarded as the sign of one of Yahweh's great Old Testament miracles, came to lie alongside the holy manna and the Ten Commandments within the Ark of the Covenant.[2] When the LORD gives instructions on how to build the seven-armed candle stand (the menorah) for the tabernacle in Exodus 24:31-40, He specifies that each branch was to include almond blossoms.

Meat forks, a bronze basin and stand... the pieces were fitting the picture of tabernacle sacrifice better than I could have hoped. As far as I knew, no westerner had ever seen these items. I wondered if these were the very items that had once served in the Temple of Solomon. It seemed a far reach for the monks to make that claim, but then, these items were there, sitting right

---

2   Cf. Hebrews 9:4

in front of us. The monks insisted that their ancient writings and traditions verified these items as the genuine artifacts from the Bible.

If I had only seen one or two of these objects, I might have written them off as coincidence. Yet taken together—the cliff shrine, the pillars for blood sacrifice, the hidden tent holes, and now the basin, stand, and meat fork, along with the silver trumpets at Axum—we seemed to have uncovered interlocking pieces of a fantastic puzzle. Each of these components appeared much like those described in Scripture, and each made an arguable case for T'ana Kirkos as an ancient Hebrew haven. Together, these artifacts gave credence to the Ethiopian claim that this had been a resting place for the Ark of the Covenant.

I turned to Abba. "Would you allow me to scrape off a bit of metal from the gomer or the meat forks, to take it back to my country to test it?" I knew his answer before I asked, but I had to ask. Abba frowned and shook his head.

"No, Mr. Bob," Misgana said. "Under no circumstances can you do such a thing. These are sacred vessels."

Figure 14: Ancient objects on Tana Kirkos Island said by monks to be artifacts relating to the Ark of the Covenant (fourth century BC ?)

136

After a time, I stood and took a deep breath. I saw an enormous, white-tailed eagle gliding over the cliffs overhead. I thanked Abba for his kindness and for showing me more than I had ever expected to see. My mind was darting from one fact to another as I tried to put all this into perspective. In a word, I was stunned.

The hours had passed quickly and we still faced a long boat ride back to our departure point. Gebeyehu Wogawehu was waiting by the boat. The blazing sun dissolved into the pale green of Lake T'ana as we turned into the waves and headed south. My first visit to Ethiopia had come and gone, but there would be many more trips to come.

CHAPTER 13

THE GUARDIAN OF THE ARK

Eventually I did meet the Guardian of the Ark—the same guardian whom Birani had told me never met with anybody. After many visits with that guardian, I am grateful that he now calls me his good friend. He also adamantly assures me that the Ark of the Covenant, the real Ark, is in the Chapel of Saint Mary of Zion Church, and no one will see it other than himself. He explains that it is he who has been chosen by God to guard the Ark until the day he dies. When that day comes, a new guardian will take his place and the perpetual ritual will continue as it has in Ethiopia for more than two thousand years.

On one of my twenty-two trips to Ethiopia, I had the privilege to meet with President Negasso Gidada at the Presidential Palace. I was with Mary Irwin (wife of astronaut Jim Irwin) along with my research team. We presented President Gidada an American flag that had traveled to the moon and back, and I have been told it still hangs proudly in the palace today.

Two History Channel specials, as well as a recent Travel Channel show called "Expedition Unknown," have highlighted the amazing story of the Ark in Ethiopia. There are certainly many stories I could tell of my activities in Ethiopia, but one particular trip remains close to my heart. I've saved this story for last, because it involves my son Brandon and a trip we took when he was just sixteen years old.

This was my second expedition to Ethiopia, and Brandon had joined me as I traveled to set up a medical clinic.

The appalling health situation I had seen in Ethiopia during my first trip had deeply bothered me, and I wanted to do something about it. A friend of mine named Doctor Gaba joined me in my concern, and together we worked to take a team of volunteers, medical supplies and large stores of medicine into the war-torn country. Dr. Gaba was as well-seasoned medical missionary and expert, and his assistance was invaluable. Most of the people in Axum had never seen a doctor, let alone had access to modern medicine.

A local man offered us a small building in which to set up our clinic, but it turned out to be nothing more than shack. Still, it was something, and we used it to set up a line of tables that were soon spilling over with well-guarded supplies. It was a rudimentary and somewhat sparse attempt at a clinic, but that didn't matter to the people of Axum. To them it was the Mayo Clinic.

Doctor Gaba stood stoically the day we opened our little clinic, wearing a crisp white lab coat and a stethoscope slung around his neck. With a deep breath and a nod he signaled the front door to be opened, and we all braced for the mass of crushing humanity to pour in. Within seconds, the clinic filled to capacity. I was thankful that we had team members with some medical experience, but we were quickly overwhelmed by the sheer numbers of poor people. They pressed in with outstretched arms, pleading desperately for our help.

Toward the end of the day, my young son's senses were stunned beyond emotional capacity. He had never seen so much human need, and the day had absolutely drained him. Dr. Gaba was far more seasoned than the rest of us, and he kept working hard as the rest of us became physically and emotionally exhausted. At one point, a boy of about twelve made his way past all the people and ended up at my son's feet. The child held the draping, emaciated body of his brother—a tragic form who looked like a skeleton wrapped in brown skin. The twelve year-old tenderly laid his sick brother at Brandon's feet and begged for help. All Brandon could do was tug on Dr. Gaba's lab coat to draw attention to the sick child, but Dr. Gaba was simply far too overwhelmed as it was.

Brandon had come from a world where pizza was a simple phone call away, where regular medical checkups were routine. He had never faced starvation or waited without hope for medical care. In Ethiopia, he faced the jolting realization that some people in our world scratched by in abject poverty. Some people entered our little clinic with no legs and had to drag themselves across the floor. The blind, the deaf, and the horribly deformed walked through our doors. They came with hope into our stifling hot room filled with flies, oblivious to the offensively sour body odors that would make most westerners gag.

Brandon could do nothing to help the boy with his dying brother, because the clinic was overrun with more and more people as the day went by. There was a constant cacophony of desperate and pleading people begging for help, and that night Brandon's emotions collapsed with the weight of it all. He sat in our hotel room with his back to the wall, and he sobbed convulsively because he could do nothing more to help these desperate people.

In that moment, I knew I had sheltered him quite a lot. I had protected him from the horrific realities of third world countries. It was an out-of-sight and out-of-mind sort of thing, but in that moment Brandon's life was changed forever. His heart has been marinating from that experience to this very day, and the rare compassion he has for all people is a legacy of that moment.

Today, there is a new school attended by more than a thousand students in Axum. My good friend Barry Hudson and others helped me to raise the money for its construction. If you visit that school today, there is a stone marker of appreciation with my name on it. I am more proud of that plaque than I could ever describe in mere words. A new medical clinic has also been built in Axum quite recently. It has a modern reception area, with exam rooms and even a pharmacy. Barry Hudson and his wife Elizabeth, along with help from me and others, worked to make that clinic a reality.

There is still great poverty and desperation in Ethiopia, but I'm grateful that God has allowed us to provide some mercy to the people of Axum. That clinic is a source of blessing today, and it just happens to be near the bunker-like building where the Guardian remains in constant vigilance as God's earthly "keeper of the Ark."

MALTA AND THE LOST ANCHORS OF PAUL

CHAPTER 14

THE MUNXAR REEF

I woke early in my seaside hotel. The sea air flooded my senses in the soothing quiet of a cool morning, and after a quick breakfast I walked along the shore of Marsaxlokk Bay. I was on the small knuckle of the island called Malta. Malta is perched like a jewel in the Mediterranean Sea, just south of Sicily, and it is here that Paul had a shipwreck, as described in Acts 27:27-44. In the first century, a crippled vessel was blown to the coast of Malta in a raging storm, and its four anchors were cut free from the boat just before it bottomed out near the shore. While the wooden pieces of that ship had certainly long succumbed to the elements, I wanted to know if the four anchors "left in the sea" could still be found under those coastal waters.

I made my way along a narrow, winding road bordered on both sides by terraced fields and crumbling rock walls. A traditional, one-seat Maltese surrey clattered up the road alongside me, pulled by a spirited chestnut horse. The driver, hunched forward, snapped the reins against the animal's lathered neck and shot me a grin as he passed. I waved a casual hello and did a double take when the driver jerked back the reins and, supposing I wanted to talk, stopped the horse; its hooves skidded across the slick asphalt.

For an awkward moment I just stood there, unsure of what to say. Finally, I stammered a clumsy Maltese greeting I'd heard the locals use and began trying to use impromptu hand signals to ask him the way to St. Thomas Bay. He nodded cheerfully, pointing me toward a small dirt road snaking up the ridgeline. "Thank you," I said and bowed slightly.

With a quick snap of the driver's reins, the man and his horse were off. I made my way up the road to a foot trail that crested on the cliffs overlooking St. Thomas Bay. I had become infatuated with Malta's gorgeous scenery, and I gazed down with pleasure at the morning sun reflecting off the shimmering sea. Malta's ever-present fishing boats trolled up and down the shoreline, fishing for the amberjack and bream that schooled around the reef.

Unlike Marsaxlokk Bay, St. Thomas was neither quaint, charming, nor anything that would be used as a tourist attraction. It was a simple, workingman's fishing village with small fishing huts and tiny homes dotting the shoreline. It did have a nice sandy beach with a rock seawall behind it, and fishermen had long spread their nets there to dry in the early morning sun.

As a prisoner on his way to Rome for trial, Paul had survived a terrible shipwreck when his ship had been crashed and ripped apart in a Maltese bay. This was one of the last prospects in my search for a bay that fit that biblical narrative.

But striking a place where two seas met, they ran the ship aground; and the prow stuck fast and remained immovable, but the stern was being broken up by the violence of the waves.

Acts 27:41

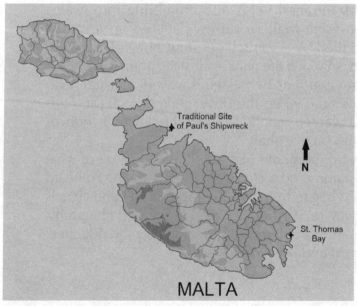

Figure 15: A map of Malta showing the locations of both the traditional site of Paul's shipwreck and an alternate site at St. Thomas Bay where Roman-age anchors were located, according to the descriptions in Acts 27:27-44.

Traditional Site of Paul's Shipwreck

N

St. Thomas Bay

MALTA

I pulled out my Bible and nautical maps and read again the account of Paul's shipwreck. I started where the sailors—on that stormy dark night—initially "sensed" they were nearing land. I followed the account verse-by-verse, retracing and reviewing everything.

> Now when the fourteenth night had come ... about midnight the sailors sensed that they were drawing near some land.
>
> Acts 27:27

I looked out into the bay. Here, as everywhere on Malta, the shoreline sat broken in sections by high rock cliffs and jagged outcroppings. Yet I noticed a difference. To this point in my search, I had yet to find a place where the sailors that dark night would have heard a thunderous roar of waves breaking over a reef. But here, stretching out and guarding the approach to St. Thomas Bay from the southeast, was the Munxar Reef—a rock protrusion extending a mile and a half out to sea. Judging from its size and peculiar angle from shore, it seemed to fit what was required by Luke's narrative.

> And they took soundings and found it to be twenty fathoms; and when they had gone a little farther, they took soundings again and found it to be fifteen fathoms..
>
> Acts 27:28

Sitting down, I spread out my navigation charts on the ground and examined the waters surrounding Malta, and then I re-checked the contour lines and recorded depths of the approach to St. Thomas Bay. From most angles, the depth changes on the sea floor were abrupt, but a ship approaching here from the southeast would have found a gradual slope rising from the depths of the Mediterranean to a shelf running alongside the Munxar Reef. Here I could see that the depths closely matched those mentioned in the book of Acts. It was also the one place on Malta where, as one old man told me, two seas came together. That was important. It was the only place I'd seen where, during a violent gale, the waves would crash together over Munxar Reef.

This was also likely why Paul told the sailors to all remain in the ship and not attempt a landing in the ship's little landing boat.

Paul said to the centurion and the soldiers, "Unless these men stay in the ship, you cannot be saved." Then the soldiers cut away the ropes of the skiff and let it fall off.

Acts 27:31-32

Luke's narrative tells us that as the morning came on, Paul encouraged all the sailors to eat some food, since they'd been fighting the storm for fourteen long days. Then, after it was morning and they could see their situation, they completely lightened the load by dumping all the wheat they were carrying.

And when they had eaten enough, they lightened the ship, and cast out the wheat into the sea.

Acts 27:38

As I sat on the cliff overlooking St. Thomas Bay, I imagined I could see what the men aboard Paul's ship might have seen, if this was indeed the bay where they had crashed. My landward view of the bay provided an interesting perspective. Perhaps it allowed me to see something of what the terrified sailors saw from the deck of that Alexandrian freighter.

They waited until the morning to land the ship. As the wind drove them into the bay, sharp, rising cliffs towered off to their left and sheer rocks threatened them to their right. Their storm-tossed nightmare had run its course; their fate seemed sealed. To challenge the malevolent sea anymore would mean destruction. Their only hope was direct the ship past the crashing waves on the reef and thread the needle of opportunity between the cliffs to their right and left. They would come to scuttle the ship in the bay. Luke was an eyewitness to it all and described the final events:

When it was day, they did not recognize the land; but they observed a bay with a beach, onto which they planned to run the ship if possible. And they let go the anchors and left them in the sea, meanwhile loosing the rudder ropes; and they hoisted the mainsail to the

*wind and made for shore. But striking a place where
two seas met, they ran the ship aground; and the prow
stuck fast and remained immovable, but the stern was
being broken up by the violence of the waves.*

Acts 27:39-41

Luke's formal education and his training as a medical professional allowed him to spell out perfectly the predicament in which these men found themselves. When Luke says, "if possible," in describing their chances of making it past the reef, he pulls from an extremely rare Greek phrase in the New Testament. In the Greek, Luke's combination of words actually indicates the "least likely" chance of completing the maneuver. Luke was saying in effect, "They observed a beach, onto which— though probably not possible—they planned to run the ship."

They cut their four anchors from the stern, left them in the sea, and then they went for it. It is not difficult to realize whatever Luke saw from the deck of the huge wooden freighter that miserable morning offered the sailors little optimism at actually reaching the beach. Still, he and the others knew they would have to go for it to have any chance at all.

I watched the lazy fishing boats drift on pristine waters on a calm, sunny morning, and I struggled to transport myself back in time and imagine the sailors' gloomy prospects that day. Yet, from where I stood, the only obstacle that could have elicited such despair from Luke and the sailors was the Munxar Reef. Surely they could see the massive swells smashing and breaking and roiling on the reef directly in front of them. The power of waves colliding together on that reef would cut them to ribbons. I had the advantage, of course, and from shore could see that the reef was in fact punctuated by a few breaks and deep cuts—any one of which might have allowed a smaller, shallower craft to squeeze through.

When we read the King James Version, it actually sounds like they didn't cut off the anchors at all, but that they committed *themselves* to the sea. This is not a good translation. The Greek is very precise, and the word "themselves" is not original in the Greek. It was the anchors that were committed to the sea.

149

In verse 20, the sailors had given up hope of being saved. Here, in verse 40, Luke uses the same word for the anchors. They were given up. There could be no doubt the ropes had been cut and the anchors left in the sea.

When they threw out the last of the grain from the belly of the ship and cut those anchors free, their goal was for the ship to ride higher in the water in the hopes of passing over the shallow reef. As the massive ship lurched forward, freed from the grasp of the anchors, frantic sailors in the bow hoisted the one remaining foresail to the still-formidable wind. The massive freighter was only a two-master. The large main mast amid ship, held by a wide mizzen yard, was probably down. If that was the case, the smaller sail mounted in the bow area, on the foremast, was now all they had to sail the ship.

As they approached the reef, every man on board must have braced himself, waiting for the inevitable, dreadful impact from the submerged reef that was under the crashing waves directly in their path. The freighter went headlong into the fuming wall of colliding whitewater—the "place of two seas" —converging in a violent tempest upon Munxar Reef. The sailors knew that to impact the reef, list sideways, and capsize outside the bay would mean death for all but a lucky few. Their only real hope of survival lay in riding the storm swells through the narrow rift of the reef and try, beyond hope, to somehow make it to shore.

As I stood there overlooking the sea, I imagined the roar of wood crashing into rock, the cacophony of splintering timbers, crashing waves, and screaming men. They apparently hit the reef with such force that the bulk of the ship "stuck fast," stranding the crew at the critical, desperate threshold of safety. They had gotten far enough across that the bow of the ship remained temporarily whole as the incoming storm waves from opposite directions began to pound the ship's stern to pieces. The lives of 276 men became the responsibility of one man alone—the centurion Julius.

And the soldiers' plan was to kill the prisoners, lest any of them should swim away and escape. But the centurion, wanting to save Paul, kept them from their

purpose, and commanded that those who could swim
should jump overboard first and get to land, and the
rest, some on boards and some on parts of the ship.
And so it was that they all escaped safely to land.
Acts 27:42-44

As with modern military units, the Roman army drilled its soldiers to respond instantly to any crisis, and the sinking of a ship at sea would be no exception. In this case, however, the pride and power of the Roman state superseded a mere prisoner's safety, and as the waves ripped the ship apart and men prepared to swim for shore, a real chance existed for prisoners to escape. Rome's policy of "death before escape" kicked in, and the soldiers on board prepared to hastily execute the prisoners. The centurion, wanting to spare Paul, stepped in and saved everybody, soldiers and prisoners alike.

Julius ordered those who could swim to head first for shore; then he gave the order for everyone else to abandon the doomed freighter and make for land on pieces of debris. Apparently Julius was one of the last men, if not the last man, into the sea. The huge waves that mercilessly pounded the vessel provided shattered flotsam—boards, beams, and broken masts—upon which the stragglers floated to shore.

From my protected clifftop perch, I watched the small waves gently lap upon the beach of St. Thomas Bay. There was no storm, and I gazed down on calm waters. That night two thousand years ago, though, men groped, gasped, and slowly, one by one, pulled themselves ashore despite the violent waves and wind. The soft sand beach there gave them salvation after two weeks of enduring a brutal ship-tossing storm.

The Maltese natives awakened that morning to the sight of a monstrous freighter breaking apart on the reef, and it must have been an incredible sight. As they watched—perhaps from the same place I was standing—one pitiful form after another slowly crept up the sand, and collapse from exhaustion. The Bible tells us that all 276 men made it safely.

I stared down again at the nautical maps and the Bible before me. The words from Luke, penned so long ago, now spoke to me of a place where "two seas meet" here at this obscure Maltese shoreline. Suddenly the biblical narrative converged and came to life in a swirl of compass points and images, pointing me to the place where, I surmised, the anchors came to rest on the seabed floor. The monumental question arose in my mind: could I possibly find those four anchors?

It was my last day in Malta; my flight was leaving in a few hours. In that moment, I knew what I would have to do: return to Colorado, regroup, recruit some expert divers and return to hunt for the lost anchors of Paul, which I hoped were hidden under the blue waters of the reef before me. It would take me a full year to return to this beautiful island of intrigue, but the results would satisfy my mind and deeply touch my heart.

Over the next twelve months, I began assembling a research team to join me in Malta. If I wanted to properly explore the reef and seabed beneath Marsaxlokk Bay, I needed experienced divers. I had no idea what to expect from Malta's coastal waters, with its peculiar tides and currents, and I would need people trained in undersea exploration if I had any chance of finding Paul's sea anchors. A friend of mine gave me the name of Jean-François, whom he said would be the perfect teammate for this potentially dangerous expedition.

Jean-François La Archevec was a master diver who hailed from Canada, and he now served as a dive superintendent based on the HMCS York in Toronto. I was told Jean-François had been involved with the diving expeditions that located the Edmund Fitzgerald, the ship that famously sank in November 1975 and was forever memorialized in the song by Gordon Lightfoot. Jean-François was also involved in locating the downed Swiss Air Flight 111, which crashed into the sea near Halifax, Nova Scotia in September 1998.

I called up Jean-François for an interview, and, without hesitating, he told me that he would love to dive in Malta. He told me in his strong French-Canadian accent, "It will be a welcome break from the cold waters of Canada!" He then gave me another name, one of a Canadian sailing specialist named David Laddell. Laddell owned a company called Sea-Ex, and he possessed both the equipment and the time to go searching for Paul's lost anchors. He also readily agreed to join our team.

In the meantime, I had independently recruited Dr. Mark Phillips, a PhD in Religious Studies, whom I asked to coordinate our research efforts and to act as a liaison with the international scholarly community. The addition of Dr. Phillips' wife, Angela, and friend Mitch Yellen rounded out the team that we needed for the next phase of our search.

WHAT TONY FOUND

Upon arrival back in Malta in September of 2001, we eventually made our way to St. Thomas Bay and visited the Aqua Bubbles Diving School. We passed a group of men carrying a load of empty cylinders into the shop, and we watched as they clanked them down on the concrete floor of the shop. The place smelled of the sea and rubber suits, and it rippled with loud conversations as divers described their days beneath the waves. They compared the merits of their discoveries, the beautiful clarity of the water or the exotic fish that swam by. A compressor in the corner of the shop hummed like a miniature jackhammer as divers swapped stories, laughed, and soaked in the contagious, fraternal atmosphere of sport diving, Maltese-style.

Since the oceans cover roughly 71% of the earth's surface, what made me think that I, not even a certified diver, could find a Roman-era sea anchor on the earth's 130 million square miles of seafloor? It was a foolhardy notion, except for the fact that I possessed a treasure map called the Bible.

Standing in the dive shop, I felt the excitement of seeking lost treasure. I had no doubt that every diver who had ever visited this busy shop held out hope of one day scanning the seabed floor and eyeing some half-buried amphora jar or a barnacle-encrusted coin, or even the heart-stopping glint of a gold doubloon.

It was not gold I sought, but lead. I wanted to find the four lead anchors lying on the ocean floor, hidden under ninety feet of water, near a bay with a beach, where two seas met, on the south coast of Malta. With my maps, ocean guides, and nautical instruments, I had used concentric circles to narrow the possibilities down to one relatively small patch of earth on the sea floor. Now, with my fully equipped dive team, I would have to cover that final distance down from the surface of the ocean to the seabed.

While we waited our turn to get served by the shop's dive staff, a big, dark man with a Mediterranean face walked into the room. Everyone smiled and greeted him warmly with shouts of "Hey Ray!" This was the owner of the shop, obviously a man all the divers admired. There was something more than that. The nearly unanimous outflow of affection and respect told me this man, Ray, was almost a father figure to these people.

I worked my way through the crowd and approached Ray. As he glanced my way, I shouted above the noise, "Excuse me, I'd like to ask you a question."

"What?" Ray yelled back, distracted by the bedlam around him. "Are you interested in diving?"

"Not exactly," I replied, trying to be discreet in this salty pack of experienced divers. "I do want to ask you a question."

"What!" Ray quickly answered back in the clipped manner of a man accustomed to getting straight to the point.

Leaning forward I said, "It's about a shipwreck. An ancient shipwreck."

Ray stopped and stared at me for a moment, then said, with arched brow, "A shipwreck? I think we should go outside."

Ray, Jean-François, and I worked our way toward the door. I looked quickly around and was relieved that no one seemed interested in following. Just outside the front door, a handful of divers and employees busied themselves with washing down wetsuits and dive gear in huge tubs of fresh water. We stopped a few paces away, and I stared out at St. Thomas Bay, a ready-made visual aid for my explanation.

I introduced Jean-François as "a master diver from Canada." Then, I softly added that, "My name is Bob Cornuke. I am trying to find the location of an ancient, lost shipwreck."

Ray didn't mince words. "How old is this shipwreck?" he asked.

"It happened over one thousand, nine hundred years ago," I said.

"Ah... from olden times?"

"Yes," I gave a deferential nod.

"From Roman times?" Ray continued.

I again nodded yes.

"Well, you won't find any wreck from that long ago," he sniffed. "The wood's all been eaten up by organisms in the water."

"I know that," I said politely. "But I think maybe something from the ship may have lasted all these years."

He turned to me and said, matter-of-fact: "Do you speak of anchors? Big Roman anchors?"

"Yes," I said, startled that he had anticipated the exact objects of our search. "Yes, I believe we can find the anchors from Paul's shipwreck."

"So you want to dive in St. Paul's Bay?" he asked.

"No," I replied. "I don't believe Paul's shipwreck was in St. Paul's Bay."

"Well, I don't think you'd find them there anyway," Ray said with a shrug. "That area's been searched pretty good, and they've found no shipwreck yet."

I decided to end the secrecy of my search and told Ray of my findings, from start to finish. I explained my theory of Paul's ill-fated route to Malta, and of the Alexandrian freighter's tortured, wind-blown course from Crete down toward the coast of Libya, then up to the southeast corner of Malta, to the corner of the island where we now stood. I explained my thoughts about the bay with a beach, and suggested that St. Thomas Bay, lying directly before us, would not have been recognized as a familiar Maltese port.

"This is why the sailors didn't recognize the land and why the other locations on Malta simply do not fit," I said. I explained my opinion about the phrase "where two seas meet" and how it perfectly fit the tide profile of Saint Thomas Bay. I pointed out how the ship of Paul ran aground on the reef before breaking to pieces in the waves.

At this point, Ray backtracked to my description of the place where two seas met. "Bob, describe again the two seas. What does that mean?" In a matter of minutes, Ray had become deeply intrigued by my theory. I took a Bible out of my backpack, opened it, and read him the description from Acts 27.

He reflected for a moment on the passage, then with some excitement he said, "Right here in front of us, on the Munxar Reef, the currents come together during a storm. I have seen it many times. A huge wall of water—a white, foamy mass of colliding waves extends almost a mile and a half out into the ocean from the mouth of the bay. It looks like a huge, white snake crawling across the water."

Ray stood for a moment, rubbing his forehead as he finally understood a Bible passage he had read many times. "It is unmistakable," he added. "This really would be where the two seas meet."

I took this response from perhaps the island's preeminent diver as a great encouragement. Next, I showed Ray where the Bible describes how the sailors cut loose the anchors after a ninety-foot sounding. He sat down on a large boulder outside his dive shop. Looking out to sea, he said nothing for several seconds; then he looked back at me and—so slowly and softly I could barely make out the word, he said, "Tony."

"I'm sorry," I said, confused. "What was that?"

"Tony," Ray continued, and with obvious affection began to share a story. "When I was a young boy, I knew a man named Tony. He was a powerful man in strength, and an amazing athlete. Everyone on the island knew of Tony. He held records in shot put, discus, and javelin. He was also a diving fanatic. Whether at a party, or a wedding, or a gathering of any kind, all Tony talked about was spearfishing and diving.

Ray paused and said, sadly, "He died in the sea. His body was missing for seven years. Then, one day he was found in a cave, still in his wetsuit. His spear gun was by his side."

I could see that this was a memory almost too painful to bear, but Ray continued. "Well, Bob," he pointed lazily toward the bay. "We saw anchors out there. They were anchors from olden times, probably Roman. We brought up two; we later heard rumors from others that two more were brought up from the same spot."

It took me a moment to grasp what I heard. "Four anchors... from the same spot?" I asked.

"Yes," Ray said. "But I never even thought that these anchors could possibly be from Paul's shipwreck. After all, this is not St. Paul's Bay. This is not supposed to be the spot. But if what you're telling me is true, these anchors may be from that ship."

With a heavy sigh, Ray said under his breath, "Leave it up to Tony to find Paul's anchors." Ray paused and thought about this for a few moments. "I think he would be proud," he huffed. "Yes, I think he would be happy."

I waited for an appropriate few moments. Then I asked, "Can you take me to the spot? The spot where you found the anchors?"

"Yes. That will be easy," Ray said.

"How will you know the spot?" I asked.

"That's simple," Ray continued. "It was the area Tony called 'The Bank,' a place where we could always find the big groupers and make a little money. The day we found the anchors, they lay in the sand in front of a big cave. We would always swim down through the top of a huge crack in the rocks, and it would bring us out into an enormous cave. You could put twenty school buses inside this cave. So you can see it would be hard for me to forget. When we found the anchors, we were in front of the big cave."

"How deep is the water?" I asked.

"I don't know," Ray said. "Maybe 20, 25, 30 meters or so. But I can take you there. I will take you to the big cave."

Jean-François had been listening intently, and at this point he grinned quietly, elated to hear such optimistic news. He and I immediately made plans with Ray to meet at the dock the following morning and take a boat out to Munxar Reef—to The Bank—and dive down to the big cave where the large groupers swim.

The next morning, every person we passed on our way to the dock called out, "Hey Ray!" or "Hey, Ciancio!"—the nickname given by Tony when Ray was a young boy. Clearly something of Tony's legendary popularity on Malta had been passed on to Ray, who proudly carried the mantle of island diving icon.

The morning air felt warm and calm as we arrived at the dock and waited for the rest of our team to arrive. It was a clear day with a calm sea. We planned to boat out to the area of the big cave where Ray said he and Tony had found the first anchor many decades earlier. I tried to simply accept Ray's claim at face value, but many questions still hung in my mind. Why had Ray refused to volunteer any hint of the whereabouts of that all-important anchor? Part of me yearned to ask him outright, but I decided to hold off. I could tell by Ray's manner—friendly yet protectively aloof—that we hadn't yet established a rapport necessary to cross that line.

Something else, something not altogether unexpected, had begun to occur to me. Ray's guarded words and mildly standoffish body language communicated something distinctly mysterious, even taboo, about the whole affair of the sea anchors. It put me on guard and alerted me to be extra conscious of unspoken island code. I didn't want to sabotage the exploration by asking the wrong question at the wrong moment. I kept my expectations low and decided not to ask Ray for specifics until the timing was right. For now, he seemed willing to take us to the reef and show us around, and I was grateful for that as it was.

I had simply planned to boat out to the reef and let Jean-François, David Ledell, and a Maltese diver from Ray's shop take independent measurements of the sea floor. The idea was to determine the depth of the water where Ray said they had discovered the anchor. I wanted to know if the depth was near to the fifteen fathoms (ninety feet) that Luke had given as the depth of the second sounding in Acts 27:28. If the anchors were found at a depth relatively close to the depth where the sailors had cut loose those anchors… we could count it a significant clue.

Jean-François and the rest of our team finally came sauntering down the pier, and we began loading Ray's boat with an array of sophisticated diving gear—sleek cylinders, regulators, buoyancy compensators, fins, masks, wet suits, and weight belts. Admiring this gleaming stockpile, I couldn't help but think about how greatly the sport of diving had changed during the past century. Ray explained that early divers in the Mediterranean used flight goggles sealed in with putty, helmets that leaked or broke apart under pressure, and pressurized tanks with unreliable, non-automatic air regulators. For those adventurous first divers, even routine dives were a death-defying risk. With quantum advances in "aqualung" or scuba (Self Contained Underwater Breathing Apparatus) technology in the 1940s and 1950s, everything changed. Once scuba technology arrived on the scene, it didn't take long for serious diving to become a popular sport. As a boy, Ray would follow Tony in chasing after huge fish that brought in cash at the local restaurants.

I marveled, listening to Ray spin through his memory reel. He told us that those early Maltese divers often dived without even consulting decompression tables. Some learned basic diving techniques and principles from a British Navy diving team stationed on the island, and others got their education word-of-mouth, or from whatever reference books they could scrounge up. Consequently, most of the divers in Ray's early circle simply did not know how to avoid, much less respond to, the extreme dangers associated with all but the most routine forays beneath the waves.

Ray recalled that several of his friends tragically perished because they didn't even realize they had limited time underwater. They had stayed down too long, until their tanks were almost empty, and then suffered the deadly consequences of decompression sickness from racing to the surface. Today we call this medical condition "the bends," and it's caused by bubbles of dissolved gasses, especially nitrogen, forming in the blood of divers who rise too quickly to the surface. After swimming deep down into the water with tanks for lengths of time, it's important for divers to stop and allow the body to depressurize at particular depths as they ascend. This gives dissolved gasses time to be released from the body. Decompression tables are important, because they direct divers about how long and at which depths they need to stop and decompress.

Fortunately, many lives were probably saved because most of those early divers did not have wetsuits, and they simply got too cold to swim deep or stay down too long. Still, Ray described a number of deaths from those early years.

As technology improved, those same divers were the first to strap on modern aqualungs and penetrate the unsearched depths off the coast of Malta. In doing so, young boys and novice divers alike routinely came across rare, ancient artifacts, long lost to the sea and hidden from history for hundreds or even thousands of years. It was a secret, brash society of amateur treasure hunters, whose members may or may not have understood when the artifacts they stumbled upon had vast historical significance. Sadly, most of these early reef explorers had little regard for the value of the ancient artifacts they found, and they did little to protect, much less preserve, the rich archeological trove they uncovered.

Today, it's a different story. The government of Malta works to ensure high standards of safety as well as the protection of natural, historical, and archaeological resources. It carefully monitors all diving on Malta, and spearfishing, for one, is now absolutely forbidden. All archaeological finds must be immediately reported, and some areas of the island are off-limits to divers altogether. People cannot simply show up and strap on an oxygen tank. All divers are required to meet international licensing requirements, and they must be able to present a medical certificate, passport photographs, and a logbook before receiving a dive permit.

Ray confessed to being a rare, living bridge between those early days of diving and standardized modern diving. As one of the first to probe the deep waters of Malta, he rose to become the Technical Officer of the Federation of the Underwater Activities of Malta, and he was a current CMAS instructor. In his youth, he had been carefree, but Ray now carefully monitored diving activities on the island and helped enforce the rigid requirements set down by the Maltese government to protect the safety of other divers and the island's cultural heritage. As I listened to Ray describe those early reef dives, however, I began to wonder with some misgivings about the fate of the anchor he and Tony had found.

I also wondered if Luke, in writing the words, *"And they let go the anchors and left them in the sea,"* had ever, even for an instant, imagined anyone ever finding them. Luke wrote more words about the voyage and shipwreck of Paul than Moses had included in the entire Creation account in Genesis. As we climbed aboard Ray's boat and cast off the lines, I saw in the world around me Luke's careful narrative being infused with new life.

NINETY FEET DEEP

"Ready?" Ray asked, and in an almost simultaneous motion, he cranked the engine to life and slammed the throttle forward. The sudden movement jolted us back as the big brass propellers bit into the sea. Within five minutes, we circled over the dive site on Munxar Reef, peering over the side into the crystalline, glass-smooth water. Ray carefully leaned over the side and scanned the seabed, searching for familiar landmarks. All I could make out was a great, dark mass of the reef, ready to rip apart an unsuspecting ship in a storm. Suddenly, Ray turned off the engine and grabbed an iron anchor attached to a long, coiled chain. Casually tossing it over the side, we waited as the chain rattled to a jerking stop a few seconds later.

"This is it," Ray said, securing the anchor chain. "We're over the big cave."

The dive crew slipped on their short summer wetsuits and busied themselves with the careful ritual of readying their gear, securing their regulators, turning on their air, and checking and double-checking their regulators and gauges. With the smooth symmetry of hundreds of repetitions, they donned vests, weight belts, fins and masks as naturally as children dressing for school. Soon they were sitting side-by-side on the gunwales, waiting for Ray's signal. With a thumbs-up from Ray, they leaned backward and splashed into the sea. They righted themselves almost immediately on the surface, and as they bobbed, they cleared their masks. The other divers gave Ray a thumb's up, and all four rolled forward into the deep. I watched as their finned feet waved downward and disappeared into a swirl of bubbles.

Ray led the slow descent through a big crack in the rock, a fissure spiraling down into a large cave that opened up to the area where Ray said they found the anchors thirty years earlier.

From the cave, they swam out onto a sandy stretch of seafloor, where tufts of grass swayed in the white sand. Jean-François settled on the bottom, where gentle currents fanned the green seaweed. He unlashed a depth indicator attached to a lanyard on his arm and read the gauge, then he looked up at Ray and flashed an "OK" sign. Nodding in approval, Ray pointed up and the four divers started their slow ascent to the surface. The whole event took just that long. They took the depth reading and paddled gently upward toward the boat.

Popping through the surface, Jean-Françoise pulled the regulator from his mouth, looked up at me and grinned. "The place where the guide showed us, it registered about ninety feet on the bottom."

Ninety feet. I stared down at the ancient reef lodged into bottom of St. Thomas Bay, anchored there century after century. My mind instinctively traced back through the steps of the biblical narrative, and I replayed the sequence of Paul's shipwreck. From directly above, I could easily see that, in a storm, the sea would gather and converge into a fierce wall of water on the long strand of reef. I turned to scan the shoreline. High white cliffs framed the harbor to its left, and on the other side of the narrow island I saw nothing but jagged cliffs terminating at the open sea. If the sailors had anchored at this spot, they would have had no option but to try for the shore and the protection of St. Thomas bay before them. Everything seemed to fit, even the depth of the sea. Rolling out my nautical map, I triangulated the sector from the outer marker buoy and quickly determined that it precisely lined up with my earlier calculations of where the crew of Paul's ship would have likely jettisoned the four anchors.

That was the moment that, in my mind, everything fell neatly into place. That moment marked the first time that I actually believed we were floating over the exact spot of the fateful shipwreck. An exhilaration washed over me that I hadn't felt in years, and with it countless unanswered questions. First, where was the anchor Ray and Tony had found? Would Ray ever tell me, or would I have to look for answers elsewhere? What about the other anchors? Did they still lie somewhere below, buried in the sand, or had some other divers found them? These questions would have to be answered, because I needed hard evidence of the anchors themselves in order to validate my theory of Paul's shipwreck.

CHAPTER 15

TONY

ack on shore, Ray sat down on a wooden bench, wet suit
and all, communicating with his body language that it
wasn't time to leave. Perhaps now would be a good time
to ask him more specifically about the anchor.

"Would you mind telling me in more detail about Tony and
the anchors from the Munxar?" I asked simply.

"Where do you want me to start?" he answered.

"Start with Tony if you could," I said. "How did you come
to know him?"

"Well, Bob," Ray began, speaking softly. "Tony gave me
the nickname of 'Ciancio' when I was just thirteen years old,
when I started working for Tony. Well, not working for him,
but sort of just helping around the dive shop. I serviced dive
equipment, painted cylinders. Every now and again, to thank
me, Tony would take me on a dive. Yes, he was a father figure,"
Ray smiled, "always steering me in the right direction, keeping
me from bad friends."

Though still soft spoken, Ray had suddenly become quite
animated. I saw he loved talking about Tony. Diving out on the
Munxar, where they had once spearfished together, had clearly
dialed up a mountain of emotion—and loosened Ray's tongue
in the process.

"My father left when I was very young, so Tony became...
truly, my Dad," he told me. "Tony and his wife Margaret sort of
adopted me. Many nights I would sit in their living room and
listen to Tony tell dive stories into the night, about the sea and
spearing the big ones." Ray went on to describe Tony's great
athleticism. "He was very powerful, with broad shoulders,

and stocky. He was also kind of hairy." Ray chuckled then, rubbing the top of his head playfully. "Tony had no hair on the top of his head. He lost his hair very young."

In spite of his physical power, Ray said, Tony was the gentlest of men, "a man who would rather discuss things than use his fists and strength." Ray paused often, reflecting on his friend's unique character, his gentle dominion. "No one challenged Tony," Ray said with pride. "No one needed to. Anyway," he concluded happily, "that's how it was with us. I would lug the cylinders to the boat. When the cylinders were empty, I would fill them from the compressor. I would do whatever needed to be done, fix wetsuits, whatever."

He continued, "The first time Tony took me out to sea, I waited in the boat for him and his dive buddies to surface. But I got a little too excited. I thought, 'I'm sure I can dive. I'll go down and have a look and see what Tony and his friends are doing.' Tony always had spare gear on the boat, so I just grabbed a big twin set of cylinders and put on Tony's spare weight belt, which had ten kilos on it." Ray laughed and patted his growing midsection. "I was a little scrawny guy then. I probably needed only something like four kilos.

"Well, I threw the cylinders on my back and strapped on that heavy weight belt. I was so heavy I should have made a hole in the boat, and I didn't have fins. I didn't have anything but the weights, the tanks, and the regulator. I went down to the bottom like a rock. Not knowing any different, I thought, 'Hey, this is normal.' So I started walking on the seabed. Tony swam over, grabbed me, and dragged me up to the surface. Tony probably saved me that day. I was so laden down with lead that I doubt I could've swam back to the surface."

Ray went on to say that Tony always ranked as Malta's best, hands down. He won almost every competition held on the island to test technique and accuracy, and (true to form, I thought) even occasionally dropped out to give the other divers a chance.

Suddenly Ray looked serious, almost sullen, at the memory of Tony's bravado. "Any time those of us who dived with Tony watched him enter those caves, we knew it was too dangerous.

166

When the caves were too narrow, Tony would sometimes take his tanks off, breathe some gulps of air, and go inside after a lobster or injured fish. We were secretly afraid he might get stuck and..." Ray's voice perked up. "But that was Tony. Bigger than life, the kind of man that legends are made from." He rubbed his hands together and, with a faraway look in his eye, added softly, "I think we all believed Tony couldn't die."

Ray's voice trailed off. He stared at the ground and kicked sand at a small crab that was inching toward him. The high noon sun sparkled across the vast dark sea. Staring off at the distant horizon, Ray recalled the day he heard that Tony was missing. It was December 17, 1978 when Ray got the call. It was too horrible to describe. "Everybody who knew Tony loved him," he continued. "The news spread across the island like wildfire. Night had come, and Tony had not returned from a day of diving alone. Most of his friends, his diving buddies, all rushed to the spot where he was last seen, but it was too late to dive and no one was organized. There were no local diving

Figure 16: Tony (left) was the man everyone loved and respected.

teams to help in the search. It would be his friends. His friends would need to find him."

Ray's eyes were wide now, and I could see he was no longer sitting beside me in his mind. He was back in 1978. "The rescue volunteers waited throughout the night and the early morning. The next morning, all of them met at Tony's dive shop in Cresta Quay. It was painful to watch Tony's wife Margaret and his children endure it all. People came from all over Malta and registered their names as volunteers. They decided on grid searches, some were even drug behind boats as they peered down into the water, but no sign of Tony was found. That went on for a whole month … nothing." His voice registered mild disgust at the searchers' futility. "Over a hundred people participated in the search, and then they all gave up. It was as if the sea had swallowed Tony."

I sat there in the sweltering heat, utterly transfixed. Tony had been to Ray as Jim Irwin had been to me. These men had introduced us to new worlds, launching us into our life's passions. Then, like Jim who died at sixty-one, Tony was suddenly gone. I could feel Ray's heartache, even 25 years later.

Seven years passed, he said, and all hope of finding a trace of Tony drifted away. Then, in 1985, a young American diver named Chris Chapman took a dive on Zonqor Reef. Chapman had come to live on Malta, and he loved to fish. On this particular day, he followed a large grouper into one of the caves beneath the reef. Once inside the cave, he angled up through a chamber that opened into a black, cavernous hole in the rock.

Ray said, "No one had gone that far into the cave, because it looked like it ended. But Chris saw the grouper go up, and so he followed it. He saw a gap that opened into another small cave. This fellow was very slow and careful," he added, explaining how many divers have perished in the caves of Malta from simply moving too fast and carelessly. Without realizing the danger, they stir up the silt and instantly become disoriented. They swim around blindly, unable to find their way, until their air runs out.

Ray paused for a few seconds before continuing. "As Chris moved into the hidden cave, he suddenly saw another diver. Later, he told me that he instinctively thought, 'Oh look, there's

Tony,' as if nothing had ever happened. But then he remembered that Tony was dead." Here Ray's eyes grew narrow. "But, of course, it was Tony. That was the cave where Tony had died—and he was still there, lying flat on his face, still in his black wetsuit, gray cylinders with a red cylinder boot, his fins on, everything still as it was."

Ray still seemed to be in a state of disbelief. "He just floated... still in the dark cave... his spear-gun lying in the same spot where he dropped it." Once Chapman realized what he was looking at, Ray explained, he shot out of the cave and swam to the surface, understandably upset. After collecting himself, he returned to shore and reported it to the authorities.

THE FIRST ANCHOR

Ray's words had become forced and slow as he continued on. "I'll never forget the day we found the first anchor, Bob. We had followed the big crack at the end of Munxar and finned our way through the cave, scanning the walls for grouper. I was getting a little bit experienced by this point, and Tony was letting me swim close by him."

Early on in his apprenticeship to Tony, Ray said he had been relegated to swimming some distance behind the others. Tony had concern that, in his inexperience, Ray might move too fast and scare the big fish away. In time, Tony taught him to swim

Figure 17: A model of a first century anchor with a lead stock, in Ashkelon, Israel.

slowly, looking ahead at all times and gliding through the water unnoticed.

They had been hunting grouper the morning that they found the anchor, and Ray recalled Tony setting his sights on a big one. "Tony saw a fish, shot and missed," he said. Then Ray paused, observing, "It was unlike Tony. I knew he would be angry for missing such a big one. He went swimming off to find the spear, stopped on the bottom and then surprised me. He turned and waved me over, pointing down to an object that sat half beneath the sand, nearly hidden by the grass swirling around on the sea floor. I swam down and watched as Tony scraped his knife across the object. We could see right away that it was metal."

Only later did Ray, Tony, and some of their diving friends find out from a local historian that the anchor stock had been a part of a Roman vessel. From its size alone, the young men knew it had come from a large ship and not a small merchant or fishing vessel.

"What we found was the stock of the anchor, the metal cross piece," Ray said. "The wood and the other parts of the anchor had rotted away. All that was left was this huge piece of lead, about three—maybe four—feet long. We could see that a large section of the anchor had been cut off."

"Cut off?" I asked.

"Yes. It was cut somehow, it was half of a big anchor stock."

Ray had perked up again. Gone for now were thoughts of Tony's death. He literally beamed as he described this moment of youthful discovery with his boyhood idol. "When we surfaced after finding the anchor, Tony said that he would go for help because it was so heavy. He wanted to immediately bring the anchor up from the sea. He returned with a friend, Charlie Vella, an instructor from his dive shop."

Ray explained that when someone finds something like an archaeological treasure on Malta, it's always kept within one's inner circle, within one's group—"the guys you can really trust." He said they put two 45-gallon barrels with rings welded around the openings into the boat, then headed back out to the reef. They planned to use the drums as a lifting device, but Ray said, "I knew enough to see that it wasn't going to be easy."

Back out over the reef, they tied ropes to the barrels and suited up. Ray minded the boat while Tony and Charlie Vella dumped the barrels overboard, and then he followed them into the water. The divers let the barrels fill with water and sink to the bottom, where the trio wrestled them over to the huge piece of lead. I had assumed they wanted the anchor for its archaeological value; perhaps a reward went to those who recovered ancient antiquities. Then Ray told me the real reason they went to such trouble.

"To us divers, that lead was like gold," he explained. "But not for money. We used it for… diving weights."

"Diving weights?" I asked, shocked.

"Yes," he said, matter-of-factly. "The anchor was in half and no good to any museum, or so we thought. In those days it was very expensive to buy diving weights, and we didn't have much money. Dive weights were always sliding off divers' belts and getting lost, so there was a constant need for more weights. So we made our own from scrap lead. Any scavenged lead we could find, we would melt down and pour into molds. But even scrap lead was hard to come by, so this huge, three-foot-long hunk of lead was extremely valuable to us."

I was stunned to hear that this historic relic had been used for scrap metal. It seemed likely that it was from the very shipwreck described by Luke in Acts, and it had been melted down for dive weights. Ray continued with his tale, describing how it took the three of them a very long time to tie the anchor stock to the barrels, and then to fill the barrels with air from their cylinders. Finally, as the barrels gained buoyancy and began to rise toward the surface, the lines to the anchor tightened and, very slowly, began to budge and loosen from the vacuum grip of the sand.

"Of course," Ray explained, "the stock was so heavy it didn't go all the way to the surface." Tony and Charlie agreed the best thing to do was tow the whole, unstable, awkward contraption into shallower water. Eventually, they managed to haul the anchor on board and hide it in the protection of a cove.

"It took all our combined strength to heft it into the boat," remembered Ray. "All of us were straining to get that huge block of lead out of the water. It makes my back hurt again just to think about it. But with one last heave we got it into the boat."

They took the anchor stock back to Tony's dive shop at Cresta Quay, where they cut it up into smaller pieces and melted it down to make dive weights. From the sound of it, they had quite an operation going that day.

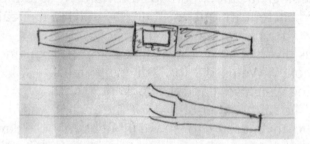

Figure 18: Anchor 1 - The hand sketch of cut/melted anchor by witness Charlie Vella.

"We took the anchor and hacksawed off sizeable chunks," he went on, describing how the hacksaw blades kept breaking. "We began chopping the lead with chisels and used gas-fed burners to melt the lead into heavy cast iron pots." Once a pot was full of the silvery lead soup, they poured it into a mold and left it to solidify until it could be popped out. "We were not used to making so many weights at once," Ray said, "but we liked the look of all the shiny new weights lying out on the floor of the shop to cool."

They marked each molded weight so that, if any should be lost and later found, they could be claimed as part of Tony's batch. Ray told me, "I hurried out and bought a small chisel and chiseled Tony's initials, 'TM,' into the mold."

Then, as if suddenly grasping the absurdity of it all, Ray chuckled and confessed, somewhat embarrassed, "In those days we didn't look upon an object as being so valuable historically. We were young and naïve. I now walk through museums and appreciate my heritage as a Maltese, and I cringe to think about how senseless we were. This object should have been preserved for its archaeological significance. Instead it went from being a priceless artifact to crude dive weights worth a few dollars each."

As I sat staring at him in silence, Ray caught my eye. He added, perhaps in his self-defense, "Fortunately, we wouldn't make that same mistake again."

Ray had already alluded to the second anchor they discovered later on the Munxar Reef. He understood that I wanted to know more about it, and he continued without pausing. Almost every detail of Ray's narrative presented Tony as its primary centerpiece, something I'd grown to expect. As I listened to Ray reminisce, I kept reminding myself that his memories of Tony remained far more valuable to him than the anchors I sought.

As with many diving tales in Malta, the saga of the second anchor began with a spearfishing excursion.

"By now we knew to keep our eyes open while we were diving for grouper," said Ray, "just in case there were any more anchors to be found on the Munxar. We didn't really expect to find another, since we had been down there so many times and had just happened onto the first one. But still, after the first anchor, I think our eyes were a little more trained to spot something unusual."

Figure 19: Anchor 2 - found by Ray and Tony in the early 70s on the Munxar Reef.

They went out again that day to the Munxar, to "Tony's Bank," where finding a fish to kill was money in the bank. Ray said, "To get to the Bank, we again had to go through the crack in the reef and into the cave. We came out the other side on our way to the same rock where we had found the first anchor, only a short distance from the cave. Anyway, we came out of the cave

Figure 20: From left to right: Bob Cornuke, professor Anthony Bonanno, and Charlie Grech.

and were swimming toward the rock, and we both looked down and saw another anchor. It was a large anchor stock, not cut in half like the first, and very close to where we had found the other one. We knew what it was right away from comparing it to the first one, so we stopped what we were doing and went straight down to it. Again, we scraped it, and again it showed metal—lead. So we went straight back to the boat and agreed that we would come back, bring up the anchor, and tow it to Cresta Quay."

They needed a different strategy for landing this anchor, because it hadn't been cut in half and it was much heavier than the first one. They would bring it to the surface with the barrels as they had before, but rather than trying to pull it into the boat; they would attempt to tow it behind the boat all the way to shore. They had almost broken their backs hoisting the first one into the boat, and they had learned their lessons.

"The day we returned for the anchor," Ray continued, "the sea was as smooth as glass on our way out. We wouldn't have any trouble locating it, because we knew that place like the back of our hand. Two other men were with us—Joe Navarro, and I think a chap named David Inglott—so I would mind the boat while they dived down to the anchor and brought it up with 45-gallon drums, like before. I remember that day very distinctly, because while I was topside minding the boat, the sea really began to pick up. You must remember," he reminded me, "I was very young, and skinny as anything. There I was, tending the boat when this strong, cold storm blew in, whipping up big waves and dropping the temperature. After a while I was desperately cold, but I couldn't leave the divers below me. I had no choice but to sit there in the boat and... wait."

Dressed lightly and ill prepared for bad weather, Ray soon found himself fighting hypothermia. By the time the barrels popped up to the surface with the anchor underneath them, Ray said he was chattering blue in the cold, wet wind. "With some difficulty I picked up the divers," he said. "But once they got on board, they could see that I was shaking uncontrollably. Tony took off his wetsuit—which could have fit around three or four of me—and wrapped it around me. Then we started trying to tow the huge anchor against the rolling sea."

Ray told me that their twenty-one-foot boat was called the "Bath Tub," and had only an old, 18-horsepower Johnson outboard for power. Straining against the wind and storm, trying to carry the group of men, the sluggish, blunt-nosed craft could hardly navigate the churning waves.

"Eventually, we decided to let the storm blow us toward the shelter of a jut of land until the wind let up," Ray said. "Unknown to us, Tony's wife Margaret had seen the storm moving in and had sent the Malta Coast Guard out to Munxar Reef to find us. So while we were fighting the anchor, the wind, and the waves, here came the Coast Guard."

The story took a bizarre twist at this point. Instead of waving the Coast Guard in to help them, they hid behind rocks where they couldn't be seen. Ray said that they were afraid of the authorities after their earlier act of vandalism against the first anchor, especially now that they were towing another piece of archaeological contraband. They knew there was a possibility they'd be arrested for stealing ancient Maltese historical treasures.

"After a while, the Coast Guard gave up and left," Ray said, looking relieved even three decades after the fact. "The storm blew over as quick as it came. So we thought we really had it made. The sea calmed down and we started tugging the cumbersome anchor back to Cresta Quay, which took forever with that huge weight behind us."

What awaited them on shore, however, was the last thing they expected.

"When we got to Cresta Quay, there were police cars everywhere." Ray raised his hands in amazement. "We figured we were really in trouble then, because we knew it was illegal to take old things, artifacts, out of the ocean. We panicked, jumped into the water, and started cutting the lines holding the barrels and the anchor. There was a point jutting out from shore where we finally got it cut loose. Then, we headed on in without our treasure, unsure what we would tell the police."

The surprise, of course, was on Ray, Tony, and their cohorts. They soon learned that when the Coast Guard returned without having any sign of Tony's boat, his wife thought they had been sunk and possibly drowned. She called the police. It sounded like something from a Keystone Cops comedy, and Ray knew it. He couldn't help smiling while he recounted that near-disaster to me.

"Everyone kept telling us how glad they were that we were alive, and that we hadn't gone down. All we wanted to do was get back out and get our anchor. Eventually the police left, and we were able to go out to where it had been 'lost' for the second time. We hooked it back up to the barrels, filled them with air, and towed it the rest of the way in."

Trouble seemed to haunt every stage of this clandestine salvage mission. At one point in their last ditch effort to retrieve the anchor, the strain of the barrels broke one of the cleats loose from the back of the boat. Tony pulled Ray out of harm's way in the last split second.

"To this day," Ray nodded toward the dock, "every time I look at that boat and see that the cleats on the back don't match, I think about Tony and the way we brought that second anchor in from the sea."

We sat in silence for several minutes until I realized that Ray had finished his story. He had invited me into perhaps the most intimate chapter of his life, and now he seemed drained. So that was it. There had been two anchors found beneath those waves, deposited from some ancient Roman ship on the southeast side of the Maltese coastline. Remarkably, I had found myself sitting next to one of the very few men on Malta who even knew about them.

Figure 21: Anchor 4 - found by "Mario" in the 60s on the Munxar Reef.

Chapter 16

The Anchor Witnesses

I knew I had to keep pressing forward. Doors had swung open and I had to keep stepping through. I now had very important questions for Ray, questions that could define the remainder of the search effort. What exactly did the anchor look like? Did it fit with a Roman/Alexandrian anchor from the time of Paul?

When I asked the first question, Ray said simply, "I'm not an expert. I don't know what year the anchor came from. It appears to be from olden times—Roman, from what others have told me."

I knew I was marching across delicate ice, but I had to ask, "Do any of the dive weights from the cut anchor that was melted down still exist?"

Ray looked at me for the longest moment, and then offered, "They may, but this was thirty years ago. Weights get lost pretty easy. Maybe some exist today, but I don't know where they would be."

"You spoke of other anchors found at this spot," I said, trying to sound casual. "Do you know if any of them exist today on the island?"

Ray sat up stiffly in his chair, looked out to sea again and said, "The only one I know of that exists today... is the one we towed into Cresta Quay." Then he slowly turned to me with a look that said, "No more questions!"

In a later conversation, Ray explained to me, "The anchors you speak of, Bob ... this could be trouble, big trouble, for anyone who possesses an ancient artifact. There are strict laws about that in Malta. There could be a big fine. It could be... jail. "

In spite of Ray's assurance that none among his old diving fraternity would volunteer information about the anchors, I asked anyway. "Could you put me in touch with Joe Navarro?" I had caught the names of Tony's two diving friends who had helped bring up the second anchor from the Munxar Reef.

Ray paused and stared off into the distance. Finally he exhaled and nodded. "I will see what I can do."

JOE NAVARRO

To my joy, I was able to meet Joe Navarro in the courtyard of my hotel, beneath a hot sun and draping palm trees. I opened with a few questions about the diving culture on the Malta and of course Tony. Joe laughed, recalling a rather bizarre incident in which Tony, fishing one afternoon near the reef, heard a succession of underwater explosions. I watched Joe's eyes grow wide as he explained, "When Tony came to the surface he saw some guy exploding dynamite in the water to catch fish. Tony shouted to the man, saying 'You almost killed me with your dynamite!' The man said simply, 'You're fishing. I'm fishing.'"

I asked Joe about Tony and the anchors Ray had mentioned. "I know of an anchor that came out of the Munxar Reef," he said, "because I was part of the group of people who brought it out." He related the episode as he remembered it, describing in detail how Tony told him he had discovered a Roman anchor in front of the big cave on the Munxar Reef, and that they all conspired to bring it up with oxygen tanks and empty barrels. As the barrels filled with air and slowly lifted and strained against the anchor, he recalled, "It felt like the anchor was protesting our intrusion. I thought the ropes were going to snap; but then it nudged from its sandy hold, and I saw this huge anchor that had belonged to the sea for so long inching its way up, at first just a few centimeters, then in a swirl of sand, like the ocean lost its grip on its prize after 2000 years. Once it left the bottom, we knew it no longer belonged to the sea—it belonged to us."

Even there—at my hotel decades later—Joe described it as, "the most exciting moment of my life, watching as the anchor rose to the surface, the bubbles from the divers and the trailing sand swirling behind it. From the bottom, I watched as the anchor was carried up into the sunlight filtering down through the surface."

With Joe's exhilaration, though, I could sense unease. I could tell that the joy of the moment had been tarnished somewhat by the sense that they had done something wrong. "As I watched this thing so old, so magnificent taken from the sea bed," Joe said, shifting in his chair, "I felt as if I was treading on something... sacred."

At that point, I explained my theory about Paul's shipwreck and told Joe I thought that anchor was one of the four that had been cut from the ship. Joe sat without speaking for some time.

"What do you think about that?" I finally asked. I expected him to pass judgment on the theory itself, but he surprised me instead with what sounded like...an apology.

He mumbled softly, "What we did was wrong, whether the anchor was from St. Paul's shipwreck or not. It belonged to the ocean... Pulling the anchor up like that was like grave robbing, like a sacrilege. I wish now that we had left the anchor at rest on the sea floor."

And then he said something I didn't expect. "I have seen the anchor since that day... at Tony's house." Then he repeated, "But it really belongs to the ocean."

Tony's house? The anchor was at Tony's house? I let the comment pass temporarily, but I would have to ask about this remark later. Joe struck me as both honest and sincere, someone who had some youthful regrets from a heady and dangerous season of life. I thanked him for the interview. He nodded and said, "I have a brother, you know. He was there when they melted the first, cut anchor. I am sure he would be willing to tell you about his experience."

OLIVER NAVARRO

Later that night, I met Oliver Navarro for dinner in a restaurant called The Black Pearl, a massive, converted wooden ship that had been built in Sweden in 1909. I'm told it was once sailed by Errol Flynn and was used as a prop in the movie *Popeye* with Robin Williams. The rustic beams and weathered planking reminded all the patrons that this restaurant once traveled the world. I felt like we were dining in the bowels of an old pirate ship.

We had barely finished introductions when Oliver reached into a small bag and lifted out a square block of lead. He placed it in the middle of the table in the dim candlelight. "I was a young man about the same age as Ray when I met Tony," he said. "The best times of my life were spent with Tony; he was an excellent man. We started doing competitions together—you know, dive competitions, spear-fishing and the like." He chuckled and said, "I couldn't keep up with him."

Oliver told me about the day when Tony spoke to him in the dive shop and said he had found something "really nice, really beautiful," near the underwater cave. Then Tony proceeded to show him what looked like a piece of stone with a square hole in the middle.

"In those days, I was maybe fourteen or fifteen years old, and I didn't know much about archaeology," Oliver said. "They all told me it was a Roman anchor that had a piece cut from it. I figured that before it was cut, it must have been maybe five feet long. They said the square hole in the middle was where the wooden shaft would have fit in."

Oliver repeated the explanation I had heard from Ray about how lead was in high demand in those days, and they had used the anchor to make small weights for diving belts. "The weights were always getting misplaced or lost beneath the waves," he said. "Always slipping from the deck of a boat, always difficult to replace."

He told me that Tony and the others decided to melt down this big lead anchor to make weights, figuring that since someone had already cut it in half, it had lost whatever value it once held. "And besides," Oliver added, "if the museum found out we had it, we would be in a bit of trouble. So one afternoon we just started cutting on this big lead thing. Ray and I cut it with hacksaw blades until our hands almost bled."

His voice grew soft like his brother Joe's. "We all needed the lead for weights, but silently I think we all felt like we were killing this thing, this thing that was two thousand years old."

The process he described certainly sounded like a primitive slaughter of sorts, with gas bottles hissing and hacksaws carving off chips that were then unceremoniously tossed into black pots for meltdown.

"Smoke was swirling from the garage," Oliver said. "We had to stand back because of the vapors. When chunks fell into the melted lead, some would splatter out. We had to use tongs to hold the molds as the lead was poured from the pots."

Oliver reached down and grabbed the weight from the table in front of me; he held it up to the candlelight.

"This is one of two weights that were given to me by Tony that day," he said. "I'm sure that others exist around Malta. Or maybe they too have been lost to the sea by careless divers. This is one of two that survive."

He set it down, and I reached over and grabbed the weight. The dense, cool mass felt much heavier than I anticipated. I remembered Ray telling me that he had chiseled "TM" into the molds that day—for Tony Macaliff-Borg. I had wanted to find one of those old weights, but this one appeared to be bare; it had no markings at all. As I pulled it close to the candle, though, I saw the letters "MT." I placed the weight back onto the table and told Oliver, "Ray told me that on the day the anchor was melted, he had taken a hammer and chiseled TM into the mold." I showed him the initials. "This one says MT."

"He did," Oliver laughed. "We all watched him do it. It surprised us all when the weights came out 'MT.' When we poured the lead into the mold and pulled out the weights, the 'TM' became the reverse 'MT.'"

CHARLIE VELLA

The whole affair of melting that ancient lead into weights raised a nagging question. When they found the first anchor, it appeared to have been cut—on the seafloor. But who would cut an anchor at the bottom of the sea?

Hoping to find a logical answer, I tracked down Charlie Vella, who had also helped Tony bring up the first anchor. We met at a seaside restaurant in beautiful St. Julian's Bay. Charlie was tanned and in exceptional shape, and he wore a short gray beard. As we talked and slowly became acquainted, he too began reminiscing about the fellowship of early divers on Malta. Charlie told me that Tony had been his P.E. teacher in school.

"I'd been getting in a little trouble," he said quietly. "Tony took it upon himself to mentor me, just like he mentored Ray and many other students." I wasn't the least bit surprised to find that Charlie held as much affection for Tony as everyone else on the island seemed to have. Like the others, Charlie had his own spin on the Tony legend.

"He was a special guy," Charlie said, "always taking students camping, helping them out, keeping them out of trouble. That's how he got me interested in diving at the Cresta Quay Dive School. I later became an instructor and then a professional diver."

Charlie told me that he had become one of the first international "saturation divers"—a commercial diver who takes on special, high-risk jobs in extremely deep, dark waters. The job had left him with some incredible memories, and for the next hour he cheerfully regaled me with tales of his "deep dives." A highly trained, experienced diver, Charlie was a man who kept his wits about him and, even on dry land, remained acutely aware of his surroundings. When he described something on the ocean floor, I had no doubt about his accuracy. As our conversation returned to the discovery of the first anchor, I mentioned to Charlie that the other divers thought the anchor had been cut. I asked Charlie why he thought they might have said that. Was it sawn in two? Had it been moved? What did he think had happened to it?

"It was obvious what had happened," Charlie said. "The anchor had literally been ripped in half." Pointing to my notebook, he said, "Let me show you."

Sliding my notebook across the table, I watched him take a pencil from his shirt pocket and begin sketching a rough image of that first anchor. Its lead had long since been melted into dive weights, but Charlie seemed to remember the anchor stock with no problem. I trusted that Charlie's picture would come closer than anything else to seeing the actual artifact that had touched that fraternity of early divers.

Charlie sketched silently, turning the page around he went. Suddenly, he pronounced his artwork finished. "There!" he said, sliding the notebook back to me.

What I saw on that small page explained everything. The picture was of a Roman anchor stock identical to the others we had discovered in our search, but this one was half gone. From Charlie's drawing, it appeared as though the anchor had been stressed, stretched, and distorted. It looked like some great, violent force had pulled the anchor apart at its weakest point, like a giant piece of lead taffy torn in two at the place where the stock was thinnest—where the wooden main shaft of the anchor had once passed though.

I sat, stunned at the drawing. An enormous amount of force would have been necessary to twist and break a thick, heavy lead anchor off its stock, and I couldn't begin to picture such violence in my mind. Charlie, however, seemed quite confident about what had happened.

I cleared my throat and asked, "What do you think it was that could have done that? What could produce that kind of force?"

Charlie didn't hesitate, having clearly thought it through many times. "It could only have been a terrible storm that was ripping at a ship out there on the Munxar," he said, raising his eyebrows at the prospect.

I let Charlie's words simmer in my mind. Was it possible; could a mere storm have produced enough force to snap off an anchor? A few moments more passed. I stared at the distorted, sheared anchor stock Charlie had sketched from memory. It was then that I realized the most likely explanation for its presence and condition on the outer Munxar.

"This was probably the first anchor thrown out as the ship tried to stop its momentum and stay off the rocks," I whispered, almost to myself.

CHAPTER 17

THE SECOND ANCHOR

I 'd witnessed the fury of the seas around Malta—the raw, grinding power of the waves that could beach a modern cargo ship and then pound it to pieces. Finally, I began to understand that every treatment of Acts 27 probably undersold what actually happened that night on the outer Munxar Reef. Today, the Gregale winds cause the most feared, powerful, and deadly storms known in the Mediterranean—and these are likely the same northeastern winds as the Euroclydon named in Acts 27:14. As Charlie continued talking about other diving exploits of Tony and his, I kept drifting back to that horrific storm described in Acts.

Paul and his companions had been locked in the grip of Euroclydon for two weeks, and the ship was still being tossed like a toy in heavy seas. As the starving, weary, hopeless human cargo held on for dear life in the darkness, they began to hear the sound of water exploding somewhere off in the blackness around them. Fighting fear and the elements, they threw out one or more lead-weighted lines that had been knotted at standard intervals, gauging the depth first at 20 fathoms, then at 15 fathoms. Their ears weren't deceiving them—they were headed straight for land. By now the roaring explosion of the shallow Munxar Reef was beside and before them, and the swells grew even taller as they stacked up on the shallow bottom. To drop anchors from the bow and let the ship weathervane all the way around would be suicide. Groups of soldiers, crewmen, and prisoners probably began working frantically on the pitching deck, moving anchors from their stowage on the bow to the far stern of the ship. They had onc chance to stop the ship in its tracks, and they just prayed that the anchors held.

We can only imagine the wrenching, crashing, terrifying impact of that first anchor, tied off on the gunwales and thrown into the raging sea. As it suddenly "bit" on the bottom and pulled the massive rope taut, the violence of it strained every board and beam on the storm-beaten ship. Certainly, it sent men flying as they worked to throw out the other anchors. Then, just as suddenly as it pulled tight, that first anchor, according to Charlie's drawing, literally tore loose, ravaged by the reef and waves. I'm sure this sent a wave of panic through the men as they struggled to heave the second, then the third, and finally the fourth anchor overboard. Only as the other anchors bit and held did the first anchor settle to the bottom. Now, however, only three-and-a-half anchors held the ship off the rocks until daylight revealed the gloomy prospects of those on the ship.

Could it really have happened that way? Perhaps. Lined up next to the countless theories on the location and nature of Paul's shipwreck on Malta, I believe it is, finally, one scenario that fits the vast preponderance of evidence. All of the physical landmarks precisely match Luke's description, from the anchors found on the outer Munxar, to the torn, broken anchor, to the depth of the sea and the presence of the reef itself.

For an object that no longer existed in its original form, these spontaneous musings about the "melted anchor" had done more to validate our search than anything I had been able to actually see and touch. From Charlie's vivid description, it was evident that some ship—not necessarily Paul's ship—had dropped an anchor in front of the Munxar Reef in a violent storm. The force of some storm, as amazing as it sounded, had torn the lead stock of that anchor in two. Which raised an interesting question. Why would the captain of any ship have intentionally dropped an anchor in front of a reef unless he had come upon the island unintentionally during a terrific storm? All other things being equal, wouldn't he seek a place offering more protection, a familiar harbor away from the violence of waves crashing upon a reef?

The fact is, a seasoned captain would have never chosen that harbor, or that reef, to drop anchor—unless he had no choice. It now seemed obvious that the anchor had been dropped from a ship that had come upon this reef without design or purpose, the captain facing a hopeless situation. He had only anchored his ship in such a deadly location, in the teeth of a formidable reef, because he had to.

Weighing these factors, I made a conclusion. If all of the anchors found near the big cave had come from the same ship, it only made sense they had been dropped during a storm. They had been cast out in desperation from a ship fighting for its very survival.

MARGARET

The following day, Ray called me at my hotel and surprised me. He said I could see the second anchor that he, Tony, and Joe had brought up from the Munxar. With no more information than that, I herded my research team into the van and drove quickly to the dive shop. There I found Ray waiting with his fiancée, Jo.

"It will be a lot quicker if I drive," Ray smiled as he and Jo slid into the front seat of the van. The Maltese landscape flew past the windows as Ray sped down unmarked country roads and through several rural villages. He only slowed when we approached a small cluster of villas, looking very picturesque in the morning sun. Ray pulled over to the road side, about one hundred yards from the villas.

"The team will have to wait here," Ray said as he parked the van. "We don't want to make Margaret nervous." In his every movement, I could sense Ray's reverence for Tony's widow as he, Jo, and I walked up to the heavy, wooden front door.

Ray knocked on the door, and after a few seconds a dignified Mediterranean woman appeared and greeted us warmly. She invited us inside, and as we entered the front parlor, Margaret hugged Ray and Jo and gave them each a kiss on each cheek, the typical Maltese greeting. Margaret poured us tea and served cake, moving with grace and elegance around the quaint cottage. I took instant notice of her kind eyes; her gentle spirit only lightly veiled the pain of her past.

After several minutes of small talk, Margaret looked over at me and asked, "Would you like to see Tony's anchor?"

Ray had obviously smoothed my way with Margaret, but I didn't want to take advantage of her eager trust. Tony's death had affected the whole island, clearly, but I knew no one had suffered as much as this gentle woman. She never expected to have an outsider like myself asking her about the old anchor, and I didn't want to trample lightly on her generosity.

"Before I do," I said with a smile, "I'd like you to know why we are so interested in the anchor your husband found." Then, I explained the research we had done. I shared with her our quickly-evolving theory about the object Tony had brought up—that it was quite possibly one of the four anchors from Paul's shipwreck.

She didn't show a hint of surprise. Instead, she answered simply and with the hint of a chuckle, "That would be just like Tony. If anyone would come across Paul's shipwreck, it would be my Tony." She grinned wide and added, "He was quite special, you know."

"That's what I have heard," I replied. "I've been told that your husband was a remarkable man."

"Yes," she continued. "I think he would be proud to know that he had been a part of such a discovery." Margaret reached out and touched me gently on the arm. "Tony found the anchor and brought it up," she said, "so it means a lot to me. I can see now that maybe it will be important to others. For me, it will always be a memento of him, something that he brought home from the sea. But..." she paused, searching for words. "I am afraid...*concerned* that if the authorities find out about it, they will come and take it away. That would mean serious trouble for me. I will show you the anchor, but I worry about what may happen."

I followed Margaret down a hallway that lead out into a sun-drenched courtyard. We stepped out under the open sky into carefully tended flower-filled gardens. Margaret gently motioned to the front part of the courtyard, and there, lying on the polished floor, lay the anchor.

It was a large slab of lead, encrusted with dried sea growth. Narrow slits in its side revealed the scars of two millennia of exposure to the constant currents of the sea. I bent down and ran my hand over the cool, leaden mass, my thoughts alive with images of sailors standing in wind and rain on the deck of a tempest-tossed ship. I imagined the desperate crew straining to throw this very anchor over the side in a final attempt to hold the ship fast before it ran aground.

"Could this really be an anchor from Paul's ship?" I asked myself. Everything seemed to add up: it was the right object, from the right place and the right era of history and even from the right depth of the ocean. I took my time examining the anchor stock, sternly reminding myself that the ancient object in front of me represented only the second anchor pulled from the waters of Munxar Reef. I lowered my hand to touch the cool lead, and in that touch I felt as though I had spanned the ages. This might be a physical connection to Paul himself. I couldn't let the emotion of the moment cloud the reality of the task before me.

I had patiently followed a path that led me to this massive Roman anchor stock, and as careful as I'd had to be, I know the journey could have been nigh impossible. I had followed a cold trail through the close-knit community of Malta. Like many indigenous cultures around the world, the people of Malta watch out for each other, protect each other, and can be as secretive as they need to be in order to take care of their own. My simple trust, the hope of friendship, and brutal honesty had brought me a great distance. Ray had opened up to me some of the most intimate, painful memories of his life, and he had trusted me enough to drive me up to the home of Tony's widow. Now Margaret offered us not only the hospitality of her home—us, complete strangers—but she presented to us one of the prized mementoes belonging to her late husband.. Here I stood in Margaret's courtyard with the anchor her island hero husband had pulled from the sea.

Kneeling beside that ancient slab of lead, I sensed that the same simple inquiry and analysis that had brought us this far would keep the plot moving forward. I explained to Margaret that I had invited a scholar along who could greatly assist my research. She thought for a moment, then said, "If it is important, he may see the anchor."

Dr. Mark Phillips soon joined us in the courtyard. Margaret had given me permission to photograph and videotape the anchor, and as I panned the camera over it from different angles, Mark literally gawked in amazement. He wasted no time agreeing that it could very well be a Roman anchor, possibly even forged during the first century. He acknowledged, however, that dating the anchor precisely lay beyond his expertise.

He turned and reminded me, "My wife and I are having dinner with Dr. Anthony Bonanno and his wife, and you must join us."

I knew of Dr. Bonanno. He was a local professor of some prestige as head of the Department of Archaeology at the University of Malta. Mark suggested we show the professor a video of this anchor and ask his opinion.

I thanked Margaret again for her kindness in allowing me this rare opportunity. I would fulfill my promise to protect her anchor and keep its location a secret. In my most enthusiastic imagination, however, I couldn't have predicted where the adventure would lead.

My scheduled stay in Malta was drawing to a close. Our investigation had moved in an entirely unforeseen direction, from sea to land. Our dive team had fulfilled its purpose, and I knew it was time to return to Colorado and regroup.

On my final evening in Malta, I joined Dr. Phillips and his wife Angela in their meal with Dr. Bonanno at the hotel restaurant. Dr. Anthony Bonanno had earned his PhD at the Institute of Archaeology, University of London and he had taught in Malta since 1971. He regularly lectured at European universities on Maltese archaeological heritage, and he had convened two important international conferences on Maltese archaeology. I looked forward to presenting my theory and hearing his response, knowing there would be unavoidable consequences to our search either way.

Mark Phillips wasted no time. Before we even ordered, he asked me to show Dr. Bonanno the video of Margaret's anchor. I pulled out a tiny video player from my briefcase, flipped up the screen and pressed "play." The LCD screen flickered to life with images of the anchor, and Dr. Bonanno immediately explained to us what we were seeing.

He said, "What you have just shown me is an anchor. To be more precise, it is part of the anchor known as an anchor stock, commonly used on large Roman vessels."

"Could this be from an Alexandrian grain freighter," I asked him.

"Oh yes," he said. "It was probably from a Roman/ Alexandrian grain freighter. It was an essential part of their equipment."

"What would you say is the probable dating of the anchor?" I inquired.

"This anchor stock," said Dr. Bonanno, "is likely to have belonged to a ship that plied the Mediterranean, possibly a grain cargo ship that used to carry grain between Rome and Alexandria, possibly around AD 60; that is, the time when St. Paul was shipwrecked on the island of Malta. This Roman anchor stock would fit well within the era of the shipwreck of St. Paul."

Dr. Bonanno's observation was electric. It was what we all hoped for, and I couldn't help noticing the smile on Dr. Phillip's face. I wished I could have enjoyed more of the evening's conversation, but I regrettably had to excuse myself from the group in order to catch my evening flight for London.

From London, I would take the early morning flight to the United States on United Airlines flight 929. The date was September 11, 2001.

CHAPTER 18

GANDER,
NEWFOUNDLAND

I could not possibly have foreseen what would occur on my connecting flight from London to Chicago.

As I made my way to the airport, through passport control and onto the airplane, I couldn't help but replay in my mind the varied and unpredictable route our expedition had taken us in searching for those anchors. Before the plane lifted off the runway, I had already started to plan my next trip to Malta.

I knew that the next phase would require good, solid detective work, which added considerably to my excitement. I had come to Malta this time with a dive team, expecting to work out of my element while my team explored the floor of the Mediterranean Sea. Now, I had a whole new strategy to pursue, one that was far more familiar to me. I planned to return to Malta and follow a small tip Ray had given me about the two additional anchors taken from the Munxar.

Could I find any remaining evidence of the melted anchor? Could I track down eyewitness testimonies concerning any additional anchors—if they existed—and earn the trust of their owners? And, most importantly, would I be able to find the common thread that connected all four anchors to that spot on the Munxar Reef where I was ever more convinced that Paul's ship had run aground?

As I was thinking about these things, I was flying at 39,000 feet above the Atlantic Ocean aboard a Boeing 777, looking at a miniature video screen on the back of the seat in front of me.

It told me we had four and half hours left in the flight. I could see from the map on the screen that we were approaching Newfoundland, on the northeast coast of Canada.

Suddenly there came such a violent buffeting through the cabin that the overhead bins popped open. Flight attendants grabbed onto the bulkheads, and the plane started to drop like a rock. There was a thunderous noise of wind and mechanical vibration, and the plane started shaking. The video screen on the back of the seat in front of me displayed 39,000 feet ... 37,000 ... 35,000 ... 32,000 ... The loudspeaker crackled on with a pilot's voice telling us that there was some kind of "situation," and he would get back to us with an update. His stream of words seemed compressed and hurried, giving the distinct impression that United Flight 929 was in serious trouble. The flight attendants pulled themselves up the aisles against the violently shaking craft and the gravity of the descent, shouting, "Put your seats up! Put your seatbelts on! Put your shoes on!"

The man seated next to me leaned over and said calmly, "We have about four to five minutes before we hit the Atlantic Ocean."

At just that moment, the captain came back on the intercom in a more controlled tone. He said, "Nothing is wrong with the aircraft, but we will have to make an immediate landing on the island of Newfoundland." The map on the screen in front of me showed the Canadian island of Newfoundland located just southeast of Greenland. Gander International Airport sits on Newfoundland, which is separated from the Canadian mainland by the Strait of Belle Isle. It's basically at the eastern edge of Canada on the Atlantic Ocean.

No one spoke. White knuckles gripped the armrests of those around me. Anxiety etched into the brows of my fellow passengers. There then came chilling words from the intercom above us. "Uh, folks, there has been an incident...a major emergency in the United States. All of the U.S. and Canadian borders are closed to approaching aircraft ... and we have been ordered to land in Gander immediately."

People started to talk. A buzz filled the airplane from one end to the other. What had happened? What emergency could be so great that it would trigger both the United States and Canada to close their borders? I heard whispers throughout the cabin suggesting everything from nuclear attack to an outbreak of war. In a matter of moments, we had become literally suspended between two worlds: the safe world we had left a few hours before in London, and the weird, surreal, unknown world ahead of us.

We continued to descend. I could feel the landing gear being lowered, creating a condition called "dirty air," a maneuver pilots use to drop the aircraft's altitude rapidly. I eventually learned that the pilot made this move as an anti-terrorist strategy. Our flight crew had no way of knowing whether we had terrorists on board, and they wanted to discourage any plans to take over the plane. One of the passengers later told me that jet fuel had been dumped, streaming from the wings—a liquid mass swirling into a trailing spray.

The landing was a blur. I saw the Newfoundland coastline and then, it seemed the wheels bounced on the runway the next moment. The engines reversed and the plane dipped down against the pressure of the brakes, and as the plane slowed, everyone aboard breathed more freely. Still, our minds rummaged through possible scenarios about what had brought us from 39,000 feet to a runway in Gander, Newfoundland in a matter of minutes.

Immediately, passengers began using cell phones to contact loved ones, to find out what had happened. One by one people began shouting out updates.

"A plane struck the World Trade Center!"

"Two planes …"

We heard "Pittsburgh" and the "Pentagon." Then we heard the word "terrorists." The man behind me turned to his wife and said, "I hope he's okay." I learned that his son-in-law was in the World Trade Center that day. The captain alerted us that we could listen to the BBC on channel eight of the console radio. Everybody slid on their headphones and listened to the reports from London of the incredible tragedy unfolding in the United States.

I realized that in my hurry to get to the airport in Malta the night before, I had not called my wife Terry to tell her of my travel plans. I had intended to surprise her at her class reunion in Chicago, so she had no way of knowing that I had been flying that morning and now sat on a runway in Newfoundland. A lady offered me the use of her cell phone, so I called Terry at her parents' house in Milwaukee. Thinking I was in Malta, she asked, "Have you heard the news?"

"Yes," I said. "I'm in Gander, Newfoundland."

"Gander?" she was startled. "What are you doing there?"

"They diverted us here because …" I attempted to explain.

"I know," she interrupted. "I know."

Not wanting to drain minutes or battery from the borrowed cell phone, I told Terry that I would need to call her back when I could.

"I'll be okay," I told her.

She said, "I understand."

As I looked out my window at the scene around us, I watched other commercial and military planes spread around the airport as one after another aircraft landed. The planes lined up along the runways and the taxiways, a growing collection of planes that displayed a vast variety of airline insignias and countries of origin. In all, some 38 large civilian planes eventually packed the tarmac, wingtip to wingtip. The entire population of Gander was 10,000, but now more than 7,000 stranded passengers from around the world sat in airliners on the runway.

Through my window, I watched as a steady stream of curious onlookers gathered behind a chain-link fence alongside the airport to witness this one-time, historical event. Just hours before, Gander had been a nondescript, anonymous little town at the eastern end of Canada. In just a few hours, it had become a refuge for people from across the world.

Our pilot promised us periodic updates, but for now we would have to "sit tight." So that's what we did. We just sat. And sat. We had landed sometime around noon, and it was a hot day for that late in the season. Then, the plane's air conditioning gave out, adding to our discomfort throughout the long afternoon.

As the sun arced low across the sky and set, we finally enjoyed some relief from the heat of our confinement.

In total, we sat on that plane for twenty-six hours, from the time we boarded in London to the time we deplaned in Newfoundland. The flight crew did their best to care for us, but it didn't take long for the plane's supplies of food and drinks to be exhausted. Soon, there was nothing left except for the contents of the liquor cabinet, which was locked for obvious reasons. Even the cups ran out, so we each wrote our name on a single Styrofoam cup, which we kept in order to get an occasional drink of water. I found it reassuring, given the horror going on in the United States, that not one person complained or caused any kind of problem.

As a side note, years later, the story of our being stranded in Gander, Newfoundland was made into a Broadway play called "Come from Away." It received seven Tony nominations.

Originally, we had all expected to disembark in Chicago, Illinois. The terror attacks made us temporary refugees and forced us to be processed into Newfoundland through Canadian Customs. We were required to enter through rigorous checkpoints where customs officials and Royal Canadian Mounted Police officers tore through our bags, one by one. Exhausted officials worked double and triple shifts in the days and weeks after 9/11, as added security precautions were made while processing great multitudes of people.

Once we cleared customs, we were each handed a small sub sandwich, a bottle of water, and a piece of cold pizza. The officials then herded us into school buses for transfer to makeshift accommodations. The 198 passengers from our plane were bussed 30 minutes south of Gander to the small fishing village of Gambo, where we were welcomed into the Salvation Army church. Workers handed everyone a blanket and told us to find a place to sleep on a pew or the floor. Our group of marooned travelers filled that little church wall-to-wall as everyone bedded down for the night.

Looking out the church window and down the road, I saw a small, white house with a satellite dish bolted on the side.

"Why not?" I said to myself.

I left the church and walked down the road and up the steps to the little house, and knocked gently on the front door. A woman answered, looked me up and down, and said, "You're one of the people from the airplanes, aren't you?"

"Yes, I am," I said, looking as dejected as I could.

"Well, you just come in and make yourself at home," she said. "We were hoping we could help in some way."

And so Harold and Madelaine immediately adopted me. Harold was an 82-year-old retired cod fisherman. Madelaine was twenty-five years his junior, and boasted of having twelve children, all of whom had moved away. She led me into the living room and said, "Can I feed you anything?"

Again, trying to look dejected, I said, "Please don't bother."

Well, that was all it took. In an instant, cod sizzled in a skillet, cookies swelled in the oven, and CNN, with all its unfolding coverage, flickered on the television.

I would spend the next five days in Gambo, amazed by the people of the town and their hospitality. Hundreds of locals brought food, clothing, and medicine to the stranded passengers. We were not allowed to take any of our luggage off the airplane, so we had nothing, not even the ability to change our socks. Yet the townsfolk of Gambo supplied everything we really needed. As I lived through those days, I thought that while September 11 unveiled the brutality of fanatics with a misguided cause, that time also showed the human kindness and generosity that can emerge during a crisis.

Five days later, we finally arrived in Chicago. There we learned that we were the last stranded United Airline flight to return to the United States. Our flight crew had labored for nearly a week, going far beyond what should have been expected of airline employees. They taxied our plane through a corridor of ground crew and other personnel waving American flags, finally delivering us to our gate and our awaiting loved ones.

We had enjoyed great hospitality in Newfoundland, but the layover also gave me time to ponder the implications of Paul's shipwreck. If we were really onto the correct location, and if the anchor at Margaret's villa was actually one of the Paul shipwreck anchors, then what would that mean to me? What would that mean to those studying and contemplating the historical truths of the Bible?

In a strange sort of way, I began identifying certain things experienced by those aboard Paul's ship. I was traveling from Malta to Chicago, and I wound up on an island called Newfoundland. Paul's ship was traveling from Caesarea to Rome, and he wound up on the island of Malta. Paul's ship carried 276 people; our airplane carried, with crew, a total of 215 people. Sensing imminent peril as we approached the island, I checked the altitude of the plane. Sensing the peril of running aground as they approached their island, the sailors on Paul's ship took depth soundings. We had dumped fuel into the ocean in order to lighten the plane during an emergency landing, and on Paul's ship they dumped grain into the sea to make the ship lighter for their emergency landing. After landfall, the natives on Malta treated Paul's group with amazing kindness; after our landing, we were treated with amazing kindness as refugees in Newfoundland. The similarities amused me.

I was looking forward to the familiar confines of my office in Colorado Springs, where I could reflect, regroup and consider everything that had happened since I first left for Malta. I would spend the next several months planning where to go from there.

CHAPTER 19

AFGHANISTAN

The chaos surrounding the September 11th terrorist attacks temporarily sidetracked my search for Paul's sea anchors. By the end of my surprisingly pleasant Newfoundland layover, a new vernacular had crept into the national vocabulary. Words like "Taliban," "Al-Qaida, "Ground Zero", and "War on Terror," now assumed a prominent place in our everyday lives. In the weeks following September 11th, our culture found itself in unfamiliar psychological terrain, with millions of ordinary citizens suddenly paralyzed at the prospect of opening an envelope, turning on a water tap, or boarding an airplane. Beyond our collective rage at Osama Bin Laden, America's focus turned to the sinister threat of a group of previously ignored fanatics living secretly among us. Images of fire, destruction, and death played out thousands of times on our television screens, and the certainty of war became a morbid fact of life.

Fear eventually gave way to cries for vengeance. Evil had had its day, but not its way. A powerful new brand of patriotism sprang to life, and our public sadness and mourning drifted irreversibly toward national resolve.

I had been home less than two months when I received a call from a man named Jerry Rose, the president of the Total Living Network in Chicago. Jerry asked me if I might be willing to travel to Afghanistan, of all places, to take part in a special film project. The Taliban's brutality had developed into a cancer that tormented people already weary from centuries of warfare, and Jerry wanted me to help videotape the ongoing relief efforts taking place amidst the falling bombs. He reasoned that millions of people would be inspired by a documentary of the aid clandestinely delivered to people victimized by their own leaders, and I had to agree. There was no specific archeological value in my going to Afghanistan, but my trip there might just save human lives.

Jerry knew that I had spent much of the previous seventeen years of my life crisscrossing the Middle East; apparently he felt that I had the skills and abilities to get us into Afghanistan and navigate our way through a treacherous situation. With a bloody war against the Taliban now raging full-tilt in that besieged country, "treacherous" seemed a monumental understatement.

Life by then had returned to a semblance of normal. I had turned my full-time attention back to the Malta project, and I was busy running The Bible Archaeology, Search & Exploration (BASE) Institute. I was also juggling several other time-consuming projects. Even though Jerry's Afghanistan adventure had worthwhile possibilities, I didn't think I could pull away for the length of time Jerry described. I recognized that his project could tell a poignant story of goodness versus evil, the kind of a tale I loved being a part of, but I didn't think I had the freedom to go. Jerry's plan didn't give me much forewarning—I'd have to leave in two weeks if I joined him. I told Jerry I would have to get back to him.

Two days later, I received a phone call from Dana Curry and Heather Mercer, two women rescued from the Taliban by Special Forces. Just weeks earlier, I had seen the two women interviewed on CNN about their arrest and imprisonment by the Taliban and their daring escape. The world had held its breath as the Taliban used these young missionaries and other captives as pawns in a savage war. I had watched the news reports during their captivity, thinking, "These young women probably won't survive."

During our phone conversation, Heather and Dana described the Afghan women who were being tortured and tormented by the Taliban, and I knew the missionaries had risked their lives in reaching out to help those women. As we talked, they shared some of the details of their amazing escape. Here again, their story struck a familiar chord. God held one of the most impossible situations of their lives in His hand, just as He had the ship full of sailors in Paul's day.

Heather and Dana said a mutual friend informed them that I might be going to Afghanistan; they wanted to know if I'd be willing to help them tell their story. In fleeing for their lives, they had left their journals in Kabul.

"Will you be going to Kabul?" Dana asked. "Could you try to find the journals we left behind and photograph the prison and the home where we lived in Kabul?"

I told them that that if I decided to go to Afghanistan, I would do my best to help them. That night I weighed the decision to go or not go. After much prayer, the answer came from my wife. Terry always shares from her heart on these matters.

"You'll never have this opportunity again, Bob," she said. "This is the event of our lifetime. Our parents had World War II; we have September 11th."

Terry never failed to surprise me. She's encouraged me to find unique ways to inspire others, even when it has involved travelling into dangerous countries filled with people who hate America. I've often joked that she has our life insurance agent on speed dial, but the simple truth is that God gave me a wife who understood that I was created for this kind of work. When I asked her why Afghanistan—especially now—she replied calmly, "Because I believe in you. I believe that you can do what they want you to do. And I know that this story will be an encouragement to so many." My wife is an amazing woman.

Just days later I kissed and hugged my family good-bye at the Denver International Airport. I could see in their eyes a deep concern, but even my children wore brave smiles. As I walked down the jet-way, I tried to think, "It will only be two weeks before I come home again."

I met up with the rest of our team in Chicago, which included a man named Joe Ritchie and his son, Noah. Joe had lived in Afghanistan as a child and was now a multi-millionaire. Both he and his brother James had appeared on the TV show "60 Minutes" the week before, telling about their incredible work in helping the people of Afghanistan. Joe would be a major part of my video assignment.

After a long flight with many connections, we arrived in Peshawar, Pakistan. A driver picked us up at the airport and sliced through traffic clogged with motorized rickshaws, pedal bicycles, and kamikaze automobile drivers. A dreary, soupy cloud of car fumes and dust particles hung in the air. The region had been without rain for three years, and the countryside had become a chalky, ecological disaster. Failing crops and devastated food distribution efforts resulted in empty-eyed stares from the starved children whose large eyes sat in bony faces. An odor of hideous, soured smog filled our nostrils and burned our eyes.

We stayed in Pakistan for several days, maneuvering through endless meandering mazes of bureaucratic red tape to secure our visas into Afghanistan. At last we received permission, and we immediately left Peshawar and drove northwest up over the treacherous mountain divide of Khyber Pass. Famous military leaders like Darius I and Genghis Khan had led their

Figure 22: Bob in Afghanistan.

invading armies across this mountain pass. As we crossed over the border into Afghanistan, we were greeted by thousands of people walking, driving, and limping on crutches. Some were even being transported on litters as they all desperately tried to escape Afghanistan. Swarms of disabled and homeless men, women, and children had congregated at the border crossing, staring helplessly through the barbed wire gates that they would never be allowed to pass through.

As we descended from the mountains, we drove along a meandering camel caravan and entered the northeastern frontier of Afghanistan. Across this vast no man's land of lawless disorder, all that remained were grief and graves. It seemed that everyone carried a weapon, whether a rifle, a pistol, or a grenade launcher. Small boys wore ammunition belts strapped to their chests, and we sensed an almost overpowering cloud of oppression. It filled the air and clung to one's skin. Generations of death and war had choked all joy and hope from these people. Children played among the carcasses of tanks and armored vehicles that littered the landscape, and the barren, dust-caked hillsides lay pocked with moon-like craters. It was like a scene from Hades.

Within a few hours, we had reached Jalalabad, which would serve as a home base during our stay. The smoky, dust-shrouded sunset brought a gloomy end to another day of the suffering that is Afghanistan. We spent the night in a mud-walled compound, where armed civilian soldiers passed by my window every few minutes. Shadows of their slow-moving forms were cast on the walls by the pale moonlight. My bed consisted of a blanket spread over a mat on the floor. A Kalashnikov rifle had been "lovingly" placed on my pillow, a gift from my Pashtun host.

The Pashtuns are mountain people, vast in numbers, comprising a major portion of Afghanistan's population. With over sixty different tribes, the Pashtuns are in constant struggle with one another for land and power, and feuds between families are often passed down from generation to generation. Unwritten codes and bizarre social rituals rule tribal conduct, but there is one custom in particular that can be traced back millennia, and that is the protection of guests. In the Old Testament, men went to great extremes in protecting visitors under their roofs, and we should realize that this attitude has not changed in the Middle East. I was a guest of a Pashtun tribal leader named Nastrula, and I was given an AK-47 because of an ancient attitude about hospitality.

Nastrula was a friend of Joe Ritchie, whose self-appointed mission was to help the Afghan people by whatever means possible. Joe had worked on numerous relief-aid projects, some of which involved repairing parks and damaged irrigation systems. I was impressed to see that Nastrula and Joe had also made important inroads to help stem the region's deadly preoccupation with heroine production.

The next day I awoke and prepared myself for a day trip to Kabul one hundred miles farther west. I was on a quest; I had to seek out the prison and find the place where Dana and Heather had left their journals. To keep me safe, Nastrula assigned me two guards with machine guns, along with a van and driver. Before leaving, however, a war correspondent from the *Sunday Times* of London warned me to beef up my armed guard, because people were constantly being attacked on the road to Kabul.

"If you go to Kabul," he cautioned, "take no less than three trucks of armed guards."

I told him I had only two young guards and an old van, and he shrugged in response, "Well then, you'll be my next story for *The Times*."

It took five, hot, jarring hours traveling through a swirling brown/orange dust storm to reach the city of Kabul. More so than anywhere else we'd visited in Afghanistan, the remnants of war dominated the landscape. Tanks, destroyed buildings, and bombed-out neighborhoods filled the horizon as far as we could see. It was a scene I had only witnessed on the news; I was now driving through Hell's back door.

Night was falling by the time I arrived at the Kabul prison that had served as Heather and Dana's temporary jail. It was really more of a brutal women's reform school, used by the Taliban to alter the behavior of women who were disobedient to their husbands, their fathers, or their faith. As Dana and Heather had discovered, the slightest offense could land a woman in this cruel compound. In Afghanistan, women could be beaten for something as minor as wearing nail polish. They were not permitted to work outside the home unescorted by a male family member. Under Taliban rule, a taxi driver was in danger of a severe beating if he dared drive a woman unescorted by a man.

So far, I had encountered no resistance from the locals, which seemed odd to me. The United States military was currently pulverizing the country, cleansing the Taliban pestilence from its midst. I'd expected that an American civilian would attract unwelcome attention. Up to this point in the journey, we had been spared any unpleasant altercations, but as I strolled toward the front of the prison, a disheveled bearded man with an automatic weapon walked over to me and stood cross-armed.

He introduced himself as a Northern Alliance commander and barked, "It will be impossible for you to enter today."

"All I want to do is take some film of the prison," I said, holding up my video camera.

"No! Forbidden!" came the gruff reply.

I had been in these situations before, and I had learned a few tricks. From my jacket pocket I removed a new watch, purchased on sale for $6.95 at a Wal-Mart in Colorado. It had a button on the side that I pressed, illuminating a pale green glow on the dial. I placed the watch respectfully in his hand and said, "This watch is my gift to you."

He took the watch, his eyes widened and after a moment he slowly whispered, "This prison is my gift to you."

Within minutes, I was videotaping Heather and Dana's prison cell, a dirty, small room located off of a courtyard. The courtyard itself was barren and dusty except for a lone tree in the middle. Heather and Dana had faxed me a map that they had sketched of the entire prison, and as I surveyed the scene, I knew I had found the right place.

Heather and Dana told me I could identify their cell, because a woman in their group had mixed fingernail polish with mud and used it to paint animal figures on the walls. We found the location of their cell, but the pictures had been whitewashed over. The Taliban forbade paintings of any kind. However, one rough drawing of an elephant remained on the back wall of the cell. (Heather later told me that someone else probably sketched the elephant drawing after their escape). The only thing that remained in their cell area was a blue strip of cloth stretched across the room to serve as a clothesline. I pulled down the blue cloth, rolled it up, and placed it in my pocket. Heather had told me that every evening hundreds of flies perched on this blue cloth, offering the women a little "entertainment" during their imprisonment.

The next day I videotaped the home where the missionaries had lived prior to their arrest. Another commander told me that the journals of the American women had been burned, so the next day at noon we left Kabul to return to Jalalabad.

As we drove through the Kabul Pass that afternoon, my driver and guards pointed out men with guns up on a ridge on the canyon walls. My driver then directed my attention to large splotches of dried bloodstains spread across the ground. "Just one month ago, this is where robbers robbed and killed four journalists," he said coldly. Gazing at the bloodstained rocks, the driver motioned discreetly toward the men on the cliffs, wrapped in turbans and holding rifles.

"Al-Qaida," he whispered. "It is very dangerous for us. We must go now."

The guns, the blood, the war, the maimed children, the insects and oppressing dust storms all produced one of the most arduous trips I've ever made. This was a foreboding land immersed in misery.

I was again drawn back in time to the Apostle Paul. "How in the world did he do it?" I wondered. He'd endured year after year of lonely, dangerous travel into hostile, alien lands. I had traveled a few thousand miles on a plane, leaving my home for two weeks, but it's estimated that Paul traveled over 20,000 miles during his various journeys—without the aid of planes, trains, or cars. Every mile he travelled, he made on foot or hooves or ancient ships. What's more, he faced dangers every place he went. As he himself wrote:

...in labors more abundant, in stripes above measure, in prisons more frequently, in deaths often. From the Jews five times I received forty stripes minus one.

*Three times I was beaten with rods; once I was stoned;
three times I was shipwrecked; a night and a day I
have been in the deep; in journeys often, in perils
of waters, in perils of robbers, in perils of my own
countrymen, in perils of the Gentiles, in perils in the
city, in perils in the wilderness, in perils in the sea, in
perils among false brethren; in weariness and toil, in
sleeplessness often, in hunger and thirst, in fastings
often, in cold and nakedness...*

2 Corinthians 11:23b-27

Paul traveled thousands of miles through warring tribal factions and dens of robbers. Through beatings, shipwrecks and hardships, he traversed that brutal and unforgiving ancient world, enduring it all, every day, tirelessly spreading a message he knew to be true. The man who once persecuted Christians was miraculously met on a roadway by his Lord and entrusted with a holy message that he would continue to spread even in the face of probably execution. He didn't hide away in the protective confines of his group, but went out into a wild and dangerous world that hated him and wanted him dead.

Here in Afghanistan I could plainly see that Heather and Dana had traveled a similar road. They had endured arrest and various persecutions in their efforts to help the women of Afghanistan. They were spit on as they witnessed their faith. There is always a price to pay when we stand up for the faith we hold dearly, and Paul ultimately died for his. In this he was content, however, and even when he was imprisoned in Rome, he told the Philippian church, *"For to me, to live is Christ, and to die is gain."*[1]

A person who converts from the Muslim to the Christian faith in Afghanistan is considered dead by their family. They are severed from family ties and cut off socially. This social segregation for accepting an alternative to the Muslim faith prevents almost everyone from proclaiming a new faith of any kind. It's not surprising to me that Afghanistan is estimated to be 99% Muslim.

---

1   Philippians 1:21

211

Paul met with similar difficulties as he worked to spread the Gospel. Many of the Jews regarded Paul as a heretic, and he met with constant opposition from his own people.

Traveling the dangerous back roads on our return to Jalalabad, I couldn't help but marvel at Paul's incredible commitment, his faith and gutsy resolve. Feared, hated, beaten, robbed, spit on—nothing stopped him. In God's plan, nothing could.

During my return flight to the United States, I mentally replayed my experiences in war-torn Afghanistan. I reached for my Bible to gain some perspective, and I found myself again journeying through the pages of Luke's narration. I lingered over the words that Paul penned from lonely outposts and prisons across the perilous ancient Middle East. During the time I had spent on the Munxar Reef in Malta and the blood-soaked plains of Afghanistan, I felt that I had come closer and more face-to-face with the man Paul than I ever had before. I realized that this man who had changed the course of history was now changing my own.

The anchor I had touched on September 10, 2001 had suddenly become something far greater than battered ancient lead. That anchor had become to me a symbol of hope, a witness to one of the greatest stories ever told, the deliverance from death of an entire ship's worth of sailors, crew, and passengers, during a terrible storm on the sea.

Staring out of the plane window, my mind traveled back to the Munxar Reef and Malta's secretive fraternity of divers. If those anchors really were the anchors from Paul's ship, then those who had lost hope in their lives needed to know. They needed to know that the words of the Bible were reliable, that they could be followed, and that they would lead us where we wanted to go. With the death and devastation of Afghanistan now behind me, I felt more inspired than ever to continue the search.

In the years to come, I would track down all four anchors from that small spot on the Munxar Reef. They had been found close to each other, spread out in about a 120-foot-spread pattern. I have been accused on the Internet of wanting to take those anchors from Malta and sell them for a tidy profit. The truth is that I raised $20,000 and bought two of the anchors, then donated them to the Maritime Museum in Malta. They are on display there today. One anchor remains hidden away on Malta by a family that explicitly wants to remain anonymous, but I did see that anchor and photographed it. I agreed to keep its location a strict secret.

Of course, as discussed before, there is one anchor that was tragically melted down and made into dive weights by the young divers who found it long ago. Today those men are older and have admitted to me they had made an immense historical error. As for me, I am blessed to own one of those dive weights. It is sitting right in front of me as I write these final words about my Malta adventures. On its oxidized grey face, I can clearly see the indelible mark of Tony's mirrored initials. I often pick it up and rub the cold lead object, thinking back to that moment in Bible history when God saved a freighter of men in a violent storm of the coast of Malta. I feel that lead weight in my hand, and I wonder whether I'm holding a bit of the past, a piece of an anchor that Paul and Luke themselves walked by as they traversed the Mediterranean Sea 2000 years ago.

TEMPLE

CHAPTER 20

UNDER THE CITY OF DAVID

E li Shukron seemed more comfortable in a darkened underground maze than under a cloudless Jerusalem sky. That was natural; he had lived in dimly lit tunnels most of the past two decades. I grasped his hands in greeting and found them unusually abrasive and vise-like. His handshake offered no display of male dominance; the guy had simply spent years of his life shoveling untold tons of soil. He had moved veritable mountains of boulders in the process of excavating world-renowned archaeological sites. It was no wonder his grip constricted around my fingers like a coiling python.

On any given day, a turn of Eli Shukron's shovel had the potential to reveal a world changing artifact. He however, was not just any archaeologist. He was the Director of Excavations at the City of David in Jerusalem. For more than two decades he had been involved in nearly every major discovery on that patch of ground, including the world-famous Pool of Siloam where John 9:6-7 tells us Jesus sent a blind man to be healed.

I had met Eli Shukron just days earlier. He had offered my research team a behind-the-scenes underground tour of the recent excavations in the City of David. Most of the world regards the City of David as merely one of the hills in Jerusalem, one that rises just south of the Temple Mount. I regard the City of David as the place where it all began, and I believe it is there and *not* on Mount Moriah to the north, that the Temple of Solomon once stood.

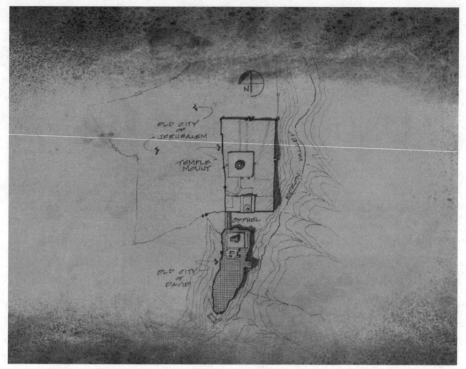

Figure 23: The Temple Mount with the City of David below (south). Note the suggested Temple placement within the City of David. Drawing by Chuck Benson.

When we wound our way through tunnels and tight passageways, I was truly amazed at the size of the dark, subterranean world. It was like a great rabbit warren with its tunnels that led into cavernous echo-reverberating caves. I was also surprised to find a mysterious underground river running its length, although the Bible makes reference to this underground water system. The history of Jerusalem could be found in those passages. Eli showed me some ancient foundation stones of Jerusalem, stones that dated to the time of the Jebusites who ruled Jerusalem in the days before David's kingdom.

As I was studying these stones, my eye caught the movement of a dim light in the darkened shadows above us to the right. A short tunnel slanted sharply upward about forty or so yards above us, and a yellow glow emanated from the dead end of the tunnel. I stepped over and craned my neck to see what was up there, and I watched as the silhouetted shadow of a man carried a sack I assumed was filled with dirt. He crossed past the tunnel opening, and then another man eclipsed the yellow glow emanating from a dangling light bulb.

This tunnel piqued my curiosity. I couldn't see much of the man other than he was wearing a hard hat and had hold of a shovel. A metal sign dangled on a chain clearly warning intruders that the tunnel was off limits, and this made me all the more intrigued. I turned to Eli and pointed up to the tunnel, but he seemed to dismiss me altogether. He ignored my gesture and turned to walk down another dark tunnel. My research team courteously followed him, all obviously interested in the straight-forward tour Eli was giving and apparently oblivious to the activities taking place in that shadowy upper tunnel.

I lingered a few more seconds, but I only heard the clattering sounds of men scratching away at rock, removing earth that had been left undisturbed for millennia. I felt my guts urging me to duck under the chain barricade to see what those men were digging up. My mind raced with possibilities. This was the same part of Jerusalem where David had crawled up a water shaft to capture the city of the Jebusites in 2 Samuel 5:8. This is where Solomon was anointed as king at the Gihon Springs in 1 Kings 1:33-45. Ancient prophets of God had walked here, maybe right where I was now standing. I wanted to know what was going on up in that mysterious narrow channel of rock. It was as if I was being pulled to that dangling light bulb up above like a moth.

As I gazed upward, I remembered that I was Eli's guest, and an echoing shout from one of my trailing team members pulled me back to reality. I adjusted my headlamp, looked one last time over my shoulder at the enigmatic shaft, and then walked down the dimly lit pathway to catch up with my group. In just a few days, Eli would willingly lead me up into that secretive shaft and let me see for myself the discoveries being made in its stone enclave. What I would see would change my life forever.

Three days later, my research team met Eli at the gift shop in the City of David National Park. He said, with an almost sly tilt of the head, "I believe you will want to see what I am about to show you." It was a simple statement, hardly befitting the monumental discovery he was about to share with us.

"What is it?" I asked, unsure of what to expect.

Eli replied with measured words, "It is an ancient underground sanctuary that dates to the First Temple period." With that explanation, he turned and walked off, rightly assuming that we would eagerly follow him. He led us in a line down the outside steps of the City of David, down the eastern embankment that faced the Kidron Valley. We passed under a canopy of shade trees, and then turned left at the bottom of the steps. Not many paces later, we found a cave carved into the wall of the cliff, and Eli led us past a dilapidated rusty fence that barely hung on its hinges. We had to inch our way down a narrow ledge with a precarious drop-off and across sand bags splattered with mud. Just before Eli took us into the cave itself, he stopped abruptly and turned. Then, he smiled widely, just as though he was about to hand me a giant gift to unwrap.

Eli had heard my theory that the Temple of Solomon, and later Herod's Temple, were not built on the hill currently known as the Temple Mount, and he was about to show me some evidence that had been hidden away since the time of King Solomon.

We descended into a cave where the sunlight could not reach, and we paused as our eyes adjusted to the darkness. There were no tourist pathways there, no hand rails, no directional signs or bright lights; it was the raw environment of an archaeological dig. The aroma of freshly churned earth wafted into our faces, earth freshly exposed to the air after a multitude of centuries.

We made our way inward, stepping over more white bags gorged with dirt. I knew that we were somewhere under the City of David, even close to its core. My heart had started to beat uncharacteristically faster. My mouth had lost all moisture, and a trickle of sweat wound down my back. I had had this same feeling before. In all my years of exploring the world for the lost locations in the Bible, I felt I had developed something of a sixth sense about these things. Something close, something perhaps just feet away, was about to change everything I had been working on for so long.

The air became moist, and the earth dampened around us as we passed deeper under the mountain. The sounds of men up ahead grew louder, and we heard talking as well as the clank of metal on metal. I knew from our position that the underground Gihon Spring must be gurgling nearby, its stream of clear water feeding the tunnel Hezekiah had dug into the rock walls as described in 2 Chronicles 32:30.

Impatience began to rise up in me, but I forced myself to remain calm. After stepping over a crumpled plastic tarp and rock debris, I entered into a series of flat-walled chambers carved out of the rock. A forest of metal support posts held up the dirt overhead, and work men below and to my left dug away in a descending lighted shaft that I immediately knew was the same mysterious tunnel that had intrigued me so greatly a few days prior. The workers paid little attention to me as they quickly moved white sacks one by one or ate at the rock with their tilling shovels.

Eli stepped close to me. It was as though he knew we shared a kindred spirit about these things, and he also knew the place he was about to show us would whirl my mind. I already felt it, and I didn't even know yet what it all meant. With a Cheshire grin growing wider he said, "Do you know where we are?"

I said nothing. My eyes, ears, and mind wondrously took it all in. Eli had uncovered this place two years earlier, and all that time workers there had painstakingly sifted through dirt and hauled it away.

Eli said, "This is a worship area. We do not know exactly what it is, but it is from the First Temple period and possibly even before." He waved his hand in a sweeping motion, "This is the only worship area in the city of David. Everything is perfect." Eli then pointed to a carved out hole in the stone floor and said, "This is an olive press to make oil." My heart and mind raced. Leviticus 21:10-12 says:

> He who is the high priest among his brethren, on
> whose head the anointing oil was poured and who is
> consecrated to wear the garments, shall not uncover
> his head nor tear his clothes; 'nor shall he go near
> any dead body, nor defile himself for his father or
> his mother; 'nor shall he go out of the sanctuary, nor

*profane the sanctuary of his God; for the consecration
of the anointing oil of his God is upon him: I am the
LORD.*

Once the oil was placed on the priest, he was forbidden
to leave the sanctuary. I was standing in an ancient sanctuary
right at ground zero, where I had logically decided the original
Temple stood, and it was conceivable that the anointing of the
priest had taken place right here. I stood in amazement.

Eli then walked over and bent down to point out a hand-
cut channel that ran straight down the full length of the room.
He stood again and said matter-of-factly, "This is a channel for
blood. As you can see, this room is raised, and it is here that
there was an altar for sacrificing small animals, such as sheep."
His words were like a jack hammer in my brain. He extended his
hand to demonstrate the direction of blood drainage, explaining,
"The blood went into the floor over there, and the animals were
tied up here."

Eli then stepped over to a corner in the stone wall and poked
his fingers through a hole in the corner edge of the stone. He
explained that this is where a ring was set to tie up the animal
being slaughtered. He smiled, as proud as though he had built
the sanctuary himself. "Everything is perfect. Few people have
been in here to see it."

Eli continued, explaining his own discovery of the place.
"I knew that something happened here, but I did not know
what. When I started to clean it, then I started to understand.
This is the place of something huge, and we are in the heart of
that area. It is an area of worship and praying, a place where
people connected with God. From what we understand, what
happened here took place during the First Temple period, and
even before." Eli later told me that the place could have existed
as far back as the time of Melchizedek.

One of my team members Bonnie Dawson had put a great
deal of effort into this project, and as Eli spoke to us in that
mysterious place, her eyes welled up with glistening tears. Eli
reiterated several times that we were in the City of David on
Mount Zion, in the very place where blood sacrifices were made.

We stood in a place where anointing oil was made to sanctify both the priests and the animals being sacrificed. What's more, this place was situated right at the Gihon Springs.

Bonnie could not contain her excitement, and in her exuberance I thought she would jump into Eli's arms. It was an uncharacteristic burst of emotion from staid Bonnie when she stepped over and gave Eli a quick kiss on his cheek. "This is all so amazing, so very amazing," she told him. Then she rubbed a knuckle across each eye and wiped tears from her cheeks. They were tears of joy, brought on by the moment's gravity. A moment later, Bonnie blushed with embarrassment at her expression of emotion, but Eli seemed to blush even more, and we all laughed out loud.

The moment brought us back to the realization that we were all humans, and we were possibly stepping on the very stones that priests and prophets had once trodden smooth. This very place might be the environs of the holy Temple, a location that had been lost for nearly two millennia.

I asked Eli, "How close are we to the Gihon Springs?"

He said, "We are ten meters, about thirty feet. You have everything together here, close to the spring, close to the water, living water. We know that the place of worship to God was close to the water, close to the spring." He paused, "This is the foundation of the earth that connects with God." According to the Talmud, the "Eben Shetiyyah" was the stone on which the Ark of the Covenant rested—and the stone on which the world was founded.[1]

As he continued to show the team around, Eli pointed out two small recessed areas about the size of a walk-in closet with a low ceiling. One of the spaces was empty, but the other had an upright stone stela about the size of a cemetery head stone. There was no

Figure 24: Underground close to the Gihon spring. Photo courtesy of Eli Shukron.

---

1   Yoma 54b

223

Figure 25: Image of an underground worship area that is close to the Gihon Spring (possibly dating to the first temple period era). Photo by Eli Shukron.

writing on it. Eli said that the fact that it was still standing upright after everything else was destroyed, and after all these years, was a sign that somebody, sometime long ago, considered this upright stone to be an extremely sacred object in a very holy place.

Eli then read a verse printed on white paper. It was from Genesis 28, and I have made bold the words that *he* had highlighted for impact. What he read was a like a lightning bolt to my soul:

"He had a dream in which he saw a stairway resting on the earth, with its top reaching to heaven, and the angels of God were ascending and descending on it. There above it stood the Lord, and he said: "I am the Lord, the God of your father Abraham and the God of Isaac. I will give you and your descendants the land on which you are lying. Your descendants will be like the dust of the earth, and you will spread out to the west and to the east, to the north and to the south. All peoples on earth will be blessed through you and your offspring. I am with you and will watch over you wherever you go, and I will bring you back to this land. I will not leave you until I have done what I have promised you. "When Jacob awoke from his sleep, he thought, "Surely the Lord is in this place, and I was not aware of it." He was afraid and said, "How awesome is this place! This is none other than the **house of God**; this is the gate of heaven." Early the next morning Jacob took **the stone** he had placed under his head and **set it up as a pillar and poured oil on top of it**. He called that place Bethel, though the city used to be called Luz. Then Jacob made a vow, saying,

*"If God will be with me and will watch over me on this journey I am taking and will give me food to eat and clothes to wear so that I return safely to my father's household, then the LORD will be my God and **this stone** that I have set up as a **pillar will be God's house...**"*

Genesis 28:12-20 (NIV)

The word Bethel means, "House of God," and this city on the northern border of Benjamin, within a day's walk north of Jerusalem, was the place where Abraham and Jacob both stopped to worship God.[2] Later, the Ark of the Covenant was brought to Bethel, and the Israelites worshiped there.[3] However, that location was corrupted by calf worship during the divided kingdom,[4] and the prophets cry out against the evil done there.[5] Did priests of the LORD bring Jacob's holy pillar from Bethel to Jerusalem when they moved the Ark? *Somebody* had considered that stela of particular value in this precious room under the City of David.

Stone set up like a pillar, oil put on it, the LORD's house... it was all swirling in my head. It was at that moment that the confluence of intellect and emotion collided. I knew in my heart, though I could not say with absolute certainty, that I was actually somewhere in the complex of Solomon's Temple, exactly where I did not know.

Eli had said that there were many more areas that needed excavating. I assumed that treasures of historic significance were only a few feet away from where I stood. More excavations would follow, and I wondered what the dirt silently held in its dark, concealing embrace—treasures that would someday face the light of examination.

We were in the City of David, the place of the Temple. We were right in the well-defined precincts of the stronghold of Zion. The nearby flowing Gihon Spring had given us a precise area in which we hoped to find the object of our quest, the real location of the Temple. How could we doubt the significance of the place in which we were standing?

2   Genesis 12:8; 13:1–4; 35:1-15
3   Judges 20:18; 26–28; 21:2
4   1 Kings 12:28-33
5   Jeremiah 48:13; Hosea 10:15; Amos 3:13–4:4; 5:1–6

Chapter 21

How It Started

My search for the Temple began on July 12, 2013, before I ever met Eli Shukron. I was walking upon stone pavers in the Arab quarter of Jerusalem, where the narrow pathway of a street was lined with densely packed shops. Copper pots, pottery, leather items, brightly colored linens and ornate wood-carvings were available for sale. Swarthy men with dark, expressionless faces sat before of piles of rugs or bins of oriental spices, while others sold from tables spread with heaps of brightly colored candies. The candy might have been more appetizing if swarms of nervy flies didn't speckle the piles.

The market resonated with a myriad of rattles and scrapes and voices. Shouts of, "Hey mister please to come in my shop" added to the general bustle. The clattering sound of an old wooden cart followed close behind me, and I turned to watch a small boy shoving a wobbly-wheeled contraption piled with flat bread higher than the child could see. The boy's bread cart rolled down a lane that had seen thousands of years of human history. The stones and dirt beneath his feet had been dominated by Jews and then by Romans, then traded back and forth between Muslims and Christians and more Muslims many times over the centuries. The throbbing hooves of horses had carried an influx of conquering invaders time and again. Yet, this child pushing his cart knew only the struggle to keep his animal directed through the crowds, to sell his piles of bread.

I had walked through this part of Jerusalem before, and I enjoyed the liveliness of the daily commerce. Here I found crowds buying and selling in a form I had seen in many other parts of the Middle East, but today something felt different about it all. Muslims worked their way down the streets in old Jerusalem in ever increasing numbers. The local police estimated that many hundreds of thousands of people flooded into the constricted walkways that day. They seemed to spring from nowhere, and the rapidly swelling numbers of determined, hardened faces focused on the ground as they marched in a hurried gait. They were propelled by an apparently imperative haste. When I grinned in greeting, nobody smiled back. When I offered a "Hello," they just shouldered me aside, time and again. Eventually, I just waited for the crowds to pass by.

I later learned they were all heading toward the Dome of the Rock, the mosque that dominates the Temple Mount. The Muslims do not call it the Temple Mount, of course, but refer to that hilltop as Haram esh-Sharif, "The Noble Sanctuary," dominated by the brightly colored Dome of the Rock and the Al Aqsa Mosque. The Al Aqsa Mosque is the site where Muslims believe Mohammed ascended into Heaven. Muslims reject any claim the Jews have to the rocky escarpment as the traditional site of the holy Temple.

During that trip to Jerusalem, I witnessed two contrasting events involving Muslims and Jews in the same general sector of the Temple Mount.

That July 12th in Jerusalem was the first Friday of Ramadan, the day of prayer services at the Al-Aqsa Mosque. A video would later show the pan-Islamic group Hizb ut-Tahrir calling for the destruction of other nations. Imam Ismat Al-Hammouri used that day to chant slogans to the gathered multitudes:

"Allah is Greater!(Allahu Akbar) Let America be destroyed!"
"Allah is Greater! (Allahu Akbar) Let France be destroyed!"
"Allah is Greater! (Allahu Akbar) Let Rome be destroyed!"
"Allah is Greater! (Allahu Akbar) Let Britain be destroyed!"[1]

On Friday, I watched angry Muslims shouting out hatred toward the West. On July 16th, I watched Jews singing, arms locked together in the shadow of the Western Wall. They danced and laughed and at times wept openly. It was Tisha B'Av,

---

1   The Clarion Project originally translated the cries against the West on July 22, 2013. Also see Khaled Abu Toameh, "Extremism Escalating in the West Bank," *Gatestone Institute*, July 22, 2013, https://www.gatestoneinstitute.org/3868/west-bank-extremism

the ninth day of the month of Av, a day of Jewish fasting and remembrance. It's a fact of history that Solomon's Temple and Herod's Temple were both destroyed on the ninth of Av—the same day on the Hebrew calendar 655 years apart. Even after the destruction of the Second Temple, Tisha B'Av continued to be a day of tragedy throughout Jewish history; it was on the ninth of Av that the Bar Kochba revolt was crushed in AD 132, the Jews were expelled from England in 1290 and from Spain in 1492. Even the Jews' removal from the Warsaw Ghetto to the Treblinka concentration camp began on the ninth of Av in 1942. These worshipers gathered at the Western Wall and remembered the painful history of their people.

Tisha B'Av is a day of fasting and mourning. The Jews follow prescribed edicts and do not wash on this day or wear makeup or leather shoes or anything else that represents luxury. In synagogues across Israel, plaintive sobbing can be heard as the book of Lamentations is read out loud. It is a day of pained reflection, and people often refrain from greeting each other at synagogues as they deeply contemplate the tragedies that have befallen their people. This display of grief has been seared into the hearts of Jews for millennia.

It seemed awkward to me to be in Israel during this charged week. I was there, however, to research the location of the Temple, and thus perhaps my visit at this time was apropos.

I stood in the shadow of the massive stones of the Wailing Wall, the western wall that is said to have been the retaining wall of the Temple. As I stared at those great blocks of stone, I thought about the war and death that had been experienced on this spot. The world has many times held its breath over political tensions involving the Wailing Wall. While the Temple Mount is regarded as the third most holy spot in Islam, it is the *most* holy spot in Judaism because it is firmly believed the Temple of the LORD once stood there.

There is no piece of real estate on the planet Earth that is considered more significant or more volatile than the thirty-six acres of the Temple Mount. Some say that World War III will erupt there. More blood has been shed over disputes of ownership and control of the traditional Temple platform than any other location. For decades, the Temple Mount Faithful organization has been waiting, preparing for the day when the Third Temple will be built and the sacrificial system of Moses reinstituted. The existence of the mosques and the explosive nature of the site have prevented that dream from being fulfilled.

However, I suggest that the traditional Temple Mount is not the historical site of the Temples at all. I believe, along with Dr. Martin, Dr. Buchannan, Dr. Missler, David Sielaff, and burgeoning choirs of others, that the Temples of Solomon and Herod were really built on the hill historically known as the City of David and *not* up on the site currently dominated by the bright Dome of the Rock mosque.

DR. ERNEST MARTIN

Like so many, I always assumed the traditional Temple location was correct and I never thought to question that the Temple Mount was the actual site of the Temple built by Solomon and, later, Herod. That is, I never questioned it until I began to read the fascinating work of the late archaeologist and author, Dr. Ernest L. Martin.

Dr. Martin reminded his readers that Jesus used very specific wording when He warned His disciples of the coming destruction of the Temple. Matthew 24:1-2 says:

> *Then Jesus went out and departed from the temple, and His disciples came up to show Him the buildings of the temple. And Jesus said to them, "Do you not see all these things? Assuredly, I say to you, not one stone shall be left here upon another, that shall not be thrown down."*

Christ's words clearly state that the entire Second Temple, each and every stone, would be dislodged and tossed away. It is interesting to note that there are literally thousands of massive stone blocks set in the wall surrounding the traditional Temple Mount platform. Was Jesus wrong in His prophesy that not one stone would remain standing? Jews today at the Temple Mount will sometimes state that Jesus was a false Messiah, because the Temple's retaining wall still stands.

I don't believe that Jesus was wrong. I believe we are wrong in our layout of ancient Jerusalem. I believe that the stone walls of the Temple were indeed thrown down to the last block, and the existing foundation blocks of the Temple Mount are *actually* what remain of the fortress which housed the mighty Tenth Roman Legion (*Legio X Fretensis*).

How could we have lost the site of the Temple, the most sacred site in all history? It's because the Temple was destroyed in AD 70 and its stones were torn to pieces. After the Jews lost the Bar Kochba revolt against Rome in AD 135, they were massacred and all Jews were exiled from the city. Second century Aristo of Pella is quoted as saying:

"The whole nation from that time was strictly forbidden to set foot on the region about Jerusalem, by the formal decree and enactment of [Emperor Hadrian], who commanded that they should not even from a distance look on their native soil!" So writes Aristo of Pella.[2]

Emperor Hadrian worked to completely annihilate the Jewish identity of Jerusalem. He kicked out the Jews, he renamed it, and he even had it plowed in fulfillment of a prophecy in Micah:

Therefore because of you Zion shall be plowed like a field, Jerusalem shall become heaps of ruins, And the mountain of the temple like the bare hills of the forest.

Micah 3:12

That's how the location of the Temple could be lost to history.

When the Muslims built the Dome of the Rock mosque in Jerusalem in the seventh century, it certainly made an impression. Its imposing, high-walled fortress must have appeared the most likely Temple site for later generations. However, it's more probable that the Dome of the Rock was constructed on the platform left behind by the Antonia Fortress.

---

2 Eusebius, *Ecclesiastical History*, IV.6.3

THE ANTONIA FORTRESS

Herod the Great built a garrison in Jerusalem sometime before 31 BC, and he named it after Mark Antony. This Antonia Fortress was as big as several cities. First century historian Josephus describes the fortress in *The Wars of the Jews* as a great structure with four towers at the corners from which the whole Temple could be viewed.[3] It housed approximately six thousand men, plus the needed support staff, which might have included as many as ten thousand personnel.

Yet, not one stone of the Roman fort has ever been found in Jerusalem. That is, not one stone has been found—unless history has mislabeled the Temple Mount. The largest structure from ancient Jerusalem is most likely not the ancient Temple site, but is instead a massive Roman fort. I find it ironic that the garrison has been hiding right under our noses the whole time. If the stones of the Wailing Wall are the remaining retaining wall blocks of the Antonia Fortress, then the Temple was built about six hundred feet to the south, on Mount Zion, the City of David.

MOUNT ZION

Three thousand years ago, there was a high-walled fortification in Jerusalem controlled by the Jebusites. It was about twelve acres in size and had an estimated population of two thousand people. At that time, the present-day Temple Mount complex did not exist; it would come to be built much later during the rise of Rome. David wanted that Jebusite fortification, because it had the most precious commodity: a gushing spring of water. David took the fortification for himself and when Solomon built his Temple, that same spring was a necessary source of water for the priests to cleanse themselves before they entered the Temple. Water was incredibly important for the priests in performing their duties and maintaining cleanliness in the Temple after ritual sacrifices. Since the Gihon Spring is the only water source in Jerusalem, it can be assumed it would mark the true place of the Temple.

3   Josephus, *The Wars of the Jews*, 5.238.

David approached the Jebusite stronghold shortly after his rise to the throne. While David and his army stood outside Jerusalem, looking up at that Jebusite fortress in 2 Samuel, the Jebusite guards stood defiantly at the top of the walls and hollered down mockingly:

"You shall not come in here; but the blind and the lame will repel you…"

2 Samuel 5:6

The insult is obvious. "Ha. Even our blind and lame could defeat you!" Despite their bravado, the Jebusites lost. The next verse lets us know, *"Nevertheless David took the stronghold of Zion (that is, the City of David)."*

David loved Zion. Throughout the Psalms, we find that he praises Zion, calling it, *"The joy of the whole earth."*[4] These two locales, the stronghold of Zion and the City of David, are inexorably intertwined and are the huge keys to solving the riddle of where the Temple truly once stood.

---

4   Psalm 48:2

CHAPTER 22

THE LOCATION OF THE TEMPLE

Many years after David took the Jebusite fortress, the LORD ordered David to build an altar on that mountain. We learn in 1 Chronicles 21:22-28 that David purchased a threshing floor from Ornan the Jebusite for that purpose. A threshing floor is comprised of a level area, usually paved with flat stones. There, crushed grain is tossed into the air, allowing the wind to separate and carry away the chaff—the light husks of broken straw. The heavier, solid kernels of grain fall to ground, where the grain piles can then be collected easily for storage.

Critics will say there are no threshing floors in cities. However, the Jebusite fortress was not a normal city; it was a stronghold. The threshing floor would have been vital for use within the city walls under extreme siege conditions.

The walls of the old City of David begin about 600 feet south of today's traditional Temple Mount. Since Jews were expelled from Jerusalem for two centuries and quarantined from visiting there until the time of Emperor Constantine. This led to disagreements about the true location of the Temple, and the debate went on and on. Finally, the charismatic Benjamin Tudela won out in AD 1169 when he proclaimed the Muslim's Haram al-Sharif site as the Temple Mount platform.

THE ANCIENT TEXTS

To sort it all out, we should go back in time to see what clues the ancients, who were alive when the Temple still stood, had left us. Church historian Eusebius was born in AD 263 and had fled the persecutions of Emperor Diocletian. After Emperor Constantine converted in AD 312, we find that Eusebius became the bishop of Caesarea, as well as curator of the library there. This allowed him access to the multitude of writings of those who went before him, writings that have since been lost to us. Living in Caesarea, Eusebius was able to visit Jerusalem himself and describe its desolations as a first-hand witness. What does he say about the Temple location? He consistently associates it with Mount Zion.

The hill called Zion and Jerusalem, the building there, that is to say, the temple, the Holy of Holies, the Altar, and whatever else was there dedicated to the glory of God have been utterly removed or shaken, in fulfillment of the word.[1]

Utter desolation has possessed the land. Their once famous Mount Zion instead of being as it once was, the center of study and education based on the divine prophecies… is a Roman farm like the rest of the country. Yea, with my own eyes I have seen the bulls plowing there, and the sacred site sown with seed. And Jerusalem itself … being inhabited of men of foreign race it is even now like a quarry. All the inhabitants of the city choose stores from its ruins as they will for private as well as public buildings. And it is sad for the eyes to see stones from the Temple itself, and from its ancient sanctuary and holy place, used for the building of idol temples, and of theatres for the populace. These things are open for the eyes to see.[2]

---

1 Eusebius, *Proof of the Gospel.* VIII.3.405.
2 *Ibid,* VIII.3.406.

The prominent Christian historian Eusebius tells us that stones dislodged from the Temple were scavenged in Zion and used for the construction of idol temples elsewhere. It was the greatest tragedy that stones taken from the LORD's holy sanctuary were reused to make secular structures demeaning to God. Notice what Eusebius proclaims with certainty as the Temple's location: Mount Zion, the center of education based on divine prophesies. He placed the Temple in the stronghold of Zion.

Unlike Eusebius, first century Jewish historian Josephus was *alive* when the Temple was still standing. He gives us an important bit of information in his *Antiquities of the Jews*[3] stating that when Herod built up the Temple, he also filled in the uneven places and made the hilltop flat, and then encompassed the whole hilltop with a wall that was one stadium on each side, four stadia square. This would make the temple platform 600 feet square, according to Josephus. Incidentally that size platform fits precisely within the City of David.

Four centuries before Christ, Hecateus of Abdera, testified that the Temple was located in the middle of the city wall, which at that time was the City of David. Josephus conversely places the Antonia Fortress (with its Praetorium for housing thousands of soldiers) at the higher spot up the mountain, that is, the Temple Mount and not in the City of David:

> For if we go up to this tower of Antonia, we gain the city... since we shall then be upon the top of the hill.[4]

THE BIBLE

There are a number of pertinent verses that direct us to the City of David (Zion) as the site of the Temple:

- 2 Samuel 5:7
  Nevertheless, David took the stronghold of Zion (that is, the City of David).

---

3   Josephus, *Antiquities of the Jews*, XV.11.3.
4   Josephus, *The Wars of the Jews*, VI.1.5.

- The City of David is equivalent to the stronghold of Zion:

- Psalm 132:8,13-14
Arise, O LORD, to Your resting place, You and the ark of Your strength...For the LORD has chosen Zion; He has desired it for His dwelling place: "This is My resting place forever; Here I will dwell, for I have desired it..."

  - God's resting place is with the Ark of the Covenant, which was in the Temple in Zion. This is not just a statement of current fact, but a prophecy regarding the future. David declares by the Holy Spirit that Zion is the place that God has chosen as His dwelling place.

- Psalm 2:6
Yet I have set My King On My holy hill of Zion.

  - This is a Messianic verse prophesying the reign of Christ, the King, on Mount Zion.

- Psalm 20:2
May He send you help from the sanctuary, And strengthen you out of Zion;

  - The sanctuary is associated with Zion.

- Psalm 65:1,4b
Praise is awaiting You, O God, in Zion; And to You the vow shall be performed....We shall be satisfied with the goodness of Your house, Of Your holy temple.

  - The praise to God and the performance of vows were always associated with Temple worship, which is in Zion.

- Isaiah 2:3
Many people shall come and say, "Come, and let us go up to the mountain of the LORD, To the house of the God of Jacob; He will teach us His ways, And we shall walk in His paths. For out of Zion shall go forth the law..."

- Isaiah, hundreds of years after David and Solomon, associates the Mountain of the LORD and the house of God (the Temple) with Zion.

• Isaiah 24:23
For the Lord of hosts will reign on Mount Zion...

• Joel 3:17
So you shall know that I am the LORD your God, Dwelling in Zion My holy mountain...

• Joel 3:21
For the Lord dwells in Zion.

CHAPTER 23

THE GIHON SPRING

O ne fact about Mount Zion that fascinated me was it holds a natural spring. In 1 Kings 1:38-39, Solomon is anointed at the Gihon Spring:

So Zadok the priest, Nathan the prophet, Benaiah the son of Jehoiada, the Cherethites, and the Pelethites went down and had Solomon ride on King David's mule, and took him to Gihon. Then Zadok the priest took a horn of oil from the tabernacle and anointed Solomon. And they blew the horn, and all the people said, "Long live King Solomon!"

In this passage, Solomon is taken to the Gihon Spring, where the priest enters the Tabernacle that holds the Ark of the Covenant to get a horn of oil. There he anoints Solomon as the new king. David's tent housed the Ark of the Covenant for 38 years until Solomon moved it up to his newly built Temple at the nearby location in the City of David; the location that once held the threshing floor of Ornan the Jebusite.

The City of David was lost to historians for many centuries. In the late 1800s, however, it was rediscovered by some boys who found inscriptions within what we know today as Hezekiah's tunnel. The Gihon Spring, which feeds water to the tunnel, is described by various historical figures. The Egyptian Aristeas visited Jerusalem a couple of centuries before Christ, and he described the Temple and its springs of water. Aristeas writes to his brother Philocrates, saying:

The Temple looks towards the east, and its back is turned westwards. The whole floor is paved with stones and slopes down to the appropriate places, so as to admit of its being flushed with water to wash away the blood from the sacrifices; for many thousand beasts are offered on the feast days. The water-supply is inexhaustible. An abundant natural spring bubbles up within the temple area. There are, moreover, wonderful underground reservoirs passing description, at a distance, as they pointed out to me, of five furlongs all round the site of the temple, each with innumerable pipes.[1]

The Romans could not put so much as a toe in the holy waters of the Gihon, so they imported water for their needs via conduits from South Bethlehem. Even though scholars will say there is water at the traditional Temple Mount, they fail to note that the water there is stored in huge cisterns, which are fed from two aqueducts, which were built during the time of the Hasmoneans (the Maccabees). Both the First Temple and the Second Temple were in operation for centuries before those aqueducts were piped in.

The first century Roman historian Tacitus records that the Temple at Jerusalem had a natural spring of water that welled from its interior. He also noted that the Antonia Fortress in Jerusalem sat visibly up on height, saying:

An inner line of walls had been built around the palace, and on a conspicuous height stands Antony's Tower, so named by Herod in honor of Mark Antony. The temple was built like a citadel, with walls of its own, which were constructed with more care and effort than any of the rest; the very colonnades about the temple made a splendid defense. Within the enclosure is an ever-flowing spring.[2]

Again, the Gihon Spring is the only "ever-flowing" source of

---

1   *The Letter of Aristeas*. This letter has been assigned to the Pseudepigrapha by scholars who doubt its author's claim to be a courtier of Ptolemy II Philadelphus (281-246 BC). At the same time, the letter is safely dated to the second century BC when the Temple still stood, and Josephus refers to it extensively.
2   Tacitus, *Histories*, V.11,12.

water in Jerusalem. Joel 3:18 tells us that a fountain shall flow from the House of the LORD. It's clear that a water source once bubbled up in the Temple area, which is an important fact in working to narrow down the Temple site.

> And of Zion it will be said, "This one and that one were born in her; And the Most High Himself shall establish her. Both the singers and the players on instruments say, "All my springs are in you."
>
> Psalm 87:5,7

Because of all the blood sacrifices, the Temple absolutely required a ready of water source to keep the sanctuary and instruments and priests clean. We read in 1 Kings 8:62 that Solomon sacrificed 22,000 bulls and 120,000 sheep when he dedicated the Temple. With so many animals being slaughtered, the severed veins of those beasts would spray blood like a flailing garden hose. Lots of water was needed to wash the blood away, and the Gihon Spring offered the necessary ready water source.

It is interesting that a Second Temple period arch has been found above a stone staircase that descends to the Gihon Spring, giving evidence that the spring was in service at the time of Herod's temple. Ahron Horovitz surmises in his book *The City of David* that the Gihon Spring served as an entrance way to those coming to purify themselves before entering the Temple.[3] It makes far more sense to purify oneself immediately before entering the Temple, rather than having to walk another quarter mile up to the traditional Temple Mount to enter the Temple. If the true Temple site was in the City of David, then worshipers could wash and immediately enter in to offer their sacrifices, or to pray and seek the LORD.

The gurgling water of the Gihon Spring became a nexus of historical and biblical pronouncements. When Eli Shukron gave us that precious peek under the fill dirt of Mount Zion, just yards from the Gihon Spring, I felt the awe of walking into a holy world. It was the hidden tomb of the sanctuary where priests had once sacrificed animals to the LORD. We all sensed that we were trodding on sacred ground.

---

3   Ahron Horovitz, Eyal Miron, ed., *The City of David: The Story of Ancient Jerusalem* (Brooklyn: Lambda Publishers, Inc., 2009), 213.

OUT OF THE CITY OF DAVID

After I published my book *Temple*, in which I detail my research into the true Temple location, I received a firestorm of criticism. I wasn't surprised by resistance to the new ideas we offered. I recognized that it's shocking to suggest that the Temple was on Mount Zion all along, and that remnants of Solomon's Temple are still hidden under the City of David. This position forces the conclusion that the Jews praying at Wailing Wall have been praying toward huge stones that supported the walls of a Roman Fort—and not the Temple! Tradition is a powerful thing, and I knew this revolutionary theory about the Temple site would ignite the wrath of an army of staid traditionalists. I expected resistance, but I would never have guessed how vile the attacks would be.

After *Temple* was published, I was vehemently attacked on the Internet for daring to question the traditional Temple Mount site. I thought I would clear things up by offering suitable answers to our detractors. I've been amazed, however, at the unwillingness of certain critics to honestly consider any alternate ideas. No amount of new information will move those whose feet are cemented into position; they wish to stay in the safe harbor of mutual consent and not venture out into the choppy sea where new theories stir the water.

As Thomas F. Torrance once wrote, "The tragedy apparently, is that the very structures of our churches represent the fossilization of traditions that have grown up by practice and procedure, and they have become so hardened in self-justification that even the Word of God can hardly crack them open."[4]

I would like to include here the one criticism that I hear most often. Those who reject the Mount Zion location for the Temple commonly cite 1 Kings 8:1-6, in which Solomon has the Ark brought up to the Temple from the City of David. This passage is often used to argue that the Temple could therefore not have been *in* the City of David. Scholar and Biblical translator Dr. William Welty offered me an excellent answer

---

4   Torrance, Thomas F., "The Radical Consequences of Justification," *The Scottish Journal of Theology* 13, no 3 (1960): 237-246.

to this issue, and I want to present it here for your edification:

> 1 Kings 8:1 tells us that Solomon gathered together the
> elders of Israel, including all the heads of the tribes and
> the leaders of the ancestral households of the Israelis, to
> meet with him in Jerusalem so they could bring up the
> Ark of the Covenant of the LORD from Zion, the city of
> David. An examination of the larger context, including
> the five verses that follow this passage, demonstrates
> that the Temple was, in fact, located in the City of
> David. The verse isn't discussing the Temple location.
> It's discussing the location of the Ark of the Covenant,
> which, according to verse 1, was being stored in the
> City of David, which is where we say the Temple was
> located. This verse establishes, and does not refute, the
> City of David location for the storage place for the Ark.

> 1 Kings 8:1 also tells us that the Ark was brought up from
> the City of David, not to store it in the Temple, but to
> remove it temporarily from the City of David so that it
> could be used for a special dedication, a one-time end-
> of-life-cycle ceremony for the ancient, but now outdated
> Tabernacle. The closing ceremony was so large there
> wasn't space to hold it in the Temple. This is so is readily
> evident when one reads the next four verses:

> *2So all the men gathered together to meet with King
> Solomon at the Festival of Tents in the month Ethanim,
> the seventh month. 3All the Elders of Israel showed
> up, and the priests picked up the ark 4and brought it,
> the Tent of Meeting, and all the holy implements that
> were in the tent. The priests and descendants of Levi
> carried them up to Jerusalem. 5King Solomon and the
> entire congregation of Israel that had assembled to be
> with him stood in front of the ark, sacrificing so many
> sheep and oxen that they were neither counted nor
> inventoried.*

The Ark, the Tabernacle (called the "Tent of Meeting" in verse 3), and the implements used in the Tabernacle sacrifices, were all brought up from the City of David, not to be placed in the Temple in Jerusalem, but to be used in a one-time, final closing ceremony with the Ark of the Covenant using the old Tent of Meeting apart from the newly constructed Temple. After this date, the Tabernacle fades into history and is never mentioned again. What happened to it nobody knows. The closing ceremony for the Tabernacle was so vast that no inventory was made of how many animals were sacrificed (verse 5). At the conclusion of the ceremony, which **did not** take place at the newly finished Temple but rather in Jerusalem, verse 6 tells us:

> After this, the priests brought the Ark of the Covenant of the Lord to the place prepared for it, into the inner sanctuary of the Temple, under the wings of the cherubim in the Most Holy Place.

This verse tells us that after the ceremony described in verses 2-5, which required that the Ark be brought up to Jerusalem from the City of David to a place large enough to accommodate the closing memorial service for the now-to-be-retired Tabernacle, the Ark was returned to the Temple's Most Holy Place, which was back in the City of David. To sum up, far from deconstructing the City of David view for the Temple location, 1 Kings 8:1-6 affirms it.[5]

Why is this important? What should prevent the Jews from worshipping at the Wailing Wall during the centuries to come? It's important, because a large number of Jews have been longing to rebuild the Temple of the LORD after nearly 2000 years. The traditional Temple Mount is solidly controlled by Muslims, who reject any Jewish right to the site. If the Temple was indeed located in the City of David, however, then the Jews will have the freedom to build the holy sanctuary after so many long centuries of waiting.

There are a number of Bible passages that require the existence of a Third Temple. We believe that the Temple will be rebuilt near the end times, because Jesus, Paul and John all

---

5   William Welty, personal correspondence. Biblical text is from the ISV Bible translation.

make reference to it.[6] 2 Thessalonians 2:3-4 states:

Let no one deceive you by any means; for that Day
will not come unless the falling away comes first,
and the man of sin is revealed, the son of perdition,
who opposes and exalts himself above all that is called
God or that is worshiped, so that he sits as God in the
temple of God, showing himself that he is God.

Clearly, the man of Sin cannot sit in the Temple of God, pretending to be God, if there is no Temple. We also find that Jesus warns all those in Judea to escape to the mountains when the Abomination of Desolation enters the Holy Place:

Therefore when you see the 'abomination of
desolation,' spoken of by Daniel the prophet, standing
in the holy place (whoever reads, let him understand),
then let those who are in Judea flee to the mountains…
For then there will be great tribulation, such as has not
been since the beginning of the world until this time,
no, nor ever shall be.

Matthew 24:15-16, 21

The "holy place" is code for the Holy of Holies in the Temple, and the Abomination of Desolation in Daniel refers to desecration of the Temple. The Scriptures are clear the Temple will be rebuilt and will be contaminated by the Antichrist, but we take hope in the fact that Christ has the victory.

I am simply an ex-cop who sees the evidence others have often ignored or passed over. I hope my research will shed new light on an old archaeological blunder, and the true location of the Temple will be uncovered. One day, we will see the Temple erected over the place where the remains of Solomon's Temple have remained hidden for centuries.

---

6   Matthew 24:15; 2 Thessalonians 2:4; Revelation 11:1-2

GOLGOTHA

CHAPTER 24

THE HILL OF THE SKULL

C hallenging the traditional location of the Temple has opened for me a world of possibilities about other important sites. For instance, if the First and Second Temples were built in the City of David, then that opens wide a passageway in determining the correct site of Christ's crucifixion.

Since the time of Emperor Constantine, Christians have visited the Church of the Holy Sepulchre in the northwest part of Jerusalem's Old City as the traditional site of Christ's death and burial. In the nineteenth century, an alternative spot called Gordon's Calvary north of the Old City was proposed and embraced.

I believe the location of the Temple and the location of Christ's crucifixion are inescapably tied together by the Bible's narrative. By sliding the Temple south a thousand feet into the area of the Gihon Springs, we should slide Golgotha south as well. How so? The Centurion officiating the crucifixion of our Lord was in

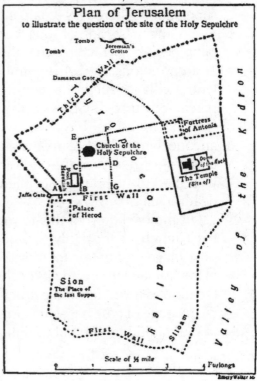

Figure 26: Map of Jerusalem designating site of Gordon's Calvary and Church of the Holy Sepulchre. Source: 1911 Encyclopedia Britannica.

a position to see the Temple veil tear in two, which means the hill of Calvary had to have been in a location east of the Temple.

Golgotha. Calvary. Both of these words derive from the word for "skull"—in Hebrew and Latin respectively, and the Gospel writers translate the location of Christ's death as the "place of a skull." Before we go off on the final adventure to find where Christ was crucified, I would like to first examine the two traditional sites that have claimed to be Skull Hill. I believe both sites are fraught with problematic assertions and geographical misinterpretations.

In the fourth century, Roman Emperor Constantine proclaimed that his mother Helena, through visions and dreams, had discovered the precise location where Jesus had been killed on the cross. A magnificent church was soon built in Jerusalem upon that very spot. It was known as the Church of the Holy Sepulchre, and it exists to this day.

During the ensuing Middle Ages, a dark shadow of fear and superstition spread across Europe. Barbarians ravaged Europe, and the breakdown of civilization led to rampant illiteracy and superstition. There was a palpable fear of the church hierarchy, of missing mass, and of soul-searing confessionals. Most of all, people were terrified of what they considered to be a vengeful and capricious God. If lightning spit out of a brooding sky, whole villages might be sent into a panic, cowering under a perceived curse of God's punishing wrath. It was a time when staid ecclesiastical directives were not to be challenged, and anyone who dared to try was labelled a blasphemer. Those accused of heresy were often tortured until they recanted or were tied to wooden posts piled with straw to face a hideous death by fire.

In the backdrop of this terror, superstition, and ignorance, the Church of the Holy Sepulchre became the uncontested pilgrimage destination for those seeking Calvary. The leadership of the Roman Empire and its ecclesiastical hierarchy certified the location as the place of the crucifixion and burial of Christ, and the passage of time has sealed that vault of tradition. Proponents of the traditional site fail to notice that the Church of the Holy

252

Sepulchre is not east of the Temple, whether on the Temple Mount or in the City of David.

On the other hand, the Garden Tomb near Gordon's Calvary is lovely and tranquil, and I've enjoyed my many visits there, but it's based on false assumptions made by the famed British officer Major-General Charles Gordon. In 1883, the war hero boldly challenged the holy pedigree of the Church of the Holy Sepulchre. While living for a time in Jerusalem, Gordon observed what he believed was a skull-like formation in a rock cliff near the Damascus gate. This rock formation suggested itself as the "place of the skull" and conversely Christ's execution location. Due to Gordon's status as a war hero (and his legendary death in Khartoum) the designation of the site steadily gained acceptance. Since Gordon was also a Protestant, his alternate site for Calvary appealed to the Protestant faithful.

As popular as Gordon's Calvary and the Garden Tomb are, they have clear issues. The first is that Gordon's "Skull Hill" is soft rock that is easily eroded, and it would have had a much different appearance two thousand years ago. Archaeologist Gabriel Barkey has done extensive analysis of the Garden Tomb, and he told me it was carved out of rock before the seventh century BC. That date is very important, because the Bible says that Jesus was buried in a new tomb that had never been occupied. According to Matthew 27:60, Joseph of Arimathea had recently hewn the tomb from rock, and the Garden Tomb is therefore just too old to be the tomb of Christ.

Figure 27: Skull Hill from the south, circa 1900.

Today, both Gordon's Calvary and the Church of the Holy Sepulchre are visited by swarms of enraptured tourists, and certainly these visitors have come to the right place: Jerusalem. And even in visiting these two locations, the visitors are stepping into historically significant spots; the original Church of the Holy Sepulchre was built by Emperor Constantine and has been visited by countless pilgrims, and it's been destroyed and rebuilt on several occasions throughout Jerusalem's colorful history. However, it is unlikely that the church, in all its struggles and glory, sits over the spot where Jesus was crucified. Both of these specific sites are fraught with certain fatal historical, geographical and scriptural difficulties that make them unlikely to ever hold the uncontested title of *Golgotha*.

During the Middle Ages, many ancient holy places were labeled without the care of research or good evidence. If an esteemed cleric offered his blessing on a location, that was often sufficient to bring in multitudes of faithful pilgrims. It was only a matter of time before another cathedral would rise out

Figure 28: Photo of the traditional Golgotha rock face by Cornuke, 2014.

Figure 29: The Church of the Holy Sepulchre in Jerusalem.

of the dust of the Holy Land with little evidence for its ties to a major historical event.

Archaeology in recent times has offered a wide range of information on ancient places, and cities like Jericho, Hazor, Capernaum and Nazareth have been uncovered and excavated. The Pool of Siloam has been found, and a stone naming Pontius Pilate was found at the archaeological site of Caesarea Maritima in 1961. There is plenty of evidence to support the Biblical narrative. The errors crept in, however, because during the times of great illiteracy in Medieval Europe, people weren't necessarily reading the Bible narrative. Therefore, some popular tourist destinations are justified, and others are not.

THE SEARCH FOR GOLGOTHA

I took a very long journey to seek out the true location of Calvary. I followed faint voices from antiquity and, most importantly, Scripture's magnetic compass to chart the way.

255

All along my journey, I found vast wastelands of man-made traditions and mangled misinformation. And yet, to the resentment of certain traditionalists, I suggest that the place where our Lord's holy flesh was once nailed to common wood is not in the spots we've long visited. I think it's ironic that the place would be where no one has ever looked before.

First, I concluded from the Bible that it was possible to see into the Temple from the hill of the crucifixion, and to see the veil had torn as Jesus died.

> *Then, behold, the veil of the temple was torn in two from top to bottom; and the earth quaked, and the rocks were split, and the graves were opened; and many bodies of the saints who had fallen asleep were raised; and coming out of the graves after His resurrection, they went into the holy city and appeared to many So when the centurion and those with him, who were guarding Jesus, saw the earthquake and the things that had happened, they feared greatly, saying, "Truly this was the Son of God!"*
>
> Matthew 27:51-54

> *When the sun was darkened, and the veil of the temple was torn in two. And when Jesus had cried out with a loud voice, He said, "Father, 'into Your hands I commit My spirit.'" Having said this, He breathed His last. So when the centurion saw what had happened, he glorified God, saying, "Certainly this was a righteous Man!"*
>
> Luke 23:45-47

The centurion in charge of the detail is named by specific rank, and he and his men are recorded as having personally felt the effects of the earthquake that occurred. Matthew also tells us that they *observed* the things that were happening. This term of description utilized by Matthew is an inclusive, but nevertheless a general term, that encompasses:

1. The earthquake;
2. The shattering of the rocks that had sealed some of the

tombs, due to the earthquake, along with an attendant resurrection of individuals;

3. The growing dark of the sun for a period of about three hours, an event that could not have been a solar eclipse, since the crucifixion took place during a full moon of the lunar cycle, and because the period of darkness lasted far beyond the few minutes of totality normal in an eclipse;

4. The tearing of the Temple veil from top to bottom.

In order for the centurion and anyone else who was at the crucifixion site to observe the veil being torn into two pieces from top to bottom, he would have had to be standing on a hill or elevated area east of the Temple. Archaeologist Eli Shukron told me at a conference in Washington D.C. that the crucifixion site should be "east of the Temples" whether they were actually located in the City of David or upon the traditional Temple Mount.

Neither the traditional Church of the Holy Sepulchre or Gordon's Calvary fit the required line-of-sight criteria. Both locations were west or north-west of the Temple during the time of Christ, and no observer would have been able to see into the Temple, as did the centurion at Christ's crucifixion.

In the 1873 edition of the *Palestine Exploration Fund Quarterly*, explorer Dr. Hutchinson suggests that Christ was crucified east of Herod's Temple near a well-traveled road entering Jerusalem. The Scottish doctor went on to say years later, "I am now prepared with further reasons for believing that our Lord was crucified (and necessarily buried) to the east of the city."[1] Most all sin offerings were sacrificed east of the Holy Place of the Temple. The sacred red heifer used for purification was sacrificed outside the camp,[2] and the nearest gate was east of the Temple. This is important, because Hebrews 9:13-14 associates Jesus Christ with the purification offered by that red heifer. Hebrews 13 reminds us that, like the animals sacrificed

---

1   R.F. Hutchinson, "Further Notes On Our Lord's Tomb," *In Palestine Exploration Fund Quarterly Statement*, (1873).
2   Numbers 19:2-3

outside the camp, Jesus also suffered and died outside the gates of the city:

> For the bodies of those animals, whose blood is
> brought into the sanctuary by the high priest for sin,
> are burned outside the camp. Therefore Jesus also,
> that He might sanctify the people with His own blood,
> suffered outside the gate. Therefore let us go forth to
> Him, outside the camp, bearing His reproach.
>
> Hebrews 13:11-13

There are, in fact, many biblical references for the sentencing of criminal acts occurring on the east side of the sanctuary, dating back to the time of Moses.

- Women who were accused of adultery were taken for judgment "before the Lord" at the east entrance of the sanctuary (Numbers 5:16-31).

- Aaron's two sons were judged "before the Lord" east of the sanctuary (Leviticus 10:1-7).

- Korah and his Levites were given their punishment east of the Tabernacle (Numbers 16:41-50).

- Sin offerings of the bull and goat on the day of atonement were made east of the Temple and burned to ashes (Leviticus 16:27)

- The scapegoat was led into the wilderness east of Jerusalem (Leviticus 16:20-22)

- The ashes of the Red Heifer were burned east of the Temple (Leviticus 4:12)

These judgments were followed with the same east-of-Temple theme during the time of Christ. It remained vital to religious leaders that judgments take place east of the Temple, because doing so would demonstrate that God was bearing witness to the punishments that were exacted there. The entrance to the Tabernacle and the Temple always faced east. Jesus Christ claimed to be the Son of God, and He was crucified for it. He would have logically been crucified as a severe punishment east of the Temple.

CHAPTER 25

THE SILWAN VILLAGE

The Silwan village is one of four hillocks comprising the Mount of Olives. When I stood on the City of David and looked east, I saw the Silwan perched on a hill about six hundred feet across the Kidron Valley, and I knew I had to investigate it. When I was able to do first-hand investigation of the hill structure on which the Silwan was built, I found cliffs hidden from view behind tightly packed homes. What's more, this two hundred foot long cliff area is believed to have been split open by an earthquake during the time of Christ, thus exposing many stone cut graves, just as Matthew 27 describes.

However, it turned out that getting access to the Silwan village was not so simple. It became a great challenge, because the Silwan is in Palestinian control. In fact, the first few times I tried to get into the Silwan, I was rebuffed by local youths throwing rocks.

I didn't give up, though. After several attempts, I finally made it into the entrance of the village. I was met there by a small emaciated dog tethered to a stone wall that was festooned with Islamic graffiti. I whistled softly to the trembling animal, but it seemed as if the tight collar had almost strangled the poor creature. I reached down to loosen the leash, and the mutt surprised me by wagging its tail, excited to be offered some of the attention it craved. However, a shadow approached from behind me, and the dog quickly curled into a cowering posture.

I watched as a teenage boy walked up and gave a sweeping kick to the dog's bony rib cage. He glared at me and spat out in an Arabic accent, "What are you do here?" Hatred curled up the muscles in his ruddy face. A blind, visceral disgust defined his expression, and I searched without success for a hint of empathy. He could not tell by my appearance whether I was Jewish, but my skin color and western clothes offered him enough cultural reasons to loathe my presence. Most importantly, I am sure his enmity towards me erupted from the simple fact that I was not one of his people. He knew I was not a Muslim, and that was all he needed to know for the moment.

In the more extreme Islamic communities, Israel and the United States are often referred to as the Little Satan and the Big Satan. This attitude has not existed throughout history, but in more modern times a vehement hatred has often boiled over. Thus, before I even had a chance to say hello to this young man, a crowd of teenage boys gathered around me with hardened stares and aggressive postures. The youths circled me, pulled out cell phones and inched closer.

I knew I had to respond quickly. I grabbed a wad of Israeli Shekels from my vest pocket, because money has a tendency to soften even the hardest individuals. I waved the bills toward the young men and said, using my best Arabic accent for added effect, "I want to see the stone high wall with the broken open tombs." I pointed resolutely, "I know it's over there... somewhere?"

Everything went awkwardly quiet. The boys stared with expressions that clearly communicated growing aversion. "Not possible to enter" one boy murmured. Another tried to snatch the bills from me, but I yanked them out of his reach. "You will get money when I see the cliff wall," I snapped back. The second lad glanced at the other boys, looked me over again, and then waved an arm, shouting hard, "Follow, mister." He led me to a house that held the geological secrets I sought deep beneath its concrete footings.

I already knew what was behind that home. Old explorer reports and photographs dating to the late 1800s had given me information that I wanted to investigate for myself. The young man gave a knuckled wrap at the door and was soon answered by a young boy. A man with a silver beard stood behind the boy's right shoulder with an initial expression of confusion. The old man then waved me off and started to shut the weather-scarred door. I earnestly asked, almost pleading, for him to let me see the split-open tombs in the cliffs behind his house. The man stopped closing the door and nervously looked up at the buildings looming around his home. His eyes were searching all the people in the windows as they glared down at us. He quietly whispered, "I have neighbors that will not like we are talking." The creaking door shut in my face before I could offer a word.

I was turned away by the Palestinian owner of the house this time. However, I would be back. I knew I would eventually see the mysterious cliffs shrouded behind this home and I hoped I would find additional clues hidden there. I had pushed risky boundaries before in my Bible research projects in foreign lands. Sometimes my persistence had gotten me what I wanted, and other times it turned out badly. I hoped here that repeated attempts to see those cliffs would provide me with the information I sought.

On my next attempt to explore those cliffs, I tried driving into the Silwan village at night with a Palestinian driver, but he was so terrified that he almost crashed. He was shaking so badly, he barely managed to get me back to my hotel. I had a similar experience with another driver when I tried driving into the Silwan. He was so unnerved that he hit a few overflowing trash containers along the way.

It was later on that particular day that I met my Israeli friend Jacob in the Old City of Jerusalem and started with my new plan to enter the Palestinian village. I had a healthy amount of money with me: a commodity that had gained me access into other off-limit locations. Jacob warned me repeatedly that my mission was impossible and foolhardy. Nevertheless, Jacob is a loyal and courageous friend who has stuck himself out for me. He told me that if I was determined to get into the Silwan, he knew a Palestinian driver who was willing to take us there. The Palestinian had told Jacob that my scheme was irrational, but he was willing to let me try.

Jacob was well aware that I had been forced back in the past by teens throwing rocks. He also knew that most of the people who live in the village disdain all Jews and Americans, and they are unwilling to allow any strangers to enter into their domain.

Nevertheless, a plan was made, and the next day Jacob and I met with the Palestinian driver, Sammer. Sammer was a swarthy man with a stocky build and short, muscular arms. He nervously chain smoked and always seemed to have a cigarette dangling from his stubby, nicotine-stained fingers. He told me that he once saw a gun smuggler shot by the police in the Silwan. After the shooting, helicopters whirled above as the police sealed off the Silwan. A riot erupted as a result.

I asked Sammer if he was worried about going into the Silwan again. He took a long drag from a cigarette. Then, he exhaled a plume of grey smoke and coughed a raspy, guttural cough into his cupped hand.

"Why we are doing such thing?" he asked.

I told him I wanted to get a photograph of the cliff area behind the houses.

Sammer tossed his cigarette to the ground and crushed it with one grind of his shoe. He looked at me oddly, coughed a chest-clogged wheeze one more time, and said, "You pay me now because you may not be able to pay me later."

We all got into Sammer's car, and within minutes we had pulled into a gift shop at the base of the Mount of Olives. A thin man approached our car, his high cheek bones shadowed by a curled baseball cap pulled down tight. I later learned that he was the owner of the gift shop and, more importantly, he owned three homes in the Silwan. It just so happened his homes were the very ones set in front of the cliffs that I wished to see.

I have no idea how Jacob or Sammer managed to get in touch with the man, but it was a tremendous help that they provided the opportunity to meet and talk with him outside the glaring eyes of the village.

Jacob, Sammer, and the willowy man with his baseball cap all talked as men characteristically do in the Middle East: loudly, with waving animated arms. I passively waited in the car, thinking I'd best keep my mouth shut for the time being (which is a difficult thing for me to do).

After getting an explanation of my intent, the gift shop owner with the baseball cap walked over to me. I stepped out of the car and stood up, extending a hand in greeting. He did not accept my handshake, and I dropped my arm. He scrutinized me then, looking me over intently from narrow, pinched eyes. His wondering gaze fell upon the ring I was wearing on my right hand. It was an expensive ring with an ancient silver coin set into a heavy silver band. He stuck out his lower lip for effect and grumbled, "Two hundred dollars and that ring."

I answered, "If you get me to see those cliffs, I will give you the ring, no problem."

In retrospect, I probably could have negotiated a better deal. I had already taken five trips to Israel in just over a year, though, and each of those times I'd been thwarted in my efforts to see those cliffs. I did not want this exceptional opportunity to slip past me, and the money and ring were a price I was willing to pay to do business with this man.

Sammer drove us all up into the village, and we soon found ourselves driving down a narrow, twisting street, ending by the western wall of the Silwan. This aesthetically impoverished neighborhood had long been known as an enclave of murderers, thieves, and malcontents. In the 1800's, the famed explorer Charles Warren wrote, "The people of Siloam [Silwan] are a lawless sect, credited with being the most unscrupulous ruffians in Palestine." Today, the Silwan is not so different than it was centuries ago.

Our van stopped in front of a crumbling concrete wall spray-painted with Islamic symbols and stained with bleeding rust. I slowly opened the car door, its hinges squeaking loudly in protest. As I stepped from the vehicle, broken shards of glass crunched under my boot, but that wasn't the only sound I heard. Distant shouting began to grow less distant as a commotion moved toward us.

A nearby heap of burning trash wafted sour smelling smoke our way. A sudden gust of hot wind sent the smoldering haze up past second story windows, where women wearing head scarves glared down at us. The sounds of commotion came from down a narrow road strewn with garbage, where a group of teenage boys and a few men appeared, clearly agitated, if not angry, in their advance.

263

A large man suddenly stepped toward me from between the buildings, and the pack of teens scattered like a startled flock of birds. The man was wearing old rubber sandals, sweatpants, a T-shirt sullied by grease, and a curdled scowl that extended down to his bulging neck. I had been told that this was a man not to be trifled with, the man who had the final say in all things pertaining to the Silwan.

All indications told me this surly Palestinian was the head of the village, and I had paid well to meet him. He ponderously strode up and stopped only when he was face to face with me. He was awkwardly close as he breathed out "Whuu you wunn?" There was no handshake, none of the pleasantries associated with meeting somebody new. The hefty man stood expressionless in front of me, his head cocked to one side and his arms crossed and feet widely planted.

I asked, as calmly as I could, for his permission to see the cliff area which was hidden from view behind a row of nearby homes. All he offered back was a resolute stare of distrust and the same repeated English words "Whuu you wunn?" They were hard to make out from the viscosity of his thick Arabic accent.

I realized I needed to give him more to help him understand. After some time explaining the seemingly unexplainable, I am sure he did not understand it all, but he allowed me inside the walls. It was comforting for me to finally be in the nefarious neighborhood, especially under the protection of this village leader. At least, that's what I'd gathered from Achmed, the home owner who was the newest owner of my ring.

I hurriedly dug into my pocket and fumbled to remove my cell phone, which contained several pictures of the Silwan dating back to the 1870's. The images on the small screen showed the village long before the place was choked with houses and scattered with so much refuse. The man took my phone, pulled it close to his probing eye balls, and fixated on it a long moment. To both my surprise and relief, the hint of a faint smile ripened across his ruddy face.

The local youths, along with some men, started to appear again—it seemed out of nowhere. A crowd pressed in behind our host to see the phone's vintage imagery. They tried to identify where their homes were now located in relation to the old photos, and I began to find the swelling crowd tilting in favor of my presence. A few boys chuckled in delight, and one man even patted me on the back as he pointed proudly at the historical imagery of his neighborhood on the luminescent face of my phone.

I was both pleased and relieved when the village leader shrugged his broad shoulders, dipped his head, and gestured for me to follow him. I took his motion as a sign granting me permission to see the cliff area. I felt sure that if I tried to tell him why this particular cliff was so important to me, he would never believe me, so it was just as well he didn't ask. If my heart was not racing enough, it now shifted to a different gear. That's exactly what I didn't want to happen. I needed to stay focused, as this would probably be a one-time visit, and a short one at that.

I walked closely behind the man as he marched down a fence line and maneuvered through the gap between houses. Off to my left, we startled a pit bull who lunged at me, straining against his stout chain and thick, leather collar. The dog was shaped like an engine block covered in brown fur, and he displayed a set of glistening teeth. I walked on and noticed off to our right, a pair of mangy, rib-thin cats hissing.

The smoldering smoke, the barking dog, the hissing cats

Figure 30: Author pointing to split open tomb in the Silwan Village.

265

and the boys shouting behind us, made for an otherworldly experience. However, I was not concerned with the cacophony of distractions, because I was actually standing at the foot of the stone cliffs I had come so far and had spent so much time and treasure trying to see. I was in the very shadow of those cliffs of the Silwan village. I gazed up at the ancient split-open tombs, and found my mouth as chalk dry as the cliffs.

Could this be the place described in the Bible, where the tombs tore open in the earthquake on the day of Christ's death? Would this place reveal to me where Christ was crucified?

I could clearly see that these stone cliffs were literally torn open from a violent tectonic event, exposing the back cavities of tombs. I felt the verse in Matthew was screaming at me. It looked as if a giant hand had grabbed the front portion of these tombs, and then yanked the face right off, leaving the back half exposed. I later learned that those cliffs were situated in a stratum of fine grade limestone. It is hard and resistant to the elements of wind and rain. But, the limestone is also easy to chisel away, thus the reason for all the tombs there. Some books have proposed that the change in the cliffs is due to poor quarrying methods by the Romans. That's a bizarre concept, because Romans did not quarry stones from around any tombs, especially if those tombs were Jewish. No, the cliff faces had obviously collapsed away as the result of a natural force—a force like an earthquake.

I felt as if I was following bread crumbs that led to a discovery of unimaginable value. I could see a cliff face had come to degradation from a violent earthquake, and all that was left was a fractured pile of swirling dust. Many times as a cop, it was the small, seemingly trivial pieces of evidence that would lead to a suspect's apprehension. That's why every detail requires careful scrutiny when making an investigation. In the Silwan village, I believed I needed to maintain that same laser-like attention. While the face of the cliff had been clearly damaged in a violent event, I saw that there were deeper holes in the face, holes with chisel marks, holes where bodies once lay. I also noticed that the stone slabs which held the bodies in the tombs were very narrow, less than a foot in width. The chiseled marks were only in the tomb areas, and the rest of the upper rock wall had no chisel marks. I saw nothing to suggest that quarrying had been done in the area where the rocks had obviously split apart.

In the entirety of the rock bluff, I counted eleven exposed, open tombs. The tombs were carved into about two hundred feet of horizontal cliff. The cliff varied in height along those 200 feet, but I estimated that the cliff face was 30 feet tall. How exciting! I knew I might actually be looking at prima facie evidence of the most notorious crime ever committed. Did I dare hope that I was standing where a completely innocent man was sacrificed in the place of the guilty so long ago? Was the Son of God killed right there? Right above my head?

The Gospels tell us a centurion stood in charge of the crucifixion event that killed Jesus. He certainly had no idea he had walked onto the stage of the most important human drama the world had ever witnessed. He had seen many people crucified, and Christ's crucifixion should have been just as common as all the others...except for what happened when Jesus breathed His last.

I imagine the centurion standing ramrod straight, in leadership stance, as he officiated over the executions. A transverse crest marked his helmet. Metal greaves covered his shins and a sword hung on his left hip. He held a vine stick in his right hand, ready to thrash any soldier that failed to explicitly follow his commands. The military leader was a hardened soldier. He had certainly seen plenty of death by the time he had reached the status of centurion, whether he had spilled men's blood on the battlefield or impaled men on crosses for breaking Roman laws. This centurion's name is not recorded in the Bible, but when Jesus died, that soldier felt the powerful rumble of the earth below his feet and saw the rocks split. He saw the tombs open, and the dead return to life. And the centurion became a believer in the righteousness and deity of Jesus the Lord. As he watched these things, his words became eternal as he spoke: "Truly this was the son of God."

I stood in the Silwan village and considered that centurion's vantage point. From this hilltop across the Kidron Valley, the centurion could have watched the curtain on the east side of the Temple split down the middle from top to bottom.

267

Figure 31: Actual photo taken of the Silwan hillside by Auguste Salzmann (1824-1872) Jerusalem, 1854.

I am an evidence guy, and I always want to see the proof. Doubting Thomas was also an evidence guy, but upon seeing the wounds in Christ's side and the holes in His wrists, he fell to the ground and said, "My Lord and my God!" I am sure mere photos will not evoke the awe I felt that day. I doubt those cliffs would cause all the doubting Thomas-types to drop to their knees and affirm the Bible. But, for me, looking at the actual chisel marks of those split-open tombs, and staring at that hilltop, I had to agree with Thomas and call out to Jesus, "My Lord and my God!"

FIRST CENTURY BURIALS

I have no doubt that those cliffs on the ridge of the Silwan were once a cemetery cut into stone. There was a feature on that hill that I found most puzzling, but which also fit the scene of a cemetery. Three round niches had been cut into the cliff face, quite high off the ground. Eventually I learned that these had been created as receptacles for cinerary urns, which were common two thousand years ago. The niches were three by two feet in size, chiseled out of the stone in order to accommodate burial urns. In the time of Rome these were called *columbaria*, after the Latin word *columba*— "dove"—because they resembled pigeon holes or the compartmentalized housing of a dovecote.

In Jerusalem during the Herodian era from 35 BC to AD 70, it became common for families to engage in a burial practice called *ossilegium*. The Jews buried their dead on a shelf in the tomb and returned a year later when only bones were left. The bones were then placed in stone boxes called *ossuaries*, which were then interred in the

Figure 32: Columbarium niches in stone to hold funeral urns. The rock cliff was split open to expose the the three niches shown here just as the Bible describes.

family tomb in special niches. One ossuary might hold the bones of several family members. The niches in the cliff wall at the Silwan therefore fit the customs during the time of Christ.

There were many options for disposing of the dead in the first century. The rich could afford elaborate funerals with paid mourners, women who wailed loudly in a convincing, sorrowful display of lament. Those who desired a grand sendoff might arrange singers and dancers and even mimes to entertain the mourners that had come to their burial show. The upper class members were not necessarily buried immediately, but might have been laid in-state in the atrium of their homes. A man who had served in the military or a government office would be dressed in clothes with the insignia of the highest office he'd obtained during his life. He'd be honored by a procession through the main streets with people singing, dancing and,

269

of course, hired women crying. The entourage of the deceased might even stop to hear an oration, after which the burial or cremation took place outside of the city.

In cases of cremation, a close relative would light the funeral pyre. In some cases, actors wearing masks would imitate the greatest achievements of the deceased or dress in honor of relatives who had obtained high public office.

Burial for paupers was much different. Time was not wasted on disposal, and the poor might be unceremoniously tossed into pits in the city dump. It was therefore common for many of the lower classes to belong to a funeral club, in which a small monthly fee in life ensured even the poor a funeral and proper burial at death. For most, whether rich or poor, cremation was the most popular choice. The cremated ashes were placed in containers of cloth, pottery, glass, metal, wood or gold and marble chests. The container of ashes was then placed in a niche, the *columbaria*, cut into rock tombs.

As I stood at the cliffs and examined the tombs that had been broken in half, I could see many of these internal niches exposed. Columbaria were designed to be hidden forever in the silent darkness of a tomb. These columbaria had been exposed to the daily cycles of sun and moon for centuries upon centuries. The niches, without argument, once held cinerary urns that were filled with the ashes of the dead, but they had been exposed by an earthquake, and they lay before me as enticing evidence of a holy, Biblical event.

One bit of encouraging news to my theory came after I asked Dr. Paul Feinberg, professor of Geology at Hunter College in New York, to examine the cliffs in the Silwan. He gave a detailed analysis that included his observations about the chisel marks, the location, the geological attributes of the limestone composition of the cliffs, and the ancient black and white photographs of the area. He offered me the following conclusion:

> The cliffs with the exposed tomb cavities align exactly as one would expect from the Biblical narrative. In the book of Matthew it states, the earth shook, rocks were

split open, tombs were opened, and many saints who had died were brought back to life. There is no doubt that the tombs were once intact, as one would expect from any tomb; however, these tombs in the Silwan were all split open.[1]

Though it excited me, Dr. Feinberg's report didn't conclusively confirm that these particular cliffs were involved in the crucifixion. However, it did at least offer a picture *consistent* with the events described in the Gospels. Ongoing research is being conducted on Golgotha as I write these words, and I look forward to more thrilling news on this location in the future.

---

1   Paul Feinberg, personal correspondence.

CHAPTER 26

THE LIGHT TO OUR PATH

I n all the years of my life, I have more than fulfilled that drive for adventure I had after I left the police department. I often think that it's a bit of a miracle I'm still alive. I can't say for sure it was all my "calling," but maybe we don't live our lives in the explicit—but the implicit. As Oswald Chambers wrote in *My Utmost for His Highest*: "There comes the baffling call of God in all our lives also. The call of God can never be stated explicitly, it is implicit. The call of God is like the call of the sea, no one hears it but the one who has the nature of the sea in him."

Whether I was called to each adventure, I can't say. The one thing I know for sure is that the nature to *explore* definitely lives within me.

I have written much in this book about the travels I made on my roads to various discoveries. I hesitate to use the word "discovery" here, because God reveals what He wants to whomever He wants for His purpose and His glory. But I believe God does want us to continually seek and search for greater knowledge. I recognize that each of these locations, from Noah's ark to Mount Sinai, to Paul's anchors to the site of Christ's crucifixion, have traditional roots planted by men with agendas. It is my goal to try and cut through the tangle of misinformation propagated by this ancient democracy of the dead. I'm humbled and awed by the thought that God might have used me to reveal certain objects and places, inexorably connected with historical events described in His Word. I believe that searching for lost locations in the Bible will certainly encourage many in their faith, and that is the goal dear to my heart.

More than twenty years ago, a man contacted me to let me know that he would do whatever it took to destroy my ministry because I dared go against an opinion he held dear. I had written that Mount Sinai was in Arabia, and it seems he believed the holy mountain of God was in the Sinai Peninsula. True to his word, he has spent the past two decades negatively critiquing every book I have ever written. He even sent in a critique of my book *Golgotha* to a national magazine before I had even come close to completing the book.

Ossification is a huge problem in the Christian community today, and it is pervasive across denominational boundaries. Like the bone boxes of ancient Judea, some people seek to protect their personal views with all the hardness of a limestone ossuary, unwilling to even consider new ideas that challenge staid tradition. My findings may be correct, or I may have missed something, and I welcome warm debate about these things. However, I have found some critics so aggressive in their disfavor against any challenges to their traditional views that their vitriol destroys any attempts at calm debate. Some contrarians consistently reject those who offer new ideas and insights, as though the very act of questioning their personal position is sufficient to create enmity. They prefer the safe harbor of mutual consent with others who agree with them and then take demeaning shots at all others with alternate ideas.

In all my explorations, I only wanted to find out what is true. I tried to find the real locations of places the Bible describes, based on what the Bible actually says and not the ancient surveys set rigidly into place by tradition. My heart has always been to dig up the truth. If people disagree with me, that's certainly acceptable. However, I believe it's imperative that the heart of all parties be in the right place before boisterous haggling begins. It's more important that our hearts are in the right location than whether we determine the correct location of Noah's Ark or any other ancient treasure.

Those of us who serve Jesus Christ are not enemies. We are all brothers and sisters, purchased by the blood of the Son of God. When we approach these issues, we should do so with an attitude of love and respect for each other. I think that Christians can start on common ground, even when we disagree about certain issues. For instance, we can disagree about where the event at Calvary took place, and yet agree in complete solidarity that Christ was crucified exactly as the Bible describes. We can agree that two millennia ago, God sent His only begotten Son to willingly give Himself to a gruesome and horrifying execution. On a lonely hill in Jerusalem, the Son of God died for us, and three days later He rose from the dead. No matter our differences, we can agree about that!

THE CURSE AND THE BLESSINGS

Sin is systemic in our world. It is a part of life, and we all falter and stumble into immorality at times. We have all failed and fallen short of the glory of God, as Paul states in Romans 3:23, and this sin blemish separates us from a relationship with a pure God. Sin is destructive and it leads to death. It requires a harsh solution, and that's why Jesus was willingly and brutally slain. He was our sin offering. If we believe in Jesus Christ and make Him Lord and Savior of our lives by confessing our sins and repenting of them, we can escape condemnation and find complete forgiveness. Christ's shed blood is the only solvent that can wash away the stain of sin. It's the only collateral we can use to get into heaven. It's in Him that I trust, and it's His Word on which I completely depend.

I have challenged many traditions in this book, and my hope is that I've added valuable information to the ongoing narrative and measured debate. I have traveled to places I believe make good candidates for Mount Sinai, Noah's ark, the Ark of the Covenant, the Temple, Paul's anchors and Golgotha, but the Bible will always be the final mediator; and I trust that truth will ultimately prevail in time. The Bible is the precisely calibrated roadmap and X often does mark the spot. God is real, and if I'm wrong, we'll be able to find it in the Bible.

The Lord has left His fingerprints all over the landscape of history, and the evidence of His miracles and wonders are out there waiting to be discovered. In your search for truth, I urge you to always trust in God's word as a lamp unto your feet and a light unto your path. Jesus said in John 14:6, *"I am the way, the truth, and the life. No one comes to the Father except through Me."*

My wonderful wife Terry, my children, my entire family and some very special friends all helped make these adventures possible. I get the screen time, but there have been a multitude of people behind every trip I've taken, without whom I'd never have left Colorado. The list is far too extensive to mention every person who deserves notable recognition for his or her gracious help to me. I offer you all, and you know who you are, my deepest gratitude and more thanks than words could ever convey.

And if, perchance, this book encourages someone to head out to solve some ancient holy mystery, I pray you safe and successful travel mercies. Maybe we will meet along the dusty road of some distant land, a Bible in one hand and a compass in the other. I will certainly offer you these words: "Keep searching, because secrets can't be kept forever."

For there is nothing hidden which will not be revealed, nor has anything been kept secret but that it should come to light.

Mark 4:22

ABOUT THE AUTHOR

BOB CORNUKE

A former police investigator and SWAT team member, is now a Biblical investigator, international explorer, and author of eleven books. He has participated in over seventy expeditions around the world searching for lost locations described in the Bible. These journeys include searching for Mount Sinai in Egypt and Saudi Arabia, looking for the remains of Noah's Ark in Turkey with astronaut Jim Irwin (the eighth man to walk on the moon) and researching ancient Assyrian and Babylonian flood accounts in Iran. He has followed ancient accounts of the Ark of the Covenant from Israel to Egypt and across Ethiopian highlands, and, most recently, his research team found the probable location of Paul's shipwreck off the coast of Malta. This find has resulted in the accounting of what many are saying are all four anchors, as described in Acts 27. His most recent adventure is sparking international controversy. Chronicled in his new book Temple, Bob makes the assertion that the Temples of Solomon and Herod are located in the City of David and not on the traditional Temple Mount platform. Bob has appeared on National Geographic Channel, CBS, NBC's Dateline, Good Morning America, CNN, MSNBC, Fox, ABC, History Channel, Travel Channel, Ripley's Believe It or Not, and for two years was the host of the weekly Television show, Gutsy Christianity, on Direct TV with the National Religious Broadcasting Network (NRB). During U.S. bombing strikes, in Afghanistan, Bob completed a dangerous photographic video assignment. He is now the President of the Bible Archaeology Search and Exploration (BASE) Institute located in Colorado

Springs, CO. He also serves as special adviser for the National Council on Bible Curriculum in Public Schools and was invited by the President's staff to conduct a Bible study for White House personnel. Bob has earned a Masters of Arts in Biblical Studies and a Ph.D. in Bible and Theology from Louisiana Baptist University, but his children believe that his most notable accomplishment, to date, is having his findings featured as a question on a Trivial Pursuit™ card. While serving as a crime scene investigator, assigned to major crime scenes, Bob earned invaluable training and experience in investigative and scientific research techniques. He has now turned his investigative skills toward Bible archaeology, using those skills and ingenuity to unlock the doors to sites that often go against traditional archaeological presuppositions. Originally sought out by astronaut James Irwin (Apollo 15) as a security adviser, Bob was later recruited to join the expedition as they searched for the remains of Noah's Ark in Eastern Turkey. His assignment was to provide protection for Irwin's team as they operated in the Kurdish-terrorist held region, but, upon completion of the Mount Ararat expedition, Cornuke and Irwin found themselves colleagues and close friends. Bob later became vice president of Irwin's "High Flight" Foundation, an exploration consortium dedicated to the search for lost Biblical locations and artifacts. Several years after Irwin's death, Cornuke founded BASE Institute to expand on the Mission of his mentor and friend. Bob also sits on the Academic Advisory Board for Koinonia Institute. When not traveling the world, Bob lives in Colorado with his wife and children. From a majestic hillside near Pikes Peak, an expedition landmark for explorers from yesteryear, Bob directs the modern day efforts of the staff and volunteers of the Bible Archaeology, Research & Exploration Institute.